WORLD PEACE

VOLUME NINE

POLITICS AND PEACE

Suresh Chandra Mallick
Pritam Mallick

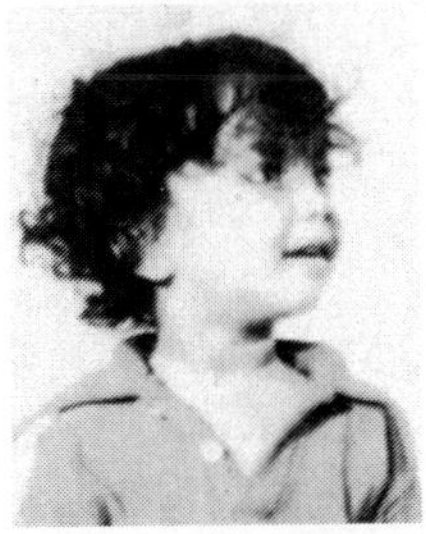

POLITICS AND PEACE

Institute of Development Studies and Policy research,
Pritam Bhawan, 93 Dharma Vihar, Khandagiri,
Bhubaneswar 751030 (Orissa), INDIA

ISBN: 978-81-924851-8-8

First Edition - 2013

E-Publication Price: US $ 4

Dedicated to

Ms. Julia Gillard
Former Prime Minister of Australia

PROLOGUE

The manuscript on WORLD PEACE Volume Nine highlights on 'Politics and Peace'. The study is intended to ascertain whether there is any possibility of clean governance by politicians even in democratic countries. Today, politics has become a business in all the developing countries. They assure false promises to the voters; bribe them in elections; and if they win, they act as the coronet of the constituency. They forget the promises and indulge in kickbacks, and black money for self improvement.

A government in all developing countries takes all steps to get loan from funding institutions for economic development. This becomes an opening for the corrupt politicians to amass huge wealth for private use. The state bears the burden of foreign debt but corrupt politicians realize huge funds through corrupt practices at the cost of the people and the country. These people cheat their own country, where they are born, live and die. They also cheat those poor people, who die without food, medicines and clean drinking water.

World Peace is possible provided the politicians do justice to the people.

In the Twenty-first century most of the politicians are more worried for self respect, self achievement, and they forget that they are not kings and monarch of yester years.

Now in all democratic countries, there is moral crisis. This is now of endemic and epidemic proportions, threatening to destroy our social fabric, and reduce us to a version of anarchy, unless we have already crossed the border. India, the greatest democracy in the world faces mass uproar for days together in front of Parliament. People maim, strangle, and abort, torture other men, women, children and animals. People cheat, lie, intimidate, corrupt and brazen it out. Our justice system is outdated, cumbersome, ponderous, over burdened and altogether easy to subvert. Our conscience is dead.

People of most of countries have achieved success in education, research, technology, and cooperation. The corporate, rich people and educated people want more and more benefits from the society; but they are not thinking for the hungry masses. Why the democracy system created selfish people to rule the state? Why more than one billion people are hungry?

This speaks that politics; politicians and policy adopted by the government are not moving in the right direction. There is rise of terrorists, Maoists and Naxalites in many countries. Some countries are frightened because of war. But the governments are not solving the causes of poverty, rich-poor gap, farmers' suicides and climate change. The governments are fighting against the ill- effects of disaster and misfortune.

In this study we have observed that the world is moving towards destruction, but still there is possibility that we could award peace to all. In the first chapter, political philosophy and political thought have been discussed to pave the way for discussion. Chapter II explains the nature and ideology of political parties in USA, Germany, China, India, South Africa, and Sri Lanka.

Chapter III has included political problems in Africa, Myanmar, South Africa, Chile, Tibet, Nepal and Middle East. Poverty and injustice are rampant in all the developing countries. Chapter IV highlights political unrest, political instability and political turmoil. The sufferers come to street to express their demands. In these developing countries practically anarchy rules the state. If the Members of august houses are purchased and sold, who could save the people and the country? Chapter V discusses how politics could have avoided war in the past and would avoid war in future. Chapter VI focuses that an efficient and effective foreign policy is necessary in this twenty-first century and beyond. Chapter VII explains that if the President and Prime Ministers of all countries change their mind and desire to award peace, it would be possible. The advices rendered by HH Dalai Lama and M K Gandhi would assist the world leaders for assuring PEACE to the people and the world. The U N should take the lead to award peace to all.

We are grateful to Wikipedia, Google in search and a number of Newspapers for collection of facts on corruption. Journals and Internet enriched this manuscript. We acknowledge the contribution of authors, who have written articles, research papers, reports, resolutions, and books on politics. They have contributed tremendously for political problems of the entire world and suggested measures for improvement. The authors are grateful to Mrs. Bina Mallick, Priyam Mallick and Priyambada Mallick for their cooperation during preparation of the manuscript. We will appreciate for constructive criticism aiming at improvement of the subsequent editions of the book. We will be happy, even if a small step towards world peace is contemplated through this endeavour.

January 1, 2013 Suresh Chandra Mallick

CONTENTS

Chapter I

POLITICAL PHILOSOPHY

The real differences around the world today are not between Jews and Arabs; Protestants and Catholics; Muslims, Croats, and Serbs. The real differences are between those who embrace peace and those who would destroy it; between those who look to the future and those who cling to the past; between those who open their arms and those who are determined to clench their fists. ----- William J. Clinton (1997)

Democracy is the best form of governance. Necessarily it directs the government to award justice, safety and peace to the people. The government must accept the responsibility to manage the state with right programs, right policies and right choices to see that every one is safe and lives in peace. Government is not a business house where it would do business at the cost of the voters or citizens. The government must try to award peace to all. The government must act as the family head of a state. In a democratic country, social problems are also political issues. Again political issues direct economic factors to prominence such as poverty, foreign debt and infrastructure development. But neither the government nor the voters emphasize on policies on equality, safety, and peace.

Why does the government undertake anti-people activities? Why there are strikes, uproar, indiscipline and discontentment among the people? Why the government forgets election manifesto and neglects in governance? Why the government neglects millions of hungry people? This means that Members of the Parliament are not the true representatives of the people and are elected through black money, corruption and false promises. In many countries few people or families have captured state power for generations or for decades. A corrupt government breeds poverty, hunger, disparity in income, suicides, Maoism, Terrorism, and faces internal and external threats. A government should award justice to the people and follow right path of governance and progress.

Why the political parties collect money from the industrialists, mine-owners or foreign companies? Why the bank accounts of political parties are not audited? Why the election commission does not deny the same persons to contest elections after two terms in a house? Why murderers, anti-socials, income tax cheats, black marketers and dismissed government employees are permitted to contest in elections?

The political parties could be the most useful devices to do justice to the people provided the election is free from corruption. The president of each political party must be clean without any black spots in his (her) life; the party account must be audited each year; and the Party president cannot hold two posts.

A politician should be at par with voters in practice. He/ she cannot be above the law of the country. Political corruption has derailed democracy, bureaucracy and judiciary. It has caused military rule in countries. Unless clean people enter into politics, World Peace would be delayed for decades.

Political party

Political party is an association of like-minded people that seeks to exercise political power. Although politics, as an activity, has been practiced for thousands of years, political parties seem to have been largely a product of the 19th century. Although the US constitution contains no reference to parties, the Republican and Democratic parties became essential elements of the political system, reflecting the country's history, social and economic structure. The one-party state, in which party and state institutions became enmeshed, was the distinguishing feature of the political system established in Russia by Lenin (and later Stalin) after World War I.

Edmund Burke defined a political party as 'a body of men united for promoting by their joint endeavours the national interest, upon some particular principle for which they are all agreed'. Political parties may also be defined as agencies of political mobilization, which seek to exercise power directly. The political party defers from pressure groups which act as agencies of political mobilization and do not seek to exercise power directly but to influence its exercise.

Burke's definition is an important reminder that parties are often, though not always, based on ideological differences. Thus the Tories were identified more closely with the monarchy, the established Church, and the status quo, the Whigs with moderate social and political reform and *laissez-faire*.

With the development of a mass electorate, especially as a result of the Reform Act 1867, the recently emergent Conservative and Liberal parties began to form extra- legislative organizations. Despite attempts by Joseph Chamberlain, in the cases of the Liberals, and Lord Randolph Churchill, in the case of the Conservatives, to give the mass party organization some control over the parliamentary parties, the extra-legislative organizations remained subordinate to the latter. In the meantime other groups formed extra-legislative parties in order to secure representation in Parliament, the most notable instances being the various groups, which eventually came together to form the Labour Party. Nonetheless, despite its extra-legislative origins, its parliamentary leadership has for the most part controlled the Labour Party, although the Labour Party Conference has exercised a significant influence from time to time.

Types of political parties

Parties developed in a similar way in the United States, with the eventual formation of the Republican Party and the Democratic Party, and in most Western European countries. Such parties were, to varying degrees, committed to some form of democratic government. Other parties, however, rejected Western liberal democratic values and sought to establish authoritarian regimes. Notable among these were the fascist parties, which secured power in Italy and Germany between the two World Wars, and the communist parties in the Soviet Union, Eastern Europe, Mainland China, parts of Southeast Asia, and Cuba.

Parties may therefore be distinguished by their basic ideological commitment to the type of regime they seek to establish, but within that commitment they may be further distinguished by their degree of radicalism or conservatism, often referred to as **Left** and **Right**. Such terms are, of course, relative. Communist parties, Labour parties, and Social Democratic parties are generally parties to the left of centre; Conservative, Liberal, and Christian

Democratic parties are generally to the right of centre; but the relative position of the centre tends to vary from country to country. On the whole, for instance, the political centre is further to the left in Western Europe than in North America. The ideological underpinning of parties may also include nationalism, regionalism, religion, ethnicity, language, culture, and so on, so that ideological classification tends to be complex.

Parties may also be classified according to the way in which they are organized. Membership, for example, may be open to anyone sympathetic to the party's policies and willing to pay a small subscription, or it may be limited and controlled. Power within the party may be highly centralized or dispersed and the membership may merely endorse the decisions of the leadership or it may have a meaningful impact on the determination of party policy. Finally, in systems, which allow electoral competition between parties, parties may be classified according to the sources of their electoral support, which may be based on various socio-economic differences, such as class, religion, ethnicity, and region.

Party systems

Parties may also be classified according to the type of party system in which they operate. The most useful classification is based on the extent to which a party system is competitive. Thus in the former Soviet Union the Communist Party was the only party that legally existed and there was no open electoral competition between candidates from rival parties for election. Such a system is known as the one-party system.

In other countries, such as India, electoral competition may exist among a number of parties, one of which, in this case the Congress party, governed continuously for 50 years; these are known as one-party dominant systems.

In countries such as the United States, vigorous electoral competition exists between two major parties, each of which wins office from time to time, hence the nomenclature 'two-party system'. Western European countries, however, have multiparty systems involving electoral competition between three or more parties. The reasons why the degree of electoral competition, where it is permitted, varies are extremely complex. There is a partial association between the existence of two-party systems and the simple plurality electoral system, which tends to discriminate elect orally in favour of parties with the larger electoral support, but it is misleading to attribute multiparty systems to proportional representation systems which, as their name implies, give each party a number of seats in the legislature in proportion to the vote it receives.

In general, party systems are a reflection of the cleavages in the society in which they exist. A widely fragmented society, such as France, exhibiting many deep social cleavages, is likely to have a fragmented party system, which reflects those cleavages, and, where it is used, proportional representation serves only to reflect them more accurately in electoral competition. Ironically, for most of its modern history France has not used proportional representation. More homogeneous societies, such as Britain, are more likely to produce a two-party system, although it is important to point out that if proportional representation existed in Britain no party would normally win a majority of the seats in the House of Commons. This is not to say, however, that proportional representation would necessarily alter the fact that electoral competition is primarily two-party.

There may also be important historical reasons why a two-party system exists, in that the parties may represent traditional lines of cleavage, as in the United States. Moreover, institutional factors may also be important: British government has institutionalized the roles of government and opposition, for instance, whilst the fact that the chief executive power of the United States is vested in a single person is regarded as an important factor in the creation and maintenance of a two-party system simply because the office of President cannot be divided. In France, for instance, the creation of a similar executive under the Fifth Republic has encouraged the parties of the Left to unite in support of a single candidate for president in opposition to their Gaullist rivals.

Party government

The chief significance of political parties is that in many, though not all countries, governments are formed by parties and may be opposed by other parties seeking to replace the government. In some cases, as we have seen, it is by a single party, sometimes in a competition in a non-competitive situation. In other cases the government may be a coalition of two or more parties in multiparty systems, since often no party has a majority of seats in the legislature.

It is important, however, to distinguish between those instances in which the party is the basis of the government in that the existence of the government is dependent on the strength of the party. In many cases the government exists with support of other political parties. In countries as disparate as France and the United States the former is the case, but in countries in which power is invested primarily in a single person, political parties, where they are allowed to exist, may only serve to support the regime. In either case, however, parties are important means of seeking to legitimize the actions and policies of governments, thus acting as agencies of political mobilization.[1]

Political Philosophy

Political philosophy is the study of such topics as liberty, justice, property, rights, law, and the enforcement of a legal code by authority: what they are, why (or even if) they are needed, what makes a government legitmate, what rights and freedoms it should protect and why, what form it should take and why, what the law is, and what duties citizens owe to a legitimate government, if any, and when it may be legitimately overthrown—if ever. In a vernacular sense, the term "political philosophy" often refers to a general view, or specific ethnic, political belief or attitude, about politics that does not necessarily belong to the technical discipline of philosophy. Political philosophy can also be understood by analysing it through the perspectives of metaphysics, episternology and axiology thereby unearthing the ultimate reality side, the knowledge or methodical side and the value aspects of politics. Then it gives insights into the various aspects of the origin of the state, its institutions and laws.

Many political parties base their political action and election program on an ideology. In social studies, a political ideology is a certain ethical set of ideas, principles, doctrines, myths or symbols of a social movement, institution, class, and or large group that explains how society should work, and offers some political and cultural blueprint for a certain social order. A political ideology largely concerns itself with how to allocate power and to what ends it should be used. Some parties follow a certain ideology very closely, while others may take broad inspiration from a group of related ideologies without specifically

[1] Helicon Publishing 2009, Research Machines p/c

embracing any one of them. The popularity of an ideology is in part due to the influence of **moral entrepreneurs**, who sometimes act in their own interests.

Political ideologies have two dimensions:

(a)**Goals**: How society should function or be organized.
(b)**Methods**: The most appropriate way to achieve goal

An ideology is a collection of ideas. Typically, each ideology contains certain ideas on what it considers to be the best form of government (e.g. democracy, autocracy, etc.), and the best economic system (e.g. capitalism, socialism etc.). Sometimes the same word is used to identify both an ideology and one of its main ideas. For instance, "socialism" may refer to an economic system, or it may refer to an ideology which supports that economic system.

Ideologies also identify themselves by their position on the political apectrum (such as the left, the center or the right), though this is very often controversial. Finally, ideologies can be distinguished from political strategies (e.g. populism) and from single issues that a party may be built around (e.g. opposition to European integration or the legalization of marijuana).[2]

Political Organization

A political party is a political organization that typically seeks to influence government policy, usually by nominating their own candidates and trying to seat them in political office. Parties participate in electoral campaigns, educational outreach or protest actions. Parties often espouse an

---

[2] Wikipedia, the free encyclopedia

expressed ideology or vision bolstered by a written platform with specific goals, forming a coalition among disparate interests.

The type of electoral system is a major factor in determining the type of party political system. In countries with first past the post voting systems there is an increased likelihood for the establishment of a two party system. Countries that have a proportional representation voting system, as exists throughout Europe, or to a greater extent preferential voting system, such as in Australia or Ireland, three or more parties are often elected to public office.

Political parties are funded by contributions from party members, individuals and organizations which share their political ideas or who stand to benefit from their activities or governmental public funding. Political parties and factions, especially those in government, are lobbied vigorously by organizations, businesses and special interest groups such as trade unions. Money and gifts to a party, or its members, may be offered as incentives.

The French political scientist Maurice Duverger drew a distinction between cadre parties and mass parties. Cadre parties were political elites that were concerned with contesting elections and restricted the influence of outsiders, who were only required to assist in election campaigns. Mass parties tried to recruit new members who were a source of party income and were often expected to spread party ideology as well as assist in elections. Because cadre parties could not expect great loyalty, many have become hybrids, maintaining elite control while expanding membership. Socialist parties are examples of mass parties, while the British Conservative Party and the German Christian democratic Union are examples of hybrid parties. In the United States, where both major parties were cadre parties, the introduction of primaries and other reforms has transformed them so that power is held by activists who compete over influence and nomination of candidates.

Klaus von Beyme categorized European parties into nine families, which described most parties. He was able to arrange seven of them from left to right: Communist, Socialist, Green, Liberal, Christian Democratic, Conservative and Libertarian. The position of two other types is Agrarian party and Regional / Ethnic parties. Other political parties are Islamic political parties, such as Huzb ut-Tahrir.

Political Thought

The history of political thought goes back to antiquity. The political history of the world, and thus the history of political thinking by man, stretches up though the medieval period and the Renaissance. In the Age of Enlightenment, political entities expanded from basic systems of self - governance and monarchy to the complex democratic and communist systems that exist of the Industrialized and the Modern Era, in parallel, political systems have expanded from vaguely defined frontier-type boundaries, to the definite boundaries existing today.

The process includes Antiquity, Medieval Islam, Medieval Europe, European Renaisance, European Age of Emlightenment and Industrial and Modern Era.

Plato and Aristotle are the pioneer political philosophers in the world. Plato's Republic and Aristotle's Politics secured the two Greek philosophers as two of the most influential political philosophers.

Industrialization and the Modern Era:

Karl Marx and his theory of Communism developed along with Friedrich Engels proved to be one of the most influential political ideologies of the 20th century.

The industrial revolution produced a parallel revolution in political thought. Urbanization and capitalism greatly reshaped society. During this same period, the socialist movement began to form. In the mid-19th century, Marxism was developed, and socialism in general gained increasing popular support, mostly from the urban working class. By the late 19th century, socialism and trade unions were established along with members of the political landscape. In addition, the various branches of anarchism and syndicalism also gained some prominence, particularly in Spain and France. In the Anglo-American world, anti-imperialism and pluralism began gaining currency at the turn of the century.

World War I was a watershed event in human history. The Russian Revolution of 1917 (and similar, albeit less successful, revolutions in many other European countries) brought communism - and in particular the political theory of Leninism, but also on a smaller level Luxemburgism (gradually) - on the world stage. At the same time, social democratic parties won elections and formed governments for the first time, often as a result of the introduction of universal suffrage. However, a group of central European economists led by Austrians Ludwig von Mises and friedrich Hayek identified the collectivist underpinnings to the various new socialist and fascist doctrines of government power as being different brands of political totalitarianism.[3]

Education and the Value of Justice

As an account of political organization on the larger scale, Plato's defense of an aristocratic government was unlikely to win broad approval in democratic

[3] Wikipedia, the free encyclopedia

Athens. He used the characters Glaucon and Adeimantus to voice practical objections against the plan. They are especially concerned (as Plato's Athenian contemporaries may well have been) with some of its provisions for the guardian class, including the participation of both men and women, the elimination of families, and the education of children.

Most fifth-century Greeks, like many twentieth-century Americans, supposed that natural differences between males and females of the human species entail a significant differentiation of their proper social roles. Although Plato granted that men and women are different in height, strength, and similar qualities, he noted that these differences are not universal; that is, for example, although it may be true that most men are taller than most women, there are certainly some women who are taller than many men. What is more, he denied that there is any systematic difference between men and women with respect to the abilities relevant to guardianship—the capacity to understand reality and make reasonable judgments about it. Thus, Plato maintained that prospective guardians, both male and female, should receive the same education and be assigned to the same vital functions within the society.

In addition, Plato believed that the interests of the state are best preserved if children are raised and educated by the society as a whole, rather than by their biological parents. So he proposed a simple (if startlingly unfamiliar) scheme for the breeding, nurturing, and training of children in the guardian class. (Note that the same children who are not permitted to watch and listen to "dangerous" art are encouraged to witness first-hand the violence of war.) The presumed pleasures of family life, Plato held, are among the benefits that the higher classes of a society must be prepared to forego.

Philosopher / Kings

A general objection to the impracticability of the entire enterprise remains. Even if we are persuaded that Plato's aristocracy is the ideal way to structure a city-state, is there any possibility that it will actually be implemented in a human society? Of course there is a sense in which it doesn't matter; what ought to be is more significant for Plato than what is, and philosophers generally are concerned with a truth that transcends the facts of everyday life.

But Plato also believed that an ideal state, embodying the highest and best capabilities of human social life, can really be achieved, if the right people are put in charge. Since the key to the success of the whole is the wisdom of the rulers who make decisions for the entire city, Plato held that the perfect society will occur only when kings become philosophers or philosophers are made kings.

Only those with a philosophical temperament, Plato supposed, are competent to judge between what merely seems to be the case and what really is, between the misleading, transient appearances of sensible objects and the the permanent reality of unchanging, abstract forms. Thus, the theory of forms is central to Plato's philosophy once again: the philosophers who think about such things are not idle dreamers, but the true realists in a society. It is precisely their detachment from the realm of sensory images that renders them capable of making accurate judgments about the most important issues of human life.

Thus, despite prevalent public skepticism about philosophers, it is to them that an ideal society must turn for the wisdom to conduct its affairs properly. But philosophers are made, not born. So we need to examine the program of education by means of which Plato supposed that the future philosopher-kings can acquire the knowledge necessary for their function as decision-makers for the society as a whole.

Structure of Human Knowledge

Since an ideal society will be ruled by those of its citizens who are most aware of what really matters, it is vital to consider how that society can best raise and educate its philosophers. Plato supposed that under the usual haphazard methods of childrearing, accidents of birth often restrict the opportunities for personal development; faulty upbringing prevents most people from achieving everything of which they are capable, and the promise of easy fame or wealth distracts some of the most able young people from the rigors of intellectual pursuits. But he believed that those with the greatest ability—that is, people with a natural disposition fit for philosophical study—must receive the best education, engaging in a regimen of mental discipline that grows stricter with every passing year of their lives.

The highest goal in all of education, Plato believed, is knowledge of the Good; that is, not merely an awareness of particular benefits and pleasures, but acquaintance with the Form itself. Just as the sun provides illumination by means of which we are able to perceive everything in the visual world, he argued, so the Form of the Good provides the ultimate standard by means of which we can apprehend the reality of everything that has value. Objects are worthwhile to the extent that they participate in this crucial form.

So, too, our apprehension of reality occurs in different degrees, depending upon the nature of the objects with which it is concerned in each case. Thus, there is a fundamental difference between the mere opinion we can have regarding the visible realm of sensible objects and the genuine knowledge we can have of the invisible realm of the Forms themselves.

In fact, Plato held that each of these has two distinct varieties, so that we can picture the entire array of human cognition as a line divided proportionately into four segments.

At the lowest level of reality are shadows, pictures, and other images, with respect to which imagination or conjecture is the appropriate degree of awareness, although it provides only the most primitive and unreliable opinions. The visible realm also contains ordinary physical objects, and our perception of them provides the basis for belief, the most accurate possible conception of the nature and relationship of temporal things.

Moving upward into the intelligible realm, we first become acquainted with the relatively simple Forms of numbers, shapes, and other mathematical entities; we can achieve systematic knowledge of these objects through a disciplined application of the understanding.

Finally, at the highest level of all, are the more significant Forms—true Equality, Beauty, Truth, and of course the Good itself. These permanent objects of knowledge are directly apprehended by intuition, the fundamental capacity of human reason to comprehend the true nature of reality.

The Allegory of the Cave

Plato recognized that the picture of the Divided Line may be difficult for many of us to understand. Although it accurately represents the different levels of reality and corresponding degrees of knowledge, there is a sense in which one cannot appreciate its full significance without first having achieved the highest level. So, for the benefit of those of us who are still learning but would like to grasp what he is talking about, Plato offered a simpler story in which each of the same structural components appears in a way that we can all comprehend at our own level. This is the Allegory of the Cave.

Suppose that there is a group of human beings who have lived their entire lives trapped in a subterranean chamber lit by a large fire behind them. Chained in place, these cave-dwellers can see nothing but shadows (of their own bodies and of other things) projected on a flat wall in front of them. Some of these people will be content to do no more than notice the play of light and shadow, while the cleverer among them will become highly skilled observers of the patterns that most regularly occur. In both cases, however, they cannot truly comprehend what they see, since they are prevented from grasping its true source and nature.

Now suppose that one of these human beings manages to break the chains, climb through the torturous passage to the surface, and escape the cave. With eyes accustomed only to the dim light of the former habitation, this individual will at first be blinded by the brightness of the surface world, able to look only upon the shadows and reflections of the real world. But after some time and effort, the former cave-dweller will become able to appreciate the full variety of the newly-discovered world, looking at trees, mountains, and (eventually) the sun itself.

Finally, suppose that this escapee returns to the cave, trying to persuade its inhabitants that there is another, better, more real world than the one in which they have so long been content to dwell. They are unlikely to be impressed by the pleas of this extraordinary individual, Plato noted, especially since their former companion, having travelled to the bright surface world, is now inept and clumsy in the dim realm of the cave. Nevertheless, it would have been in the best interest of these residents of the cave to entrust their lives to the one enlightened member of their company, whose acquaintance with other things is a unique qualification for genuine knowledge.

Plato seriously intended this allegory as a representation of the state of ordinary human existence. We, like the people raised in a cave, are trapped in a world of impermanence and partiality, the realm of sensible objects. Entranced by the particular and immediate experiences these things provide, we are unlikely to appreciate the declarations of philosophers, the few among us who, like the escapee, have made the effort to achieve eternal knowledge of the permanent forms. But, like them, it would serve us best if we were to follow this guidance, discipline our own minds, and seek an accurate understanding of the highest objects of human contemplation.

An Educational Program

Having already described the elementary education and physical training that properly occupy the first twenty years of the life of prospective guardians, Plato applied his account of the structure of human knowledge in order to prescribe the disciplined pursuit of their higher education.

It naturally begins with mathematics, the vital first step in learning to turn away from the realm of sensible particulars to the transcendent forms of reality. Arithmetic provides for the preliminary development of abstract concepts, but Plato held that geometry is especially valuable for its careful attention to the eternal forms. Study of the (mathematical, not observational) disciplines of astronomy and harmonics encourage the further development of the skills of abstract thinking and proportional reasoning.

Only after completing this thorough mathematical foundation are the future rulers of the city prepared to begin their study of philosophy, systematizing their grasp of mathematical truth, learning to recognize and eliminate all of their presuppositions, and grounding all genuine knowledge firmly on the foundation of their intuitive grasp of the reality of the Forms. Finally, an extended period of apprenticeship will help them to learn how to apply everything they have learned to the decisions necessary for the welfare of the city as a whole. Only in their fifties will the best philosophers among them be fit to rule over their fellow-citizens.

Kinds of State or Person

In order to explain the distinction between justice and injustice more fully, Plato devoted much of the remainder of *The Republic* to a detailed discussion of five different kinds of government (and, by analogy, five different kinds of person), ranked in order from best to worst:

(a)A society organized in the ideally efficient way Plato has already described is said to have an **aristocratic** government. Similarly, an aristocratic person is one whose rational, spirited, and appetitive souls work together properly. Such governments and people are the most genuine examples of true justice at the social and personal levels.

(b) In a defective society, on the other hand, the courageous soldiers have usurped for themselves the privilege of making decisions that properly belongs only to its better-educated rulers. A **timocratic** person is therefore someone who is more concerned with belligerently defending personal honor than with wisely choosing what is truly best.

(c) In an **oligarchic** government, both classes of guardian have been pressed into the service of a ruling group comprising a few powerful and wealthy citizens. By analogy, an oligarchic personality is someone who's every thought and action is devoted to the self-indulgent goal of amassing greater wealth.

(d) Even more disastrously, a democratic government holds out the promise of equality for all of its citizens but delivers only the anarchy of an unruly mob, each of whose members is interested only in the pursuit of private interests. The parallel case of a democratic person is someone who is utterly controlled by desires, acknowledging no bounds of taste or virtue in the perpetual effort to achieve the momentary satisfaction that pleasure provides.

(e) Finally, the **tyrannical** society is one in which a single individual has gained control over the mob, restoring order in place of anarchy, but serving only personal welfare instead of the interests of the whole city. A tyrranic person, then, must be one whose entire life is focussed upon the satisfaction of a single desire at the expense of everything else that truly matters. Governments and people of this last variety are most perfectly unjust, even though they may appear to be well-organized and effective.

Although Plato presents these five types of government or person as if there is a natural progression from each to the next, his chief concern is to exhibit the relative degree of justice achieved by each. The most perfect contrast between justice and injustice arises in a comparison between the aristocratic and the tyrranic instances.

Justice is better than Injustice

Thus, we are finally prepared to understand the full force of Plato's answer to the original challenge of showing that justice is superior to injustice. He offered three arguments, each of which is designed to demonstrate the intrinsic merits of being a just person.

First, Plato noted that the just life of an aristocratic person arises from an effortless harmony among internal elements of the soul, while the unjust life of a tyrranic person can maintain its characteristic imbalance only by the exertion of an enormous effort. Thus, it is simply easier to be just than to be unjust. This argument makes sense even independently of Plato's larger theory; it is a generalized version of the fairly common notion that it is easier to be honest than to keep track of the truth along with a number of false stories about it.

Second, Plato claimed that tyrranic individuals can appreciate only pleasures of the body, monetary profits, and the benefits of favorable public reputation, all of which are by their nature transitory. Aristocratic people, on the other hand, can accept these things in moderation but also transcend them in order to enjoy the delights of intellectual achievement through direct acquaintance with the immutable forms. This argument relies more heavily upon adoption of Plato's entire theory of human nature, as developed in *The Republic* and other dialogues; it is likely to influence only those who have already experienced the full range of intellectual advantages for themselves.

Finally, Plato resorted to myth (just as he had at the close of the *Phaedo* by imagining that justice will be rewarded with steady progression in a series of lives hereafter. This "Myth of Er" isn't philosophical argument at all. Even if it were literally true and demonstrable that the just are rewarded in the afterlife, that would be only an extrinsic motive for being just, not a proof of its intrinsic value.

Although it is a masterly treatment of human nature and politics, *The Republic* was not Plato's only discussion of these significant issues. His dialogue Gorgias includes an eloquent appeal on behalf of the life of justice and personal non-violence in all things.

The *Statesman* devotes extended attention to the practical matter of securing effective government under the less-than-ideal conditions most of us commonly face. And the unfinished Law is a lengthy analysis of the history of Athenian political life.[4]

The Politics of Welfare

Edmund Burke wrote that "government is a contrivance of human wisdom to provide for human wants". Governments have a wide range of possible actions. Governments establish rules. Governments set the rules by which they and other organisations (like companies or charities) operate. Governments coerce. Governments can prohibit action (such as child abuse), or require some forms of action (such as sending children to school). Governments provide or purchase services. Provision means that states provide services themselves. Public housing, national health services or state education are examples. Purchasing services implies that the state accepts responsibility for ensuring provision, but that the service can be obtained from another agency.

(a) Governments subsidise: Subsidy consists of a financial inducement to act in a particular way, which may be a reward for doing things (e.g. increasing employment), a form of compensation, or an incentive to do things. Tax can be used in the opposite direction, as a negative subsidy - e.g. to deter people from smoking.
(b) Governments persuade: Examples are propaganda, exhortation and directed education.
(c) Governments plan: Governments 'steer' a society by watching and adjusting policy.

---

[4] Garth Kemerling, Philosophy Pages – Com / hy, last modified 27th October, 2001

(d) Governments produce: Like independent organisations, governments may offer services to customers - e.g. insurance, banking or commercial production. There is no rule which says that government activity has to be tax-based or financed.

(e) Ideology and social welfare: Political views on welfare are often divided into 'left' and 'right' wing views.

The positions people hold are not, however, straightforward. There is an individualistic left wing, and a collectivist right wing. Left-wingers favour social security (which enables people to buy food in the private market) rather than soup kitchens (which can be publicly provided). Many right-wingers accept the principle of institutional welfare, and many left-wingers are uncomfortable about institutional measures, like earnings-related pensions or student grants, which favour richer people over poorer ones.[5]

From the perspective of welfare, the main political positions are:

Marxism

Marxists see society in terms of a conflict between economic classes. A dominant class (the bourgeoisie or 'capitalist' class) owns and controls the means of production; an industrial working class, the 'proletariat', is exploited by them. The Marxist analysis of welfare concentrates principally on its relationship to the exercise of power. The state can be seen either as an instrument of the ruling capitalist class or as a complex set of systems which reflects the contradictions of the society it is part of. It is often argued that welfare has been developed

---

[5] Paul Spicker, "The Politics of Welfare", An Introduction of Social Policy, Wikipedia

through the strength of working-class resistance to exploitation.

Marxism is not a single doctrine; it has come to stand for a wide range of opinions within an analytical framework that is critical of 'capitalist' society. Neo-marxists argue that the state has two main functions. The first is to improve the conditions for the accumulation of capital - that is, the chance for industries to make profits. The second is to legitimate the capitalist system, by introducing measures (like welfare policies, pensions and health services) which lead people to accept the system as it stands. The requirements of accumulation and legitimation may be contradictory, and the costs of legitimation have led to a 'legitimation crisis'.

The basic objections to Marxist analyses are that the description of 'capitalism' is false; that power in society is divided, and not based in ownership; and that states which promote the welfare of their citizens are not pretending to be more legitimate - they are more legitimate.

Socialism

There are many forms of socialism. The main models, which can be found in various permutations, include representations of socialism as

(a) A general movement for the improvement of society by collective action (for example, in Fabianism)
(b) a set of methods and approaches linked with collective action, such as cooperatives, mutual aid, planning and social welfare services (e.g. the co-operative movement);
(c) A set of arguments for social and economic organisation based on ownership and control by the community (e.g. in syndicalism, guild socialism and anarchism)

(d) An ideal model of society based on cooperation and equality (e.g. Owenism);
(e) A critique of industrial society, opposing selfish individualism (e.g. Christian socialism), and
(f) A range of values, rather than a particular view of how society works (e.g. the position of the Parti Socialiste Européen in the European Union).

Socialism is misrepresented in many popular texts, which confuse it with Marxism. Marxists want to claim that socialism is just another name for Marxism; right-wing critics want to describe socialism as communism by another name, with the state running everything. Marxism was the most prominent form of socialism in the early 20th century, but socialism is not equivalent to Marxism. The Marxist analysis of society is irrelevant too much of the mainstream of European socialism, which grew from a range of religious, occupational and communal groups. Historically, socialism is strongly associated with working-class movements, and in much of Europe 'socialist' issues are closely linked with labour relations. The largest socialist group in the European Union identifies its role in terms of socialist values and principles rather than an ideal model of society.

The key socialist values are collectivism, empowerment and egalitarianism - the 'liberty, equality, and fraternity' of the French revolution, interpreted in collective and social terms. Some socialists would add to those issues of rights and democracy.

Socialism is collectivist

People have to be understood in social context, rather than as individuals. Socialism is often represented in Europe in terms of 'solidarity', which means not just only standing shoulder-to-shoulder but the creation of systems of mutual aid.

Socialism calls for people to be enabled to do things through collective action, a principle variously referred to as 'freedom' and (in recent years) as 'empowerment'. This principle has been central to 'guild socialism' and trades unionism.

Socialism is egalitarian, in the sense that socialists are committed to the reduction or removal of disadvantages which arise in society. The 'Fabian' tradition, a reformist movement, attempted to achieve greater equality through spending on social services.

Social democracy

Social democracy depends, like socialism, on the values of liberty, equality and fraternity (or solidarity). This is fused with a model of liberal democracy, based on rights.

The differences between social democrats and socialists are hazy, because their ideals may coincide in some aspects and not in others, but two are particularly important. First, many social democrats are individualists rather than collectivists; even if they accept arguments for mutual aid or the reduction of disadvantage, they think it important to stress the liberty of the individual, to develop individual rights (as liberals do), and often to restrict the role of the state. Second, some social democrats are not concerned to remove inequality, but only to mitigate its effects through social arrangements which protect people from the worst consequences of a market society. Others favour equality of opportunity, which implies the opportunity to be unequal.

Conservatism

Conservatives believe in the importance of social order. This is reflected in a respect for tradition, an emphasis on the importance of religion, and a stress on the importance of inequality - such as inequalities of class or caste - as the basis for structured social relationships. Welfare is a secondary issue, but the kinds of concerns which conservatives have are likely to impose restraints on welfare, with a particular emphasis on traditional values in work, the family, and nationhood. Welfare does raise concern where it is seen to have implications for public order - one British conservative commented, in commending the Beveridge report, that "if you do not give the people social reform they are going to give you revolution."

Christian democratic thought is closely related to conservatism, but it also has important distinguishing features. Like conservatives, Christian Democrats place a strong emphasis on order; but order is to be achieved, not primarily through state action, but by moral restraints. These moral restraints have principally in Europe reflected the influence of the Catholic religion. Catholic social teaching has emphasised both the limits of the state and the responsibility of people in families and communities for each other; Christian democrats tend, then, to favour limitations in the role of the state while at the same time accepting moral responsibility for social welfare.

Liberal individualism

Liberalism begins from the premise that everyone is an individual, and that individuals have rights. As a political position, liberalism has been important as a means of defending people from abuse by authority. Although liberalism was initially a radical doctrine, it has also been used since the 19th century to stand for a defence of propertied interests.

The central value of liberalism is freedom. All freedoms are not equally important; the main liberal values are concerned with certain particularly important freedoms, such as freedom of assembly, of speech, and of worship.

Liberals mistrust the state and argue that society is likely to regulate itself if state interference is removed. Hayek argues that all state activity, whatever its intentions, is liable to undermine the freedom of the individual; that society is too complex to be tampered with; and that the activities of the free market, which is nothing more than the sum total of activities of many individuals, constitute the best protection of the rights of each individual.

Fascism

Fascism is often represented in the academic literature as a pseudo-ideology, lacking any coherence or system of thought. This was a political position taken post-war in an attempt to deny the romantic and emotional appeal of fascist thought. Fascist ideology is based in an authoritarian collectivism. The individual is meaningless; the collectivity (the state, the nation or the race) is paramount.

Fascism has been characterised by a strong social agenda; in Nazi Germany, the desire to foster racial supremacy included extensive state intervention in society and the economy, with a stress on socialisation (both through schooling and youth movements) and eugenic policies.

Eugenic ideologies existed before fascism, and although they were discredited by their association with medical murder and the holocaust they have resurfaced in recent years. They are characterised by the nineteenth-century belief that socially constructed characteristics, like poverty, crime or sexuality are inborn, and that they will inevitably find a way to emerge unless breeding is regulated. Repeated attempts in social science have found no empirical support for the belief that such characteristics are replicated between generations.

Currently the extreme right in Europe is racialist and nationalist rather than collectivist. The Front National in France has argued for a 'national preference''. The FN mayor at Vitrolles, for example, offered a bounty for children born, for "French families" only.

The economics of the welfare state

Social policy is to a large extent dominated by economic policy, because economic policy determines the amount that government is prepared to spend. There are two main views of public spending: monetarist and Keynesian.

Monetarism is based on a view of the economy as self-stabilising. In times of stringency, it is necessary to reduce spending, on the basis that increased saving will lead to growth later. If the government does not balance its budget, there will be inflation (money will be worth less) and there will be fewer resources available to the private sector for the economy to expand productively.

Keynesians sees government intervention in the economy as necessary for the stability of the economy. Public spending is an important regulator, which can be used to stimulate the economy at a time of a slump or to damp down growth if it happens too quickly. Unemployment is unnecessarily wasteful. In the long run, Keynes argued, the economy may correct itself; but in the long run, 'we are all dead'.

In recent years both views have been supplanted by a new financial orthodoxy, which combines government regulation with market-based provision, "targeted" expenditure and balanced budgets.

The welfare state and economic performance

There are competing views of the impact of social welfare on the economy. One view, the 'handmaiden' model, sees welfare as an essential complement to industrial development: social policy helps the economy to grow by serving the workforce, providing services to industry and offering a secure basis for development. This has been the dominant model in Germany. Keynesian economics sees spending on welfare as a useful economic regulator, helping to balance the economy in periods of recession. On the other hand, both neo-liberal and Marxists have represented the welfare state as a major burden on economic performance. Public expenditure is seen as a fetter on economic growth.

There is no consistent evidence to support either view. The relationship of the economy and public spending is complex. Atkinson has brought together evidence from a wide range of opposing studies. Although developed countries generally spend more on welfare than less developed countries, developed countries with higher welfare spending do not generally do better or worse than developed countries which have less. The graph, drawn from OECD data, shows no clear, consistent pattern. Beyond the OECD, the general trend is that richer countries tend to spend higher proportions of their GDP on social protection.

The 'crisis' of welfare

The term "crisis" is used fairly indiscriminately by critics of the right and left. From the perspective of the right is undesirable and economically damaging. To Marxists, welfare is often represented as unsustainable. Neither position is supported consistently by the evidence, but as both positions are held on faith they have been impossible to dislodge.

Pierson points to three main uses of the idea of a "crisis". They are:

(a) **Crisis as a turning point.** A crisis is a period when long standing problems become particularly severe.
(b) **Crisis as an external shock**. Examples include war, problems in the international economy or the "oil crisis" of the 1970s.
(c) **Crisis as a long standing contradiction.** Marxists believe that welfare and capitalism are incompatible, and have been claiming that crises spell doom for a hundred and fifty years.

If we take "crisis" in its normal, everyday sense, as a sudden, serious problem, there is no current crisis of welfare.

The ideal political philosophy

A diagram of the political spectrum can be drawn as a horizontal line on the board and labeled the left end as "communist" and the right end as "fascist". A mark in the center of that line segment is labeled as "moderate." Half-way from the left of "moderate," is labeled as "liberal." Halfway between "moderate" and "fascist" is designated as "conservative." This diagram has become the "accepted" illustration of the political spectrum. There are two extremes — communism and fascism. But the ideal is the center. Liberalism is left of center and conservatism is right of center. The ideal is a compromise, or a happy medium between the two extremes. The ideal is directly between liberalism and conservatism.

This illustration—this diagram—is absolutely false, of course, because it misidentifies the two political extremes. But more importantly, it completely disregards the true political ideal. For this very reason, it is perilously misleading.

The nature of the "extremes"

It is very true that two "extremes" exist among all of the political systems ever devised by man. One is "extremely" good and the other is extremely evil. The good "extreme" also happens to be the only true political ideal.

The evil extreme has been practiced/enforced by every tyrant, every king, and every dictator—by virtually every "political leader" or group of leaders—since the dawn of civilization. Both Hitler (the ultimate fascist) and Stalin (arguably the ultimate communist) practiced this evil extreme. Communism and fascism is the same thing! Totalitarian socialism—in any form and to any degree—is the ultimate evil extreme.

Realistically, the only difference between communism and fascism is that communism represents international socialism and fascism is founded upon National Socialism. If your civics teacher was anything like either my public high school civics teacher or my state university political philosophy professor, then he/she may have tried to argue that communism is not an extreme. Rather, communism is an "ideal" that has been ineffectually attempted from time to time, but has never been given the opportunity to be properly and fully implemented. In my humble—largely self-educated—opinion, knowledge of both human nature and human history unquestionably refutes this very idea.

Communism, fascism, and every form of totalitarianism (i.e., any degree and every form of tyranny) represent the evil extreme of any true and honest illustration of the political spectrum. What then, represents the good extreme? What is the ideal political philosophy? If totalitarianism, tyranny is evil, then the opposite of tyranny is good. That opposite good is necessarily liberty.

True liberty

America's Founders understood the difference between tyranny and liberty. America's Founders also knew the difference between liberty and license.

In short, license means absolute individual freedom to do, to think, or to say anything and everything a person wants as long as it does not directly harm another living and breathing human being. A person is answerable only to himself. There is no higher authority than man. Liberty, on the other hand, means absolute individual freedom to do, to think, or to say anything an individual wants as long as it does not violate the Laws of Nature and of Nature's God. America's Founders knew, without doubt, that liberty comes from God. Liberty demands responsibility to the Ultimate Author of Law. License leads to anarchy, and anarchy breed's tyranny.

Both the understanding of liberty and the hatred of tyranny are clearly seen in the many writings of America's Founding Fathers—most notably, of course, in the Declaration of Independence. The Founders' understanding of human nature is abundantly evident. They wanted no part of any monarchy.

They wanted a severely limited national government so that power could never be concentrated in the hands of a corrupt few.

They demanded checks and balances among the branches of government. They established short terms of office for elected officials.

They warned the people over and over again that the political system, which they had labored long and hard, to establish, would not last long unless the people remained generally moral (virtuous), educated, and informed.

Our constitutional system

This labor of love, this political system that the Founders bequeathed to those of us who are privileged to be called as "Americans," is of course the constitutional republic. It is not a democracy. Democracy is mob rule. Mob rule is, basically, anarchy. In every true democracy, the will of the majority always crushes the will of any minority. Neither was it intended to consist of powerful, bloated bureaucracies. Centralized bureaucracies place unwarranted power in the hands of a select few and rob the liberties of the people. The constitutional republic that America's Founders established is both the good "extreme" and the ideal political system.

For the first time in human history, a political system had been established that fully understood human nature, completely rejected tyranny, and promoted—even demanded—human liberty.

A political conservative is one who wants to conserve (to preserve or to keep) the fundamental political system as it was intended from his nation's founding. A political liberal is one who wants to fundamentally alter the political philosophy upon which his nation was established. An American conservative wants to maintain the constitutional republic and every degree of liberty that it affords. However, as Paul Harvey often says, "Self-government will not (cannot) work without self-discipline."

An American liberal — often with little or no regard for individual responsibility or accountability (and certainly with no real understanding of either human nature, the evils of tyranny, or the true blessings of liberty) — seeks some form of bureaucratic (totalitarian) power in the name of "economic equality" (socialistic redistribution of wealth), "racial equality" (affirmative action quotas), "tolerance" (relativistic acceptance of even the most deviant behavior), "environmental security," or any number of other emotionally-charged issues.

Conservatives are right

An American moderate is one who seeks some safe and happy medium between conservative and liberal political ideology. After more than eighteen years of diligent research and deep philosophical thought, I have arrived at one brief conclusion regarding political ideology:

Conservatives are right, liberals are wrong, and moderates are confused. Moderates are very confused. [6]

Political Ideology

The fall of the Soviet Union and the collapse of communist economies in the late 20th century reinforced belief in capitalism. The phenomenal rise of the Chinese economy removed all doubt about its role in fuelling economic prosperity. India's own success with liberalisation has convinced its governments, major political parties, bureaucracy, big businesses, and many in civil society to abandon socialistic ideals in the single-minded pursuit of libertarian goals.

Despite the increase in the country's Gross Domestic Product (GDP), its ranking in the Human Development Index (HDI), its indices for maternal and infant mortality and its rates of under-nutrition of its people tell a completely different story. The burgeoning incomes of the wealthy increase the indices of growth; yet, these averages hide much poverty, suffering, loss of livelihoods and life. Capitalistic ideology, which has been driving recent growth, has its blind spots.

---

[6] Sam Weaver (2002), "The ideal political philosophy", Renew America, December 28, 2002

Basis of belief: All beliefs, including economic theories, stem from the ability of the human brain to recognise patterns and meaning in perceived information. People fashion particular beliefs from subjective, personal and emotional cues aided by social and historical contexts. Beliefs are constructed and then rationalized with supporting data; discarding of contrary evidence is common. Some researchers argue that beliefs determine reality and not the other way around. Yet, the most rational among us sincerely believe that we systematically sift information, identify facts and logically construct our arguments to form our beliefs.

For example, the wealthy, steeped in conservative ideology, often argue for tax breaks for the rich and reduced government spending for the poor to fuel growth. Their financial backgrounds and success in the free market colour their vision; they dismiss the lot of the poor, their lack of capital and the uneven playing field as inconsequential. On the other hand, liberals would support a priori social justice and equity arguing for higher taxes and increased government spending to improve the lives of the poor. The many arguments employed to support each of these positions are post hoc and based on particular beliefs.

Arguments with facts: Facts are used to attack opposing political rhetoric and economic theory. However, even strong arguments based on many undisputed facts are open to refutation, if they do not include all relevant information. The challenge is to include all relevant facts; ignoring some essential information can result in a false sense of confidence in our political and economic arguments. Good arguments require that we understand as many relevant facts as possible about the reality. Rational arguments based on authentic reality will be more convincing than perfectly logical opinions based on part perceptions.

Fiscal conservatives focus on average GDP figures, which increase by a disproportionate rise in the fortunes of the rich, often at the expense of the poor. On the other hand, liberals argue that trickle-down economics do not work resulting in even greater inequity, mandating governmental regulation and intervention for social justice. Ideological beliefs determine the type of selective blindness and consequent focus.

Ideological conflicts: Philosophers including Descartes have argued that we should start from obvious premises, self-evident to any rational person. However, a failure to agree on basic assumptions leads to a breakdown of rational arguments and the consequent refutation of many supposedly substantive claims. Such premises are based on mental pictures and world views, which, in our pluralistic world, are controversial. Family background and influence, schooling and education, training and work environments, friends, newspapers, television, internet blogs and diverse sources of knowledge determine our world views. Different people hold rival world views, which play a greater role than facts in reaching conclusions about politics, morals and religion.

Policymaking requires both theoretical knowledge and practical judgment for implementation. However, in pluralistic societies with different world views, mental pictures often eclipse facts. Nevertheless, identification and application of world views in policymaking requires the appreciation of exceptions to a particular world view. Such recognition and incorporation of these in planning is crucial for rational argument.

Fiscal conservatives believe in free markets, minimal regulation and small governments that maximize profit and increase capital, which they consider crucial for achieving social and economic good.

Liberals, on the other hand, focus on issues related to social justice and equity. They claim that individual aspiration and greed, in addition to capital used to maximize profits, can threaten the well-being of society and demand governmental regulation. Nevertheless, conservatives admit that some regulation is necessary while liberals acknowledge that too much control makes for bad economics. Both world views are legitimate and have valid exceptions, calling for diligence in policymaking and application.

Basis of policy:

(a) Which world view should India's policy makers subscribe to?
(b) Which facts should be highlighted to determine application?
(c) Should the fiscal stimulus to encourage economic growth give even greater tax breaks to the wealthy?
(d) Should mineral-rich forests, home to tribal people, be acquired by governments and transferred to multinationals and corporate for development?
(e) Is the world view of the tribal, who has been displaced by the clearing of forestland for mining, valid?
(f) Have the constitutional rights of farmers, whose lands are acquired by government for private housing, violated?
(g) Are the unemployed and those in extreme poverty entitled to social protection?
(h) Are the hungry and the malnourished entitled to food security?
(i) Should the poor always be required to sacrifice their lands and livelihoods for large dams to provide water and electricity to the rich?

Bias among decision makers: India's current decision makers, both politicians and bureaucrats, are products of the free market. It is no secret that members of legislative assemblies and of Parliament spend billions of state currencies to win elections. The unregulated Indian free market, with its crony capitalism of cuts, commissions, contracts and corruption, has aided and abetted their ascent to power. Similarly, many of our bureaucrats are schooled in elite capitalistic institutions. Capitalism now runs in their veins. They are not able to see, much less feel, the world of the dispossessed and disenfranchised poor.

Capitalistic thoughts are now well-entrenched habits, which accept the inequity produced by free markets as a given. The belief in the success of trickle-down economics is delusional. Reminders about the prevalent extreme poverty, significant unemployment, massive under-nutrition and chronic hunger are mere annoyances and irritations.

There is a split in the India question. Should India's economic policies focus on Shining India to stimulate growth or on the poor of Bharat to provide social, employment, food and health security? Should these policies heal the divide and reunite the country or should they focus solely on the growth story? Should India take its gaze off the GDP numbers and examine the impact of its policies on the HDI?

The people saw through the Bharatiya Janata Party's (BJP) India Shining Campaign. The United Progressive Alliance (UPA)-I's promise of an egalitarian society through its many progressive schemes — National Rural Employment Guarantee, National Rural Health Mission, Sarva Shiksha Abhiyan — paid handsome electoral dividends. However, UPA-II has moved to the right and is now defending the indefensible. It is coddling the rich at the expense of the poor. The lack of significant differences among major political parties, the Congress and the BJP, on financial and economic policies reflects the insensitivity of the ruling class to the needs of the majority.

Moving forward

The vision for a civilized society, enshrined in our Constitution, needs to fulfill the collective aspiration of the majority of its peoples. The focus on reducing poverty is a just cause. National policies and programmes should cater to the needs of the majority rather than add millions to the coffers of the wealthy. The magnitude of subsidies for the corporate sector and the scale of corruption in business dealings also suggest that the amount of monies actually available for social justice programmes exceed all expectation and only require political and administrative will for implementation.

The two very different ideologies will have to engage the big picture, focus on economic growth and on justice. The current emphasis that all ideas, including political and economic policies, be monetized needs to be replaced by an emphasis on justice and equity. Their intrinsic worth, currently measured by their impact on GDP, should be substituted by assessing their impact on humanity. Indian policymakers, driven by ideology, should also be able to see the exceptions to their conservative philosophy in order to be able to provide rational and just policies for the whole country. The magnitude of the poverty underscores the unethical position of the right-of-centre governments. There is a need for an overlapping consensus in which different groups, with different arguments, accept the centre ground. Surely, social justice and equity for millions of Indians is a worthy cause. [7]

INDIA: **Maoists bereft of Marxist Ideology**

The recent hostage crisis in Odisha has exposed the serious limitations of the far Left movement. The

---

[7] K S Jacob (2011), "Ideology, facts and the push to the right", The Hindu, September 12, 2011

abduction of functionaries of the state or the killing of security personnel or the boastful declaration of the liberated Red Corridor may garner enough publicity for gun-wielding Maoists but such strategies will definitely not help in achieving their goal of social transformation.

The society has changed a lot since the first Maoist uprising took place at Naxalbari in West Bengal in mid 1960s. New social challenges have emerged in the country over the last 50 years. The Maoist leadership has failed to demystify the complex and contradictory dialectics of social reality because leaders of the Maoist movement be it Kanu Sanyal or Charu Majumdar during mid-1960s or Kishenji of yesterday — have kept themselves away from the theory and praxis of Karl Marx.

Since Maoists in India do not really follow the philosophy of Karl Max, they have neither analysed nor understood the inherent flaws that characterised the Telangana People's Armed Struggle led by the Communist Party of India just after India got independence. The Communist Party of India abandoned the path of armed struggle because it realised after the withdrawal of peasants' struggle in Telangana that armed revolutionary struggles are completely counterproductive, even redundant, in India because people have accepted the politics of ballot.

Indians, since they actively participate in the electoral process, believe that democratically elected leaders will bring about social changes in the country. Maoists, on the other hand, have failed to understand that the level of social consciousness of the people, including the deprived, have undergone a sea change because of the ongoing democratic process.

Unlike Maoist leaders who prefer to fight guerilla wars, leaders of the Communist Party of India and the Communist Party of India (Marxists) have joined the mainstream politics, got democratically elected, formed Governments in West Bengal, Tripura and Kerala and have impacted national politics by their presence in Parliament.

The Governments ruled by Communist parties have successfully undertaken land reforms and restructuring of agrarian class relations. The Communist movements in India has brought together the peasantry, the urban working class and the lower middle-class intelligentsia on the same platform and have successfully launched struggles for better service conditions of workers and progressive legislation on social security.

This underscores the fact that Indian democracy provides enough political space for launching struggles for the rights of different social groups, including the proletariat. Therefore, the basic failure of Maoist leadership lies in the fact that they have completely misread the implications of democracy.

Further, Maoists are wrong in believing that struggles for the rights of tribals can be successful without a broad social platform. This is particularly true in a democracy like India, which is socially, politically and culturally diverse and where forming alliances with multiple social groups to achieve common goals is the norm. Precisely, this is the reason why Maosists lack any broad mass support.

Since Maoists do not Follow Karl Marx, they have not learnt the basic tenet of revolution — that lessons have to be learnt from every failed social struggle. Karl Marx declared in 1848 that the spectre of communism haunts Europe. But after its failure, he critically re-examined his theory on revolution.

Further, Maoists in India must realise that following Mao Tse-tung's ideology will not help because a Long

March, the central event in the Chinese revolution, is not possible in India as the Indian society and state are fundamentally different from that of Mao's China. Left parties in Indonesia, Malaysia, Thailand, Philippines, Burma and other countries, who are influenced by the Maoist ideology, have failed to achieve any success because they wanted to replicate Mao's revolution without understanding a simple fact that revolutions cannot be copied. Same holds true for Maoists in India.

In India, political leaders, since they are elected by the people, can claim legitimately that they represent the people and work for them. A competitive democratic politics provides an opportunity for political alternatives to contest against one another by mobilising social constituencies. Alterative levels of social consciousness can emerge and have emerged through democratic social struggles. But Indian Maoists are adopting short cuts to revolution because launching democratic struggle for people's rights requires a very sustained and patient political activity.

That Maoists in India are victims of serious limitations of their own theory was exposed during the recent 'hostage crisis' in the State of Odisha. The gun-wielding Maoists have witnessed how the poor tribals in Malkangiri turned hostile because of their deep sense of anger against the abduction of a popular district Collector. Maoists have to accept the serious limitations of politics of gun, in a functioning democracy like India. In fact, because of their slogan that 'revolution flows from the barrel of a gun', majority of landless agricultural labourers, marginal farmers, millions of deprived in rural and urban India have kept themselves away from Maoists ideology.[8]

---

[8] C P Bhambhri (2011), " Maoists bereft of Marxist Ideology", The Pioneer, March 4, 2011, friday

Chic despair

Politics' usually refers to flashy yet carefully staged electoral contests between candidates, who ordinary citizens had no hand in choosing and whose policies are filtered through the status quo biases of suave media commentators. But politics encompasses the use and abuse of power in all spheres of life, not just the voting booth or parliamentary chamber. Politics in our mass media age crucially is the quest to control the difference between what is happening and what people can be persuaded to imagine is happening. If you can plunder the hapless citizenry while inducing them to believe you thereby protect them, you win. Propaganda is the old-fashioned word for all the mandarin machinations that create a profitably self-serving gap twixt reality and delusion.

The dazed and confused citizens are informed that joblessness is lower than it is, that inflation is slower than it is that a few ragged jihadis are a threat worth wasting trillions to chase, that bailed-out banks are a social boon, and that a financier-caused downturn is over when plainly none of these daft assertions are true. Elites continue to bilk the population on the basis of messages they disseminate about the joys of savage capitalism, terrorists lurking under all our beds, and the virtue of universal surveillance. Why not? He who has the power to define the problem, after all, defines the solutions too. Privileged classes never miss a trick in steering the game their way. They triumph even when they fail, as the bailout, and the austerity-for-thee-and-not-for me regime accompanying it, demonstrate.

If you must work more hours then your parents and at less pay, and with fewer benefits, you have little time to find out for yourself what the implications of dubious policies are. So far as elites see it, the less leisure and fewer resources the citizenry enjoys, the better. In the 1970s, at the start of a ferocious corporate movement to erase every public benefit the US citizenry gained since the Great Depression, the Trilateral Commission, a club for global VIPs, issued a hand-wringing report on the 'crisis of democracy,' which rued the rise in the 1960s of nonconformist youth, meddlesome environmentalists, consumer advocates, and insolent minorities as all noxious forces interfering with elites' wise manipulation of national politics. The **'crisis of democracy'** was that unruly non-elites were taking democracy seriously by putting it into wider practice. The subsequent success of upper classes in achieving a self-enriching regressive agenda has been steady, cumulative, quiet and phenomenal, especially in the USA and UK. Politics also is about limits, about how far you can go in pursuing interests and what the costs and consequences are, and to whom.

The current US rulers believe no limits exist to a restoration of 19th century-style plutocracy. They are going for broke. Why? Because wrecking the system in 2008 worked out handsomely for them, with all benefits captured by the one per cent, with minor trickledown to the top 20 per cent, but no further down.

Since the 1960s the corporate contribution to total taxes fell from 20 per cent to under 9 per cent (with everyone else paying the difference in extra taxes or service cuts). A number of colossal firms pay little or no tax and, like especially oil companies, reap government benefits too. Taxes on the highest incomes steadily were slashed until they are a meagre third of what they were in the 1950s. Capital gains tax ~ a boon to the wealthy ~ is lower than personal tax. Few mainstream voices ask how this cunning arrangement can be justified as an incentive to invest in an economic climate starved of demand because wages are in decline for four out of five workers. Give investors everything they clamour for ~ deregulation, low wage conditions, offshore incentives ~ and you guarantee a breakdown in the system.

Wages were linked to productivity from World War II until the 1970s. Productivity rose over 80 per cent since 1983 while wages stagnated, guaranteeing an economic crisis. Workers did not have enough pay to buy the things they were producing. House inflation and easy borrowing filled the gap until the inevitable crash five years ago. Americans are missing an 80 per cent wage raise, and yet experts scratch their heads as to why the economy is stalled. You don't have to be a Marxist to notice that tycoons are determined to continue destructive policies, for it is not toxic assets that are being rescued by so-called 'quantitative easing' but a toxic economic system too. Those who question the 'magic of the market' are shunted aside.

Thus far policy debates remain confined within elite assumptions and official strictures. The reliable rulers' technique is to narrow the frame of reference. The educational institutions, and aspiring students, are told to adapt meekly to soaring expenses that exclude or indebt most entrants. Few experts mention that restoration of taxation on the rich to the levels of the Sixties, and an accompanying reinstatement of state funding, would solve the problem overnight. Reining in militarism wouldn't hurt either if the funds were diverted to infrastructure. Austerity is portrayed as if it were an act of nature, not a result of venal human schemes. This pattern stifles debate and is at work in every policy realm. Too many people believe they must submit to God-like "market reality" when the "market' really is what powerful institutions make of it. Institutions can be changed. There has never been more wealth available to improve our daily lives. It's captured at the top and more folks are awakening to the problem.

Propaganda works only so long. When the strain grows untenable, and more people are harmed, then the more things stay the same, the more they have to change. Closing the gap between economic reality and market mirage is the nightmare of rulers who prosper in a world of chic despair.[9]

In short, you don't have to be a Marxist to notice that tycoons are determined to continue destructive policies, for it is not toxic assets that are being rescued by so-called 'quantitative easing' but a toxic economic system too. Those who question the 'magic of the market' are shunted aside.

Democracy today

When a term has become as universally sanctified as democracy now is, I begin to wonder whether it means anything, in meaning too many things.

TS Eliot in 'The Idea of a Christian Society' (1940)

This was Eliot's confusion. The textbook reply to this confusion is that democracy, despite its many forms, is, in essence, a political concept that rests upon the foundation that the people are the real political authority. Democracy stands on certain principles. These are: competition among political parties, periodic elections, parliamentary government and a more or less homogeneous social infrastructure or a national identity bound together by a common language, common culture and a shared history. Democracy emphasizes commonality and homogeneity.

Defying and invalidating some of these principles, democracy has taken root in many countries in

---

[9] Kurt Jacobsen and Sayeed Hasan Khan (2013), "Chic despair", Statesman, Saturday, October 05, 2013

different geographic contexts by successfully carrying out mutations into environments where previously either democracy was nonexistent or exercised little influence.

India is not only the largest democracy but also a much admired and respected democracy in the world. Even then, India is not considered a true democracy as it has yet to develop a common and homogeneous culture and society. It is a unique example of a representative democracy that has a successfully functioning parliamentary government in the midst of great cultural diversity and heterogeneity. What India has affected is indigenization of democracy. This novelty is its gift to the world. Taiwan, South Africa, Botswana, Senegal and Nepal are just some of the case-studies of indigenous democracy. These cases have reversed many presumptions about democracy in political science, sociology, economics and international relations. These beneficial mutations are the raw materials of evolution and adaptation to changing environments. The success of these democracies will re-define democracy in political science. That is how frontiers of knowledge expand.

Apart from these country-specific indigenous democracies, a major change has taken place in the real world of democracy since 1945. This novelty is the emergence of numerous power-scrutinizing mechanisms such as human rights organizations, integrity commissions, information commissions, public interest litigation, anti-corruption commissions, Gallup polls, opinion polls, summits, forums and citizens; assemblies. The combined effects of these extra-constitutional bodies have gradually altered the political geometry and dynamics of democracy. Democracy has now come to mean much more than periodic election of representatives to a parliament. Elections still count, but parties and parliaments now have to compete with these monitoring organizations, networks and watchdogs that try to keep power on its toes. The traditional meaning of democracy as the periodic election of representatives based on the rule of one person, one vote is replaced by a democracy guided by a complex rule of one person, many interests, many representatives, both at home and abroad. Auditors-General, public enquiries, Election Commissions, Finance Commissions are constitutional bodies and adjuncts to parliaments. Other bodies operate at a distance from elected representatives. Many of these entities are served by retired government servants and their recruitment rules are not in the public domain.

Elected representatives and parliaments are required to share power with unelected representatives whose public legitimacy stems from such criteria as closeness to the incumbent government, administrative orders, media exposure and resilience in suffering. The question whether or not these monitoring bodies are effective for a functional democracy and whether they actually help to keep elected representatives on their toes are highly interesting topics of research. What is certain is that monitoring of elected representatives by unelected representatives is a sure change from the traditional concept of democracy.

There is a changing historical relationship between communication media and democracy. Ancient forms of assembly democracy belonged to an era of spoken word, backed up by laws written on stone or papyrus and messages dispatched by foot and horse. Representative democracy in the form of a territorial state sprang up in the age of print culture dominated by books, pamphlets, newspapers, telegraphed and mailed messages. With the advent of mass communication media, radio, cinema and television attained great prominence. Contemporary democracy is now tied closely to an explosive growth of multi-media. This is the age of communicative abundance. Communication can now take place through interlinked global network in real time that are affordable and accessible to millions of people scattered across the globe. The new age of communicative abundance has resulted in disaffection with political parties, politicians and politics in general. The modern communication technology has given a strong tool in the hands of people to ventilate their grievances against political parties. At the same time, the disaffection is dangerous for democracy as it can be exploited by an authoritative leader to convince people that their own interests are identical with those of the leader. Modern democracy can neither live with communicative abundance nor live without it. If the quality of democracy is to be enhanced, the structural defects of the new communication media are to be addressed by fostering new business models.

In the modern world, cross-border democracy has taken deep roots that combine to complicate and weaken the conventional mechanisms of electoral democracy within states.

Trends such as the concentration of power in the hands of global firms and the hesitation of parliamentary mechanisms in the face of globalizing markets, the disproportionate power of a few states within global bodies and the growth of supra-national institutions, agencies and networks are inhibitive for a modern democracy as they are by and large wholly unaccountable to citizens and their elected representatives. Cross-border and cosmopolitan democracy has several good features as well. Bilateral and multilateral cooperation by governments, economic networks and development corridors have combined to bring about a greater sense of interdependence and elevated the need for new bargaining mechanisms. East Asia is a critical case in point. The advantages and disadvantages of these approaches should be fully explored within a new research, teaching and public outreach agenda.

Lord Derby famously claimed to Prime Minister Benjamin Disraeli in the 1860s that the building of democracy from a scratch in hostile contexts no longer remains an impossibly daunting leap in the dark. Yet historical records suggest that successful promotion of democracy is a subject much beyond the realm of firepower, policy, strategy and foreign assistance. One study covering more than 200 US military operations including forcible interventions, peacekeeping, border control and military training, showed that democratic effects were noticeable in only 28 per cent of recorded cases.

Of the global powers, China and Russia pursue authoritarian state capitalism. These countries represent a regime alternative to representative democracies of Asia and Europe. It is projected that China is marching ahead to become a new global dominant power that will overtake the United States in economic, cultural and political matters. Once that happens, Asia will rise and the West will decline. Whether China's rise will affect the Asian democracies through ripple-effect cannot be predicted now.[10]

In 1945, there were only a dozen democracies left on the face of the earth. According to the World Forum of Democracy, electoral democracies now represent 120 of the 192 existing countries and constitute 60 per cent of the world population. Democracy as a principle cannot be applied in virtually all settings in the world. Winston Churchill felt that the respect for diversity and openness made democracy the 'Least Worst' form of government. The strongest case for its superiority lies in its ability of preventing and amending mistakes and in anticipating, defining and handling unexpected events and unforeseen consequences. Finally in a democracy, no political

---

[10] Khasnobis, H. (2013), " Democracy today", The Statesman, Thursday, November 28, 2013

party or its elected representative is indispensable. It is the people who say the last word.

In short, Democracy as a principle cannot be applied in virtually all settings in the world. Winston Churchill felt that the respect for diversity and openness made democracy the 'Least Worst" form of government.

INDIA:

Definition of Democracy has changed

Tired and exhausted after fighting a corrupt political system throughout his tenure as Karnataka Lokayukta, Justice N. Santosh Hegde said:

The trend of Indian democracy as understood to be "by the people, for the people and of the people" is indeed "governance by the elected, for the elected and of the elected".

Speaking on the topic 'Changing Trends in Indian Democracy' in the Capital, he said:

The intoxication of power has made elected representatives in the country to believe they are superior citizens of India and this arrogance is found in the manner they have come to function.

He was addressing the Third Justice HR Khanna Memorial Lecture in honour of the Supreme Court judge who was known for his courageous dissent opinion opposing the Emergency declared by Indira Gandhi government. As a consequence, he missed becoming the Chief Justice of India in 1976 when he resigned in protest over the Indira Gandhi Government's decision to supersede him.

Hegde, who retires as Lokayukta on Monday said, "The definition of democracy as it was understood was by the people, of the people and for the people?

Unfortunately the understanding of democracy has changed very much. They think it means governance by the elected, for the elected and of the elected." Hegde shared his anguish and pain, quoting a recent incident when a political functionary criticized his comment on Jan Lokpal bill by terming him "un-elected and unelectable tyrant". He said, "My experience over two decades shows that the legislature as an institution of democracy has continuously decayed. This attitude 'if I cannot serve let me not damage' did not work.

The elected representatives became officers not to serve the people but instruments to peddle power."

Showing instances of this decay, Hegde referred to statistics to suggest, "From the point of view of money spent on every election one is forced to ask whether election expenditure is an investment as elections tends to have become a business." If it is an investment, he asked, "In return what work has the Parliament done?" Statistics suggested that in the previous term of Parliament, only 107 MPs spoke, of which six spoke six times or more during their entire five-year tenure. However, there has been an increase of 17.2 per cent in the number of MPs with criminal record, while the asset value per MP has recorded over 200 per cent since the last Lok Sabha.

Scoffing at this trend of democracy, Hegde said, "Nobody can grudge their financial success, but the question remains where this money comes from and at whose cost." Issuing a guarded caution, he said, "Once people lose faith in the system, no force can save the system." The bureaucracy and judiciary too were not spared.

Though the rot in judiciary was the least of the lot, Hegde expressed serious concerns on the "selection criteria" for judges. "In fact merit and integrity alone was considered for selection of judges. That is not what is happening today...quicker the change in the selection of judges, better the change in the system." Calling the bureaucracy to be the "conjoint twin" of legislature, he said:

Of late, the relation between political bureaucracy (Cabinet) and executive bureaucracy has become that of master and servant. Fearing uncomfortable transfers, they have succumbed to pressure.[11]

INDIA: **Reform of the polls:**
Need to Make Democracy Meaningful

THE issue of electoral reform gathered momentum after Anna Hazare included the matter in his agenda. There is now a public debate to buttress the demand for suitable legislation. There are four major issues involved: to debar the tainted from contesting; the right to recall; the right to reject; and the funding of the electoral campaigns.

In a recent interview to the media, Mr. SY Qureshi, Chief Election Commissioner, said that a Bill would be introduced in Parliament's winter session, seeking to bar the tainted from contesting. He asserted that it is the "maxim of law" that the larger public good takes precedence over individual rights. However, there are certain contentious issues. The first is the nature of offence with which a person is charged. The second is the stage at which the disqualification comes into effect. There are various suggestions regarding the "nature of offence" ~ that it should be a "heinous offence or a set of offences". Instead of engaging in an exercise to identify the "heinous offence", all cases that are tried by a Sessions court should form the criteria for disqualification.

---

[11] Pioneer News Service, New Delhi, July 31, 2011

There are eight offences in the Indian Penal Code 1860 which prescribes death penalty with an alternative of life imprisonment. There are about 54 offences which entail life imprisonment with an alternative of lesser term of imprisonment. All or most of them are cases of corruption and can be tried in a Sessions court. These offences should form the criteria to determine the nature of the crime.

The next issue is the stage at which the disqualification is to take effect. Offences under fiscal laws also need to be brought within its ambit. The disqualification should take effect after the court frames the charges. If and when the accused is acquitted of the charges, he can re-qualify for electoral politics.

This has been contested by the political class on the assumption that one is "innocent till proven guilty", which means till one is convicted and such conviction is upheld by the appellate courts. This can take a decade to materialize, defeating the very purpose of cleansing public life from the influence of tainted legislators.

I am not inclined to accept the argument of "being innocent till proven guilty" because this principle is applicable to prison sentences that are ordered upon trial. It is not applicable to a quasi-criminal action of disqualification ordered by the competent authority. Therefore, these principles of criminal jurisprudence call for fresh evaluation by the judiciary to save the nation from criminal elements getting into the political structure.

A heavy responsibility rests on the judiciary and the jurists. The adversarial system of justice ~ of being innocent till proven guilty ~ is adopted by the Supreme Court. It is based on Article 20(3) which states that "no accused shall be compelled to be a witness against himself". This is an elastic interpretation. The jurists need to question several premises held sacred by the judiciary. Alternatively, the judiciary needs to speed up the trial within the maximum time-frame of one to two years in all cases in which the political class stands charged with crimes. The judiciary should not impede its own functioning on such principles of jurisprudence as "justice hurried is justice buried".

Mr. Qureshi has described the right to recall as impractical. He is partially correct, but it has one advantage. It acts as a "deterrent" and controls the working and conduct of legislators. It ensures responsible discharge of duties. It can be enforced only after the member completes half the term and the demand to recall should be supported by half of the electorate and he ought not to be recalled unless it is desired by two-third of those voting.

Neither has Mr. Qureshi given his approval to the right to reject. Yet if it comes into force, the political parties will be cautious in sponsoring the crime-tainted and to that extent; this right can serve its purpose.

These measures have a preventive effect, and prevention is better than punishment.

As regards the influence of money, Mr. Qureshi feels that a full-fledged expenditure monitory division in the income-tax department can take care of this problem. He is oversimplifying the issue. The tyranny of money power cannot be fought by bureaucrats alone. The nexus between the corporate and political class feeding each others' greed is the bane of democracy. In an interview to the BBC on 5 October this year, Jimmy Carter, the former US President and a venerated politician and statesman, spoke about the "massive infusion of corporate funds into political structures in the USA".

The story is no different in India where politicians amass a substantial portion of this money. There are at least nine methods to break the nexus:

(a) Stop financial bailouts to corporate
(b) Stop tax exemptions;
(c) write off the bad debts of banks;
(d) Abolish the income-tax department's voluntary disclosure scheme, which gives immunity from prosecutions;
(e) Speed up the contested taxes cases pending in courts for which the country needs the unstinted support of the judiciary;
(f) Ensure austerity in the election campaign. Extravagant campaigns, with large motorcades, should be deemed as an "offence";
(g) Duration of campaigns should be limited to a maximum of six weeks;
(h) Penalization of paid news;
(i) False statement of expenses must be made a criminal offence.

When candidates sponsored by political parties are reasonably honest, there is no need for extravagant electioneering that involves bribery. Such campaigns symbolize capitalism at its worst. Another major factor is that heavy corporate funding cuts into the dividends of the shareholders ~ the honest investors. Black money is the villain of the piece. As and when detected it calls for confiscation, not merely taxation. State funding is no substitute; it may not preclude the infusion of black money. Apart from corporate funding, the candidates get money from mafia gangs operating in several illegal businesses locally, corrupt bureaucrats of such departments as excise for example. Indeed, politics is big business. Under the present law, those corporate that pay bribes are accountable.

But the solution lies elsewhere - party functionaries need to be defined as "public servants".[12]

Morality in public life

THE assertion that there is an ethical foundation in public life assumes that there is a difference between ethics in private and public lives. Unlike in the past, this difference is a modern concept. For instance, Aristotle compared social existence to the bees; in Rousseau's political philosophy, there is the concept of "forced to be free" implying that the few who disagree are the deviant ones.

This belief structure continued for thousands of years because of a slow process of change and strict adherence to social norms which implies unquestioning acceptance. The individual's role within a larger societal hierarchy is well-defined and seldom violated. This long-standing societal praxis (which Durkheim calls mechanical solidarity) changed during the last 500 years because of a variety of reasons. The first was the impact of the Protestant Revolution which was largely successful because of the invention of the printing press. Subsequently, the Renaissance unsettled this age-old practice and with it emerged the new restless human being, more daring, selfish and motivated only towards glory and power. This new human being as it were is best reflected in the writings of Machiavelli. The emergence of the new human being is further strengthened by the new scientific discoveries and inventions.

By the 17th century, Hobbes propounded the philosophy of public ethics. He realised the importance of societal acceptance of do's and don'ts which would be strictly observed. The human desire

---

[12] Rama Chandra Reddy (2011), "Reform of the polls -Need To Make Democracy Meaningful", The Statesman, Bhubaneswar, November 17, 2011

for power is central to this new scheme of things, rendering Aristotle redundant. The invention of a new paradigm of politics, based on human nature, becomes essential with the assumption that if human beings are angels there would be no need for laws.

With the rise of the democratic revolution and liberal individualism, it became imperative to lay down the first principles of ethical conduct in public life in order to maintain civility and order. The process of American constitutionalism and the writings of Smith, Ferguson and Hume of the Scottish Enlightenment and of Montesquieu and Voltaire of the French Enlightenment seek to provide a larger economic, societal and political basis for such ethics. This was followed by Blackstone, Austin and Bentham within a legal framework. Bentham's greatness is that he evolved this larger and comprehensive framework both within a legal and a utilitarian order, enabling him to make liberalism the national philosophy of Britain.

The overriding philosophical framework with an ethical base and appropriate for a public space is one of the major achievements of modern constitutional liberalism. It makes a categorical and firm distinction between well-defined private and public space. This allows universal rules and values in a world of "incommensurable values", to quote Sir Isaiah Berlin. In this large detailing of a management of mega societies the realm of private life is a world of plurality where one eats, wears, and dresses according to one's choice and where one is also expected to respect similar space of others. But the realm of public space is entirely different as there is a more universalistic norm that is employed and that is expected to be observed by the overwhelming majority of the people. This larger framework of the rule of law and its implementation lies at the very root of providing an ethical framework to public life.

For instance, we are all familiar with the adage that honesty is the best policy. The question that arises is: Why is it referred to as policy and not a principle? Alternatively, if one argues that dishonesty is the best policy and vindicates that perception with successful examples, then the implication would be that the State is unwilling or unable to evolve a larger social, political and economic order which is based on rational ethical principles by which the nation is governed. To arrive at such a framework the following ingredients are essential in building an enduring ethical foundation of public life in today's world. These are:

(a) A strong State;
(b) Rule of law;
(c) Accountability;
(d) Efficiency derived out of just meritocracy, And just reward; and
(e) Social discipline.

To achieve this larger ethical foundation, it is imperative to put in place a structure of decision-making which is responsive to people's aspirations. To ensure that it does not evolve into a situation of alienated culture, it is important to create confidence in the average person that his rights and property are well secured. This can be achieved by the creation of strong and enduring institutions based on Montesquieu's theory of separation of powers and larger constitutional processes. What helps in consolidating this framework is what Meade calls property-owning democracy which implies that the overwhelming number of residents would be owners of individual property. This is a modernized and more realistic basis of organizing a well-ordered democracy than the idealized form of ownership based on a rough parity envisaged by Locke and Jefferson. This helps in creating civil society with its own rules and principles, and restricts State power with its inherent tendency to indulge in excesses.

The justness of a system and the strength of its ethical foundation are proved by the enduring institutions that are built over time within public space. The absence of such initiatives leads to decay and a crisis of the belief structure in which unethical means to an end are preferable. This leads to stagnation, inefficiency, non-competitiveness, frustration and hopelessness. Ethics in public life can be measured by the level of institutionalisation that would be achieved and the gap between achievement and desirability on a world scale. John Rawls emphasizing on reason to achieve this Aristotelian Mean has advocated the doctrine of overlapped consensus thereby ensuring a political structure which would promote a great deal of plurality of opinion but would have enough public space for smoothly operating the political life. The attainment of this level of consciousness is equally essential for achieving morality in public life. The substantive aspirations of the people can only be realised if the procedural basis of democracy remains unshaken with the strict observation of the well-established constitutional certitudes. This would have to be the rule rather than an exception.[13]

Scam and the Whistle Blowers

Of the many politicians who have taken up the task to bring the perpetrators of the 2G scams to justice, Mr. Subramanian Swamy stands out for his doggedness and an almost missionary zeal. He did not stop at merely stirring the murky pot and pursuing the matter in the courts; Swamy has now written an exhaustive account of the scam. While the massive irregularities the Telecom Ministry indulged in during A Raja's tenure as Union Telecom Ministry is now all in the public domain, and whatever is not known will

---

[13] Subrata Mukherjee (2012), " Morality in public life: And the Evolution of Political Philosophy ", The Statesman, June 24, 2012

be out in the course of the investigations, the book is relevant for two reasons: One, it is a valuable reference material for academics, commentators and students of contemporary subjects; and, two, it raises larger issues of governance in an increasingly industrialized nation, where narrow materialistic considerations threaten to outweigh the larger national good.

The author takes us into the frightening reality of how corrupt the country is perceived by international agencies and the general causes of the malaise. From fudged accounts of corporate entities to the generation and siphoning away of black money to the role of illicit funds in promoting terror activities, he gives us a quick take on the vast and seemingly unmanageable problem. Towards the end, Mr. Swamy suggests a national policy to counter it. This would involve the integration of "spiritual values and organizational leadership". He lays emphasis on the incorporation of the "evolved youth" in the plan since that alone could create a "modern mindset". But for that to happen, as he rightly points out, there will have to be a greater accountability in governance — something that the political class talks of a lot but does precious little to execute. What remains unsaid, therefore, is that such a national policy will not be forthcoming unless the people, especially the youth, compel the Government to respond.

The author has relied on a heap of material that has emerged through the investigations, including the various correspondences among Ministers and Government officials on the subject. Again, while they are all known, they help in maintaining the focus and keep the issue in perspective, highlighting the callousness of those in power in allowing the scam to take shape. The Comptroller and Auditor General's observations, too, have been used extensively, and rightly so, because it is the CAG findings that officially set the ball rolling for a probe, involving the Central

Vigilance Commission and the Central Bureau of Investigation. The latter had been rather reluctant in fully involving itself till the Supreme Court cracked the whip.

The large canvas of the scam included a number of personalities and institutions, and the author has done well to approach the issue in an uncluttered fashion. He has neatly categorized the important developments, such as those involving CAG, the Public Accounts Committee, the Radia tapes and the Telecom Regulatory Authority of India. He has also provided a chronology of the event dating from September 24, 2007, to January 25, 2008 — the time when the Telecom Ministry took the stand that no application under the Unified Access Services (UAS) would be accepted after October 10, 2007, to the questionable issuance of those licenses. Swamy puts on record that then TRAI chief Nripendra Misra had said that the Ministry had never sought the authority's views on grant of new licenses.

This is important since the Government has been saying that it had complied with TRAI guidelines. In fact, TRAI also took the position that its opinion should be sought even if the Telecom Ministry issued fresh licenses under the existing policy. Misra had also warned the Government against what is now famously quoted as "cherry picking" of the recommendations the Authority had made on the matter of issuing licenses.

A great deal of what the book contains will sound familiar to the regular readers of *The Pioneer.* The daily had been the first to break the 2G - scam through a series of articles beginning 2008-end. For more than 18 months, *The Pioneer* continued to publish one informed expose after another, detailing the murky business of the 2G - deal. The end result was that the authorities, compelled by the exposes and driven by the Supreme Court, had to take finally note and act.

There are many heroes in this tale. While Swamy is certainly one of them, he has been quick to acknowledge the others, particularly the whistle blower, Mr. Ashirvatham Achari, without whose cooperation the scam would have remained buried in the sands of time. *The Pioneer* correspondent Mr. J Gopikrishnan doggedly pursued the story, flinging aside temptations that were laid his way by those who wanted the matter forgotten. He is the other hero the author names.

While the probe is now on track and there is hope that the guilty will be eventually punished, the fact remains that a scam of this magnitude can happen again. The book provides some solutions to prevent that, but it is for the political class to wake up and recognize that. Meanwhile, we need more such whistle-blowers, news correspondents and activists.[14]

Thoughts for Twenty first Century

The world passes through a period when education, scientific progress, and all round development of people are progressing at a higher speed. But there is more ambition, more despair, more suicides, more hungry mouths and more corruption in all countries. The people have voting rights, but democracy itself is in peril. The rich countries are offering wrong advices to the developing countries for their benefits. In many countries military rulers administer the people as of yester years.

---

[14] Subramanium Swamy (2011), " Scam and the whistle blowers", The Pioneer, July 30, 2011 as reported by Mr. J Gopikrishnan

World peace is at a stake

The democracy has become a slogan than a reality. The same presidents, prime ministers and political parties rule the country for indefinite period. People need world peace, good governance and no war, no starvation deaths, no corruption, no black money to rule the state. The questions are:

(a) Who runs the government? Is it free from corruption?
(b) Why corruption cases are not finalized within a year?
(c) Why the forests and mines are to be exhausted within the shortest possible of time?
(d) Why the Election Commission is allowing people to contest in elections without verifying the candidates' eligibility and ability in making laws in the parliament, senate or assembly?
(e) Why MPLAD or MLALAD is granted to MPs or MLAs in India?
(f) Why court cases are not finalized before granting a berth to Parliament?
(g) Why assets of leaders are not verified before the election and expiry of each term?
(h) Why there are regional or state level political parties in countries?
(i) Why there are religion based political parties? And why there are sleeping political parties in countries?
(j) Why the cash registers of registered political parties are not audited?

Conclusion

The world has practiced all forms of political philosophy and the political parties have adopted these philosophies to come to power. Political philosophy in Marxism, socialism, fascism, conservatism and social democracy has proved its impact among people. But people's involvement in democracy is not practically accepted in most of the countries.

Democracy is morbid in different developing countries because the political leaders are corrupt and avail political opportunism to convert state funds into personal wealth. The leaders tell lies; stab other leaders in the back and utilize black money for purchase of votes through muscle power and money power. And democracy runs through culprits and sycophants. The wrong policies of governments widen the rich – poor gaps in democratic countries.

The governments, justice system and bureaucracy should be impartial to award justice to all. But in corrupt countries, corruption rules the state and the sufferer suffers as he cannot fight against the government.

The political leaders adopt Secularism or Communalism or Opportunism to come to power in each election and get elected by hook and crook. Votes are purchased and what not? Hence, there is rise of Maoism, Naxalism and Terrorism in poor countries.

Corruption, inefficiency, reservation, strikes, road marches, false assurances, media capture and red carpet to Foreign Direct Investment in retail sector and banking sector lead to mass uprisings in India and other countries.

The use of police force to control the mob and CRPF forces to control the Maoists and Naxalites have become the headlines of all news channels each day.

The eligibility of candidature to the august houses of countries must be chalked out by the Election Commission. Moreover, number of terms as elected members must be finalized. It is a fact that many leaders have made the political parties as corporate houses or business establishments.

The Parliament should alone make laws for the entire country and the Supreme Court must study its implications and suggest if any. The states should not be allowed to make laws. It should follow the central laws and orders. A country cannot have more agencies to make laws.

The religion based conflicts and geographical boundary disputes must be finalized within a specific period. Let the peasants of the world live in peace and achieve justice by the political, bureaucratic and judicial institutions. Let the United Nations Organization work for awarding justice to the people by ensuring peace to all and imposing restrictions on war.

Let the philosophers, world organizations, governments and intelligentsia searches for that political thought to find out a process of governance, which could establish long-term WORLD PEACE.

Let the political thinkers, researchers and voters search for a new political philosophy for a peaceful world in future.

In short, people of the world need good governance, food security and human rights to lead a peaceful life. But hunger, illiteracy, rules by muscle power still control the life of a vast majority of people even in Twenty-first century.

+++++

Chapter II

POLITICAL PARTIES IN COUNTRIES

The deaths of so many brave soldiers would not be in vain; that slavery would end as a result of the losses; and the future of democracy would be assured, that "government of the people, by the people, for the people, shall not perish from the earth." ------ Abraham Lincoln

Political parties are formed by groups of people who wish to win control of the government. In democratic countries, such groups have to win the support of the people who elect candidates from the party of their choice. Many democratic countries such as the United States and Canada have a two-party system, where two major parties compete for office. One party generally supports conservative policies and the other is usually more radical. Before **political campaigns**, parties adopt political platforms or programs, which they present to the people. The program sets out what the party plans to do if it is elected.

Role of political parties in democracy:

Many countries in the West have two or more major political parties, which fight election campaigns in order to gain control of the government. In this picture, Lyndon Baines Johnson, United States president from 1963-9, greets a crowd in Los Angeles, California, during the 1964 election campaign, in which he successfully stood as Democratic Party candidate.

In the United States, the two main parties are the Democrats and the Republicans. The president is the leader of his party. The leader of the other party is usually the presidential candidate who was defeated at the last presidential election. Parties owe their strength to their organization at a national and at a local level. Both the Republican and the Democratic parties have national committees, state committees and county committees. At precinct level, the parties generally have a precinct committeeman or precinct captain. His political campaign is to get people to vote for his party on Election Day.

Role of political parties in democracy is an interesting theme of research. Some countries have more than two parties. In most of Europe there are Christian-Democratic and Socialist parties. In Finland, France, and Italy there are strong Communist parties as well. In other countries there are various Liberal parties. Where no single party has a majority, several combine to form a coalition to form a government. Parties may bring together people of the same social class or the same religion that is one of the democracy signs.

For example, most socialist parties usually get more support from manual workers than non-socialist parties do. Christian-Democratic parties unite people who support definite Christian policies. In Africa and Asia, there are Muslim parties.

In Communist countries, the Communist party is either the only party or it dominates a coalition of several parties. In many African and Asian countries, a one-party system of government now exists. In such countries, the people cannot change the government by elections. This is sometimes a stable form of government that permits leaders to introduce strong measures to eliminate poverty. But this system can also lead to tyranny.[15]

The United States of America

Political Parties

A political party is a group of voters organized to support certain public policies. The aim of a political party is to elect officials who will try to carry out the party's policies.

A political party offers candidates for public office. It sets out positions on issues that may range from war and taxes to how children should be educated. When people in a democracy disagree about what the government should do, voters express their opinions by voting for the candidates that most closely reflect their views. Political parties provide a way for voters to easily identify a candidate's positions.

Political parties may be large or small, national or local. Large political parties generally have millions of members and supporters. In democratic election campaigns, parties compete freely for votes. Such competition is one of the hallmarks of democracy.

How Parties Began

Political parties as we know them did not begin to develop until the late 1600's. The ancient Greeks, who were pioneers in developing democracy, had no organized political parties in the modern sense. The senate of the ancient Romans had two groups that

[15] Wikipedia Com On line Encyclopedia

represented people with different interests--the Patricians and the Plebeians. The Patricians represented noble families. The Plebeians represented the wealthy merchants and the middle class. Although these two groups often mingled, at times they voted as factions, or parties, on particular issues that were important to the groups they represented.

For many centuries after the fall of Rome (AD 476), the people of Europe had little voice in politics. Thus there were no true political parties--only factions that supported one noble family or another. Political parties developed as representative assemblies gained power. In England, this change began after what was called the Popish Plot of 1678.

English Political Parties

In 1678, a rumor spread through England that Roman Catholics were plotting to kill King Charles II and give the throne to Charles' brother, James, Duke of York (who was a Roman Catholic). There was no real popish plot, but an alarmed Parliament barred all Roman Catholics from public office and tried to take away the Duke of York's right to inherit the throne. But to King Charles II, Parliament seemed to be challenging royal authority, and he struck back by dissolving Parliament.

All over England people were either for or against the king's act. Those who urged the king to call a new Parliament were called Petitioners. Those who backed the king's deed were called Abhorrers because they abhorred any attempt to control the king's actions. Before long the two factions took on other names. Petitioners were called Whigs. "Whig" was an old term for Scottish Presbyterians who opposed the government. The king's supporters were called Tories. "Tory" was originally a name given to Irish Roman Catholics who had suffered under Protestant rule. These old names took on new meanings.

The basic difference between Whigs and Tories in the 1600's was their view of what government should do and how strong it should be. Tories wanted rule by a strong king. Whigs wanted ordinary people to have more rights and gain more control of their government. In time, as Parliament took greater control, the Whigs and Tories developed into organized parties.

Political Parties in the United States

The leaders of the American Revolution did not like the idea of parties and political battles between parties. Upon his retirement from public life in 1796, George Washington warned Americans against "faction" (parties). James Madison thought parties were probably necessary, although he did not entirely approve of them. Alexander Hamilton thought that faction was a vice to be guarded against at all times. Thomas Jefferson declared in 1789, "If I could not go to heaven but with a party, I would not go there at all." Nevertheless, the men who held these views founded the first two great American political parties.

Early U S parties

Hamilton and other leaders who wanted a strong central government banded together to put over their policies. In 1787 they began calling themselves the Federalists. This was the first United States political party. In 1796, anti-Federalists gathered around Jefferson. Members of Jefferson's group called themselves Democratic-Republicans. Northern businessmen, bankers, and merchants supported the Federalists. They believed in a strong national (or federal) government. Federalists held that capital and industry were the basis of a healthy republic and that the federal government should act to protect the country's infant industries. The Democratic-Republican Party drew its followers from planters, small farmers, and artisans. These people wanted government to leave them alone as much as possible. They wanted to limit the federal government's power and leave the most power in the hands of state and local governments. In foreign affairs the Federalists generally leaned toward England, while the Democratic Republicans sympathized with Revolutionary France.

Early leaders such as John Adams, who succeeded George Washington as president, had Federalist sympathies. But the Federalists lost control of the government to Jefferson and his party in 1800. The Federalists lingered on as a minority party, especially in New England, for 20 years.

By 1820, American political life was being influenced by sharp differences of opinion between sections of the country. In time, these quarrels led to the Civil War. The slave-holding planters of the South, the frontier farmers of the West, and the manufacturing and banking industries based in the North each wanted the government to follow a different course of action.

In 1828, Andrew Jackson, a Democratic-Republican from Tennessee, was elected president. His party had great support in the South and West. Jackson changed the party's name to Democrats. People who had once been Federalists joined with anti-Jackson Democrats to form the National Republican, or Whig, Party. Between 1836 and 1852, Whigs gave Democrats strong opposition.

By 1854 the issue of slavery overshadowed all political debate. A related issue was states' rights. If a state government was in conflict with the national government, which government had the final authority? Debate over slavery and states' rights tore the parties apart. Northern Abolitionists--people who wanted to abolish slavery--left the Whig party. The Whigs also lost voters to the "Know-Nothing" Party, a new party that violently opposed Roman Catholics and foreigners. The Whig Party began to go to pieces. At the same time, the issues of slavery and states' rights divided Democrats into Northern and Southern branches. Southern Democrats strongly favored slavery and states' rights. Extremists among them believed that a state had a right to secede (leave the Union) if the national government tried to interfere with slavery.

In 1854 antislavery forces and Free Soil forces (a group founded in Buffalo, New York) formed the Republican Party. The Republicans ran their first presidential candidate, John C. Frémont, in 1856. By 1860 the voters had a choice of four major parties--Northern Democrat, Southern Democrat, Republican, and the Constitutional-Union Party, which drew some ex-Whigs. Strong antislavery feeling helped Republicans capture the presidency for Abraham Lincoln. In 1861 the Southern states seceded and the Civil War began.

Democrats and Republicans

The defeat of the Southern Confederacy weakened the Democrats, who were associated in voters' minds with the Southern cause. For many years the Republicans were the major party. They favored business interests and high tariffs (taxes on imports). The Democrats supported free trade. They attracted farmers and the immigrants who poured into the country between the Civil War and the turn of the century.

The two major parties were not so deeply divided again until the 1930's. At that time the Great Depression struck the country. The presidential election of 1932 brought in Franklin D. Roosevelt and his New Deal programs. Roosevelt Democrats thought that the federal government must actively help people who had been hurt by the Depression. Under the New Deal the government passed economic relief measures, social security, laws helping unions, and other bills. Republicans thought the government was taking too much power and moving the country toward a welfare state. They fought against governmental interference with business.

Today both parties agree in general on social security, unemployment insurance, basic foreign policy, and civil rights. The issues on which they disagree often are not goals so much as means: how best to keep the economy growing, protect the environment, and maintain a strong national defense. In general, Republicans tend to oppose government programs as solutions to national problems. Democrats tend to believe that government can and should act for good. However, the parties' views on government's role often depend on the specific issue or program in question.

U S Third Parties

The United States has a two-party system. However, nothing in the Constitution requires two parties. The Democrats and Republicans have alternated in power since before the Civil War mainly because they have put forward candidates and policies that appeal to most Americans. But minor parties, or third parties, have often played a role in politics. Third parties focus attention on issues and ideas. Sometimes they draw enough support to affect the outcome of elections. Sometimes a third party gains part of its goals by supporting a major party that promises to act on the third party's views.

After the Civil War, Americans debated issues such as women's voting rights and labor reform. New political parties helped focus attention on these issues. In 1872, for example, Victoria Woodhull became the first woman to run for president. She shared the Equal Rights Party ticket with African American leader

Frederick Douglass. In the 1890's the People's Party of the U.S.A., or Populists, drew support from laborers and farmers.

In 1912 a disagreement among Republicans produced a splinter group called the Progressive, or "Bull Moose," Party. Theodore Roosevelt, the party's presidential candidate, outpolled the Republican candidate, William H. Taft. But the Republican split only helped the Democratic candidate, Woodrow Wilson, to win the election. The Progressive Party's name was revived in the 1920's. The Progressives opposed big business monopolies and favored the interests of farmers and workers. The Socialist Party favored wider social welfare measures. It reached its greatest strength in the 1930's, during the Great Depression.

After World War II, Southern Democrats formed the States' Rights, or "Dixiecrat," Party to protest a growing movement to secure the civil rights of African Americans. The American Independent Party, led by Alabama governor George Wallace, also opposed racial integration. It was a factor in the presidential election of 1968. The Libertarian Party, formed in the 1970's, stressed individual rights. The 1990's saw the growth of the Reform Party, formed by Texas businessman H. Ross Perot. And the Green Party has formed as an outgrowth of the environmental movement. Like earlier third parties, these groups have helped focus attention on important social and political issues.

How U S Parties Work

The major U.S. political parties are highly organized. The precinct is the smallest local division. The county and state committees run the parties. Committee members may be elected at primaries, chosen at state conventions, or appointed by party officers. The two major parties also have national committees, made up of one man and one woman from each of the 50 states and U.S. territories. Every four years, parties hold national conventions. Delegates are chosen in primaries, by state conventions, or at gatherings called precinct caucuses. These delegates gather at the conventions to nominate a presidential and a vice-presidential candidate. Each party at its convention also drafts a platform. The platform is a statement of what the party stands for. If the party wins, the platform is supposed to guide the actions of the elected officials.

Parties today use computers to draw up lists of possible supporters and take public opinion polls to explore the views of voters on certain issues. They use advertising to mold public opinion and compete for favorable media coverage for their candidates. U.S. election campaigns are enormously costly, and fund-raising is a major part of the parties' work. Special-interest groups able to raise money and turn out voters for candidates they favor have grown in influence. State and federal laws control the ways political parties can raise and handle money.

Political Parties in other countries

Political parties are often a standard by which a country's political freedom can be measured. Some countries have only one political party. In China, for example, there is only one party, the Communist Party. Under such a system, people who do not agree with the party in power cannot express their objections by voting for another group. Often the ruling party holds power with the support of the army. Democracies usually operate under either a two-party or a multiparty system. Like the United States, Britain has a two-party system. The major parties are the Labour Party and the Conservative Party, though there are active third parties. Canada also has two major parties, the Conservatives and the Liberals.

Multiparty systems are common in Europe and other parts of the world. In this system, three or more parties each enjoy substantial support from voters. France, Germany, Israel, and South Africa are just a few examples. In these countries there may be many parties representing a wide range of political views. Because of the number of competing parties, it is sometimes difficult for any one party to get a clear majority of the votes. In such cases, leading parties that can agree on general policies form a coalition (a combination of parties) to run the country.[16]

Germany

Parliamentary System

The German parliamentary system has always intrigued me because it stands apart from the more popular Westminster (British) and the Presidential (US) systems. The 'list system' that supplements proportional representation (calculated through the percentage of votes polled by a party) may be complex, but is probably a more accurate reflection of the popular mandate than the 'first-past-the-post' British or Indian model or the American Electoral College system, which can enable a candidate with fewer votes than his opponent, become President. Second, political parties in Germany are state-funded, which lends an interesting dimension to the way democracy functions. This has acquired relevance in India because of persistent suggestions that elections here too should be similarly funded to curtail the excessive influence of money, which in turn fuels further corruption. Germany has a bi-cameral Parliament and has comparative balance of power between the two Houses.

---

[16] Scholastic, Teachers where teachers come first, The New Book Knowledge, Grolier online, Scholastics Library Publishing, USA / Stephen Flanders, Correspondent, Columbia Broadcasting System

Germany has 110 registered parties but only 19 are represented in the Federal and State Parliaments. The law stipulates that a party has to procure at least five percent of the popular vote to get a seat in the Bundestag, while at least one per cent is needed to claim representation in a State Parliament. Only those getting votes above this threshold are entitled to state financing. The experience of Nazi Unitarianism during Adolf Hitler's 12-year-long dictatorship (1933-45) was instrumental in pushing post-War Germany in a party-oriented and federal direction. First, Germans decided to ensure that one-party rule would never come back and accordingly drafted a Constitution that conferred legal status on political parties. Incidentally, the Indian Constitution does not have a similar provision although the Anti-Defection Act has necessitated definition of a party in the amended Representation of the People Act. Second, the erstwhile Federal Republic (West Germany) also decided to bring back a federal Constitution, which had been abolished by the Nazis. The States were given proportionate representation in the second House of Parliament, Bundesrat.

The electorate on the 'first-past-the-post system' directly chooses approximately half the seats in the German Parliament. The remaining seats are occupied among different parties on the basis of the percentage of votes polled. All parties declare the list of their nominees in order of preference prior to the elections. For example, a candidate can be named to contest a direct seat as well as figure in the party's list. If he/she wins directly, the person next in order of precedence on the party's list gets to occupy a seat in the House. As a result, intense lobbying takes place for a prime position on a party's list, somewhat similar to the jockeying that happens here for a party nomination to the Upper House.

The stipulation that only parties garnering five per cent or more of the popular vote are entitled to gain seats in the Bundestag ensures that the number of parties in Parliament is restricted to within manageable numbers, unlike India where more than 30 political parties, some with just one member, have representation in the national Parliament. Germans contend that unrestricted multiplicity of parties leads to political instability and hence that has to be curbed by law. Although complicated, how they did the calculations prior to the advent of the computer; the PR system seems to function well and has enabled parties like the Greens, for example, that don't win too many directly elected seats to claim representation commensurate to their popular support.

However, state funding of parties is an even more complicated and less popular mechanism. There is a consolidated Budget of Euro 133 million per annum to be divided between eligible parties. MPs voted this figure in 2002 but since it does not take inflation into account, the amount has fallen way below requirement. It is not a popular measure and political parties, it was confessed by all; do not have the guts to bring forward fresh legislation for its enhancement. What complicates this is the fact that parties are expected to raise their own revenues in order to get a grant from the state. So, for every Euro 100 a party garners by way of income or donation, the state contributes Euro 38. But there is a ceiling here: State grants are permissible only up to Euro 3,300 in a year for individual donations. Amounts exceeding this are subject to the ceiling; so a donation of Euro 10,000 will get the same state funding as a donation of Euro 3,300. Further, state funding cannot exceed 50 per cent of a party's annual income. In other words, parties need to exert themselves to raise money through membership fees, subscriptions to journals and events, private and corporate donations and so on.

We are familiar with the term 'State funding of elections'. But I discovered that the German model, oft quoted in this context, is not about elections alone. The state pays all eligible parties in four equal installments starting February 15 every year on the basis on voting figures and income details of the previous calendar year. In fact, the funds are used primarily for organizational expenses, not elections. As a result, parties have large buildings that function like corporate headquarters, bring out publications, hold exhibitions, conduct opinion polls, fund research and indulge in other acts to bolster their political base on an ongoing basis. Elections per se are not very expensive for individual candidates since the system in Germany revolves around parties who pick up the bulk of the tab for campaign expenses including television and print advertising.

The Germany political system was too complex for India and could work only in a country with strong firewalls to guard against corruption, manipulation of accounts and other malpractices. But the German model merits far closer attention than it has received from political thinkers and academics because it holds the key to a largely corruption free structure that may, some day, help cleanse highly extravagant and corrupt electoral systems in all developing countries.[17]

INDIA: Left Parties in India

As a system of government, communism is dead or dying, but as a system of ideas, its future looks secure in the country. Utpal kumar looks into the past and expresses his happiness for the downfall of left parties in India. He explains the facts as follows: It took more than 20 years for Indian communists to experience the tremors of the collapse of the Berlin Wall. While their counterparts across the world stood

---

[17] Chandan Mitra (2010), "From Germany With Wisdom", Sunday Pioneer, November 7, 2010

discredited, their thuggery (cheating) exposed beyond redemption, comrades in India continued to bask under unprecedented glory as late as 2008. Even today, when they have lost their strongest bastion in West Bengal after 34 years of incessant (mis) rule, there is no dearth of Marxist sympathizers, bemoaning the loss of the 'secular', Left space in the country.

This is astounding, if not outlandishly outrageous. No data, no record, not even a shred of evidence corroborates this assumption. Yet, it's a gospel truth that Left supporters ardently believe in. A State, which the Left ruled for well over three decades, may crawl at the bottom of all development indices, but communists remain spokespersons of the country's economic policy. The minorities in Bengal may be the worst-off compared to other States, including those ruled by the 'communal' BJP, yet the Left pretends to be the self-appointed guardian of secularism. It may regularly pay homage to Stalin — one of the most heinous mass murderers of the last century, one who inspired Hitler to copy his Gulag experiments at Auschwitz and elsewhere — yet the Left has patented the right to parade as the sole 'conscience-keeper' of the country. And, yes, the Left's habit of being historically on the wrong side of patriotism might be a crime in other countries, but here in India it is ironically seen as a badge of conscience — much like an Orwellian world where war is peace, freedom is slavery, and ignorance is strength.

Today, as the Left remains in power in only one State, Tripura, which will go to polls in 2013, and where the credit primarily goes to the personal integrity of Chief Minister Manik Sarkar rather than ideology, a few questions need to be answered: Is the Left now history? If so, should we celebrate it, or hold a condolence meet? And, will the decline of political affiliations associated with communism end the reverential position Marxist ideals hold in the country?

Is left history now?

Since Independence, the world of Indian communists, unlike their counterparts elsewhere, has remained so static and unchanged that at times one is left wondering if the fall of the Berlin Wall was a reality at all and the Soviet Union not a thing of the past. The scenario, however, has changed in the past two years. The political Left, which never had it as good as in 2004 when communists won 53 Lok Sabha seats at a 51.5 per cent success rate, has been witnessing one crisis after another since 2009. In 1952, the communists had won 16 Lok Sabha seats out of 39 contested; in 2009, they could just win 20 out of 130 contested. Its steep decline between 2004 and 2009 is too obvious to ignore — from winning more than half the seats contested to winning just 15 per cent. The previous lowest percentage of seats won by the communists was 21.2 per cent in 1962 at the height of anti-Left sentiment following the India-China war.

Why is the Left in such a mess today? The blame partly lies with its overconfidence because the comrades took their 2004-08 political supremacy for granted. And why not! Such was their influence back then that one would often see the stock market shudder at the slightest threat from the communists, and the Government ever-ready to change its economic policies simply to appease them. Then suddenly, the Left decided to pull the plug off U.P.A- I on the issue of the India-US nuclear deal. While the Government survived the no-confidence motion, the Left lost its hold over the Centre.

What, however, is truly damaging the Left's cause is the fact that Indian communism has turned into an anachronism. In Bengal, for instance, the demons it nurtured for three decades came back to hound the party in Singur and Nandigram. Technically, Buddhadeb Bhattacharjee wasn't wrong when he set aside 30 years of the Left's de-industrialization policy. He faltered when he took a cue from China in coercively giving industrialists a fertile, arable land without taking farmers into consideration. Even in Kerala, another communist stronghold, Marx seems an odd man out as one in four households in the State have a relative toiling in the Gulf, migrant workers who remit close to 200 billion INR (Indian Rupees) annually. How can a party so incompatible with the forces of market do well in a consumption-oriented State like Kerala?

The Left needs to introspect. Strangely, however, Marxists believe that there is nothing to worry about: Elections are lost, and there is always the next election. They seem to draw solace from Kerala where they almost pulled it off, falling short of the Congress-led UDF's tally by merely four seats. But if we look closely, it was not the Left, but the image of VS Achuthanandan, who even fought against the party on the issue of corruption, which almost managed to beat the anti-incumbency factor. This again brings us to Tripura's Manik Sarkar, who has been regarded as the "poorest Chief Minister of India", with a bank balance of Rs 13,920 in January 2008, and whose wife continues to take a rickshaw to office everyday despite her husband being at the helm of affairs in the State for three consecutive terms.

Why should we celebrate?

"The enemy is the great justification of terror, and the totalitarian state needs enemies to survive. If it lacks enemies, it invents them. Once they have been identified, they are treated without mercy. Belonging to the enemy class is enough; there is no need actually to have done anything at all," said Franco-Bulgarian philosopher Tzvetan Todorov. These words aptly sum up both the ideology and the history of world communism — from Russia to China and Cuba to Cambodia. How else could one explain the 1978 Cuban law that was adopted to prevent a crime even before it actually happened? Or, what Lenin told his colleague Zinoviev: "It is of supreme importance that we encourage and make use of the energy of mass terror," to which the latter remarked, "To dispose of our enemies, we will have to create our own socialist terror"? Or, our own BT Ranadive who ensured PC Joshi was kept languishing in a room till he got rid of the idea that India had got Independence, that communism should adapt itself to Indian ethos and realities? Indian communism, therefore, had little or no stakes in the freedom struggle. Mohit Sen recalls in his autobiography, *A Traveller and the Road*, how Indian comrades were surprised when Vietnam's communist leader Ho Chi Minh said that his colleagues were hugely influenced by India's freedom struggle led by Mahatma Gandhi and Jawaharlal Nehru. After all, for Indian communists, Gandhi and Nehru were nothing more than "the running followers of American imperialism"!

Though the Left never directly ruled the country, its impact remained remarkably visible in every aspect of administration, culture and economy. Right from the days of Partition, when Marxists provided a semblance of respectability to the idea of the country's division on religious lines, to the India-China War in 1962, when the Left's loyalty was very much in doubt, the communists have always remained on the wrong side of history. In the next decade, 1975 to be precise, a section of the Left even supported the imperious Indira Gandhi Government in its efforts to impose Emergency in the country. Not stopping there, the communists, riding against massive popular support, not only derided the Pokhran tests in 1998 but also went so far as to question the Government's war efforts during the

Kargil conflict. Why do communists behave the way they did on countless such occasions?

Most of the blame primarily lies with the alien nature of Marxism, whose decisions were mostly taken to suit the Soviet — and even Chinese — interests. If the erstwhile USSR decided to support the allies in their war efforts, Indian communists never hesitated in making a U-turn to join hands with the British Government in India. And, if Stalin thought otherwise, Indian communists wouldn't mind mending their differences with the Congress. For Indian comrades, the nature of World War II altered with changed Soviet stand on the issue. This still remains the case with most Indian comrades, with China replacing the Soviet Union as the only 'fatherland'.

The decline of the Left should also be celebrated because of its pathetic economic record. Forget West Bengal, whose share of manufacturing output tumbled from 13 per cent to a pathetic three per cent in the three decades of its rule, it was the Left's bankrupt economic policy that ensured India remained a begging bowl for most part of the last century. Harvard scholars Jeffrey D Sachs and Andrew M Warner concluded that 13 third world countries, which were open economies, grew at an average 4.5 per cent between 1970 and 1990, while the remaining 74 countries following a closed path had only a 0.7 per cent growth rate. Ironically, the phenomenon was given a Hindu name, calling the sluggish economic performance a 'Hindu growth rate'! The Left's administrative record has been no less pathetic. The communists in Bengal proceeded to politicize every possible institution, ranging from the civil services to the police. Not content with their ideological penetration of these entities, they also tampered with school and college curricula, besides appointing university administrators on the basis of their political affiliations. Worse, the Left-front Government compromised with parochialism in order to sustain its vote base when its economic policies in the State had exhausted its ability to deliver. This was evidently visible when it banned the teaching of English at the primary school level in 1982. Jyoti Basu, then Chief Minister of Bengal, advertised this as a triumph for the mother tongue. The move, in reality, was a retreat into mindless regionalism by a party that had lost its imagination. No wonder, Basu's grandchildren were sent to the prestigious La Martiniere for studies! And, it was ensured that they learnt English, and not just the mother language.

Is it all over for Communism?

Marxism has often been called a secular religion — creed complete with prophet, sacred texts and the promise of 'heaven'. Not being a man of science, as is erroneously believed, Marx founded a faith. The economic and political systems he inspired are dead or dying now. But his religion continues to flourish. No wonder, there is an attempt to revive the image of Marx, making him relevant in today's 'free' world. Some even reinvent him as the prophet of globalization. At least Lord Meghnad Desai does so. In his book, *Marx's Revenge*, he writes that capitalism's quest for profit is so dynamic that it is compelled, however inequitably, to be a transforming economic force that must flow into every nook and cranny of the world. Once all its possibilities have been exhausted — which might take centuries — the path of socialism will automatically be paved. Lord Desai further adds that Marx would have deplored the way his ideas were bent to serve the Russian revolution and Soviet Communism, because that development obstructed what capitalism was destined to do. For Desai, the revolution came far too early; it massively predated the development of Russian capitalism, which could not have done its modernizing work by 1917. *Marx's Revenge* is nothing but an apologia of the Left. It also shows how deep the impact of Marxism is even among the supporters of the open market.

Thus, as a politico-economic system, communism may be on the way out, but as a creed it remains well entrenched. The political Left may look like an endangered species, but the "spirit of communism" seems well secured in structures like the Sonia Gandhi-led National Advisory Committee. Comrades may be out of business in all States except one, but they are still running a super-government at the Centre. As a system of government, communism is on the edge, but as a system of ideas, its future looks secure. More so because the Right today — as always — disowns everything mainstream about the country. The Left, for instance, used the meanest of slang for Gandhi when he was alive; today, it has hijacked most Gandhian institutions. Gandhi, for all his follies, was closer to the Right than the Left. And, today, it's the Left that dominates the Gandhian discourse. Till the time the Right wakes up to regain its lost space, the Left will have a field day. And, it would continue to flourish as an idea.[18]

India needs political economists

Since the dawn of liberalisation in 1991, India, its people and the economy have undergone a sea change. From a $300 billion economy, we are now fast approaching $2 trillion. The government of India budget, which was one trillion INR then, is now 14 trillion INR and growing at an annual rate of 15 percent. Many state budgets are over one trillion INR. A plethora of Indian businesses are competing to be the best in offering goods and services to customers worldwide. In short, India and Indians are thriving globally in a free market economy.

[18] Utpal Kumar (2011), "Why Left should be History?" Sunday Pioneer, June 5, 2011

Unfortunately, politics in our country is mired in decadence and has been oblivious to these winds of change. Caste still remains the prime factor for political mobilization and populism is still the de facto method for converting crowds into votes. Families dominate the political landscape with very little inner-party democracy. The hierarchical and feudal mindset is predominant and merit is relegated to the background. Cash for votes is common both inside and outside Parliament and legislative assemblies.

Party manifestos promise freebies to various groups of voters during elections power and interest-free loans to farmers, gas connections and television sets to low- and middle-income homes, reservation and appeasement to minorities, laptops and tablets to students, rice and wheat to the socially disadvantaged etc. It is an endless list.

None of the parties even remotely attempts to communicate about the augmentation of resources required to implement such populist schemes. Along with handouts, a fear psychosis is created to sway community votes in favour of a political party or a leader. The result is an absence of creativity and innovation in the Indian political arena for the past two decades.

In order to differentiate it from existing political parties and fulfill its promise of a new alternative should have articulated a vision that would empower people through markets and choice. A political party championing economic freedom is sorely lacking in our political milieu and is the need of the hour.

Politics and politicians must fast forward to align their ideology to meet the rising economic aspirations of a young India. And for that to happen, the political discourse in the country needs to change from the age-old themes of social justice, reservation and secularism to social and infrastructure development, taxation and fiscal consolidation, job creation and prosperity.

The concerns of modern-day India are predominantly economic and lifting **millions out of poverty** will be the greatest challenge of the coming decades.

The upcoming election season offers an opportunity to all political parties to kick-start the change process and shift Indian political discourse to a different paradigm. To attract voters of new India to polling booths, they must deliver a reform-oriented economic message that resonates with hope and optimism in election campaigns and manifestos.

Reforms are a sine qua non for resolving much of the social, economic and fiscal malaise plaguing the country. Hence, it is imperative for political parties to explicitly formulate a long-term reform agenda that offers a clear and definite choice to voters. Agriculture, land usage and education, to name a few state subjects, require reforms from state governments. Transforming archaic labour laws, speeding up infrastructure development and tackling the ever-ballooning subsidy bills are in the domain of central government.

All parties must state their position on the most important tax reform the goods and services tax and propose a transparent political funding process that will reduce corruption, improve efficiency and boost economic growth. And they must level with the voters and be truthful about winners and losers in the battle of subsidies and taxes.

Other reforms like administrative reforms, judicial reforms, police reforms are also required to cut bureaucratic red tape. Many new issues that have cropped up since liberalisation like allocation of natural resources, inequality and urbanization pose enormous policy challenges for the coming decade.

Rapid migration of people from rural to urban areas demands that we start building smarter cities for the future. New and innovative methods must be found to balance the needs of environment and sustainable development.

And there are issues that have not been resolved since Independence from jobs for Kashmiri youth in the north to Cauvery in the south, from Assamese discontent in the east to migration into Mumbai in the west. It is essential for political parties to seek a mandate for governing on these issues and avoid future policy paralysis.

The election season is upon us. Starting with the Himachal and Gujarat assembly elections and culminating in the parliamentary election, there are a slew of them in which more than 200 million young first-time voters are expected to exercise their franchise. The fate of India is likely to unfold in the next 18 months, a defining moment for the country, its people and politics.[19]

The Politics of Dignity

The situations in Egypt and Russia have nothing in common. These two countries have starkly different histories. But having visited both in recent weeks, I can tell you that they have one very big thing in common: the political eruptions in both countries were not initially driven by any particular ideology but rather by the most human of emotions — the quest for dignity and justice. Humiliation is the single most underestimated force in politics. People will absorb hardship, hunger and pain. They will be grateful for jobs, cars and benefits. But if you force people to live indefinitely inside a rigged game that is flaunted in

---

[19] N V Krishnakumar (2012), "Time for a different politics", Times of India, October 26, 2012

their face or make them feel like cattle that can be passed by one leader to his son or one politician to another, eventually they'll explode. These are the emotions that sparked the uprisings in Cairo and Moscow. They don't go away easily, which is why you're in more trouble than you think.

Have you gentlemen looked at the homemade videos going viral around Russia these days? One of my favorites was made by two Russian paratroopers-turned-singers, posted on YouTube under the title "Russian airborne veterans against Vladimir Putin." Their lyrics were aimed directly at you, Mr. Putin, in the wake of the Sept. 24 announcement that President Medvedev would step down and pave the way for you and your party (now widely known as "the party of crooks and thieves") to run for president for two more six-year terms — 12 more years! Russians immediately started calculating how old they'd be when they might see their country led by someone other than you, Mr. Putin. It was depressing for many — made more so by the fact that Mr. Medvedev said that your "trading places" was planned long ago.

Yet no one else was consulted, and you two didn't even bother to offer a narrative as to why Putin should have 12 more years. No wonder that song by the paratroopers to Putin was all about dignity: "You're no different from me, /a man and not God. /I'm no different from you, /a man, not some hick. /We won't let you keep lying. /We won't let you keep stealing. /we're liberated troops who defended the motherland."

Aleksei Navalny, the shareholder-activist-blogger who helped stoke the rallies against you, said to me that nothing spurred the protests more than the daily experience of Muscovites having to sit in traffic while a car with a flashing blue light carrying some Putin crony behind tinted glass speeds past. "It is all about dignity," said Navalny. "Who are these people? Why don't they care about our rights? It doesn't matter at all how good a career you build. You will stand in this traffic, and these people and their sons will drive past you with their blue lights."

Mr. Putin, you have substantial achievements. During your first eight years as president, starting in 2000, you stabilized a collapsing Russia and oversaw the emergence of a big urban middle class. Admittedly, you didn't achieve this with kid gloves, and it was attended with widespread corruption and fueled by oil exports. But enough trickled down so that a real middle class of professionals and entrepreneurs emerged. They are your accidental political offspring — "maybe the first independent political class in modern Russian history," says Max Trudolyubov, the editorial page editor of the Vedomosti newspaper — and now they want a voice in their future.

Have you spoken lately to Mikhail Dmitriev, the president of the Center for Strategic Research? He has been doing focus groups since 2009, which I am told your aides were shown but didn't believe. The anti-Putin protests, Dmitriev found, were not driven by the unemployed but rather by "the highly skilled part of the Russian population" that has come to feel as though "Russian society is a two-lane highway, with one lane for the privileged individuals in proximity to state power," with its own laws or lack of them, "and one lane for the rest of the population."

Beginning in 2009, says Dmitriev, his focus groups all started indicating that this new "wealthy, self-respecting middle class," felt that "they are not recognized as deserving individuals and entitled to be treated with equal rights of everyone else." One phrase, he says, "suddenly appeared all over the country: 'We are not cattle.' " This, he says, is when he realized that "this is a matter of dignity and self-respect."

This struggle between you and your accidental offspring will play out over a long time. But, good sirs, have no doubt about this: politics is back in Russia. Watch out. You, Mr. Putin, will surely win the March presidential election, predicts Dmitriev, "but in a weakened way." The Putin brand is declining, he says. "The trend is downward. This will ensure that Putin is a weak president with declining support."

Therefore, argues Dmitriev, your only hope to remain relevant is to "set up a coalition government, including the opposition, on the basis of free and fair elections and move toward a more balanced and competitive political system." I'd listen to him this time. [20]

CHINA

White paper on political party system

The State Council Information Office published on Thursday a white paper entitled China's Political Party System. The document, composed of seven chapters and one appendix, describes that the political party system China has adopted is multi-party cooperation and political consultation under the leadership of the Communist Party of China and it plays an irreplaceable role in the country's political and social life. The full text of the white paper follows:

China's Political Party System

The political party system is an important component of modern democratic politics. What kind of political party system to adopt in a country is determined by the nature, national conditions and social development of that given country? The diversity of political party systems in different countries reflects the diversity of human civilizations.

---

[20] Thomas L Friedman (2012), "The Politics of dignity", Deccan Chronicle, February 2, 2012

The political party system China has adopted is multi-party cooperation and political consultation under the leadership of the Communist Party of China (CPC) (hereinafter "multi-party cooperation system"), which is different from both the two-party or multi-party competition systems of Western countries and the one-party system practiced in some other countries. This system was established and has been developed during the long-term practice of the Chinese revolution, construction and reform. It is a basic political system that suits the conditions of China. It is a socialist political party system with Chinese characteristics, and a key component of China's socialist democratic politics.

The Constitution of the People's Republic of China states that "the multi-party cooperation and political consultation system under the leadership of the Communist Party of China shall continue to exist and develop for a long time to come." Both the CPC and the democratic parties must take the Constitution as the basic norm of their conduct, and uphold the dignity of the Constitution and ensure its implementation.

Under China's multi-party cooperation system, there are the CPC and eight other political parties. The eight democratic parties are: Revolutionary Committee of the Chinese Kuomintang, China Democratic League, China National Democratic Construction Association, and China Association for Promoting Democracy, Chinese Peasants and Workers Democratic Party, China Zhi Gong Dang, Jiu San Society and Taiwan Democratic Self-Government League. The Chinese People's Political Consultative Conference (CPPCC) is an important institution of multi-party cooperation and political consultation under the leadership of the CPC. Based on the principle of "long-term coexistence, mutual supervision, treating each other with sincerity and sharing each other's weal and woe," the CPC and the eight democratic parties work hand in hand in developing socialism with Chinese characteristics, thus giving rise to the basic feature of "multi-party cooperation system under the leadership of the CPC, with the CPC holding power and the other eight parties participating fully in state affairs." The multi-party cooperation system shows unique political advantage and strong vitality, and plays an irreplaceable role in China's political and social life.

An Inevitable Choice in China's Social Development

China has had a long history of feudalism. From 1840 on, when the Western imperialist powers launched aggressive wars against China, the corrupt and weak feudal ruling class buckled, and China was reduced to a semi-colonial, semi-feudal society. For nearly 110 years after that, the Chinese nation was plunged into the most dangerous situation, and the Chinese people had no democratic rights whatsoever.

To change the fate of the country and the Chinese nation, generation after generation of Chinese people rose up and waged heroic struggles to save the country and the people. In the early 20th century, Sun Yat-sen, forerunner of China's democratic revolution, turned his eyes to the West for a road that would save China. In 1911, he led a bourgeois democratic revolution, bringing to an end the autocratic monarchical system that had been in place for several millenniums. With the founding of the Republic of China, Sun Yat-sen introduced a parliamentary and multi-party system in imitation of that in Western countries. Though historically progressive compared with the autocratic monarchy, the bourgeois political system soon collapsed under the onslaught of domestic and foreign reactionary forces and therefore failed to fulfill the Chinese people's fervent desire for independence and democracy. Mr. Sun Yat-sen later concluded that China could not simply copy European and American politics to govern its own society, as Chinese society was different from that of the West.

Between 1927 and 1949, the Kuomintang headed by Chiang Kai-shek exercised one-party dictatorship and monopolized all state power. It persecuted democratic and progressive forces against the trend of democratic politics and the wishes of the people. It was finally abandoned by history.

The political development of modern China called for a new political party system that suited China's national conditions. Such a historic mission fell on the shoulders of the CPC and its eight partners.

The CPC, founded in 1921, creatively combined the general truth of Marxism-Leninism with the actual situation in China, put forth the revolutionary program of "new democracy," and united all revolutionary classes to fight for national independence, the liberation of the people, the prosperity of the country, and the well-being of the people. The eight democratic parties, mostly founded during the War of Resistance against Japanese Aggression (1937-1945) and the War of Liberation (1945-1949), were rooted among the national bourgeoisie and urban petty bourgeoisie, as well as intellectuals and other patriots associated with them. These people formed a progressive force who were anti-imperialist, patriotic and demanded democracy.

In the days of tough struggles, the CPC has established and developed close relations of cooperation with the eight democratic parties and joined forces with them to fight for peace and democracy. During the War of Resistance against Japanese Aggression, the democratic parties actively joined the national united front led by the CPC and the democratic movement against the Japanese invaders, and made concerted efforts for national unity and progress and against the surrendering, splitters' and retrogressive activities of diehard elements in the Kuomintang. After the war, they, together with the CPC, continued the fight against the policies of dictatorship and civil war adopted by the Kuomintang and Chiang Kai-shek clique.

While leading the new democratic revolution to victory, the CPC established its core leadership role among the various revolutionary forces. And the democratic parties and democratic personages without party affiliation, through experience in the years of practice and on their own initiative, chose the leadership of the CPC. In April 1948, the CPC's proposal to convene a new political consultation conference and set up a democratic coalition government was warmly endorsed by the democratic parties and democratic personages without party affiliation. They made it public that they were willing to strive to build a New China under the leadership of the CPC. The convention of the first Chinese People's Political Consultative Conference (CPPCC) in September 1949 marked the formal establishment of the multi-party cooperation system under the leadership of the CPC. It also marked the beginning of the CPC, the democratic parties and the democratic personages without party affiliation working together in building the state power of New China.

After the People's Republic of China was founded on October 1, 1949, the ruling CPC further strengthened its unity and cooperation with the democratic parties and continued to push forward the theoretical innovation and development in practical work regarding multi-party cooperation. After the socialist transformation was completed in 1956, and in light of the profound changes that had taken place among China's social classes, the CPC set forth the principle of "long-term coexistence and mutual supervision," which meant that the other eight democratic parties would exist as long as the CPC exists, and that they and the CPC could supervise each other. Since the CPC was the ruling party, the other eight parties would play more of a supervisory role. Thus, the basic framework of multi-party cooperation in socialist China came into being. But after 1957, especially during the "cultural revolution" (1966-1976), the multi-party cooperation system suffered serious setbacks.

After the reform and opening-up policies were adopted in 1978, the CPC, in light of the changes in the situation and tasks, made it clear that the multi-party cooperation system is a basic feature and advantage of China's political system, and set forth the principle of "long-term coexistence, mutual supervision, treating each other with sincerity and sharing each other's weal and woe" to guide its relations with the other eight parties. It also set forth a complete set of theories and policies regarding the multi-party cooperation system, making sticking to and improving the system an important component of the theory and practice of Chinese-style socialism.

In 1989, the CPC formulated the Opinions on Sticking to and Improving the System of Multi-party Cooperation and Political Consultation under the Leadership of the CPC, thus institutionalizing the multi-party cooperation system. The First Session of the Eighth National People's Congress in 1993 added to the Constitution the words "multi-party cooperation and political consultation system under the leadership of the Communist Party of China shall continue to exist and develop for a long time to come," providing a constitutional basis for the system. After the 16th CPC National Congress in 2002, the CPC, in its effort to build a socialist political civilization, released two documents -- Opinions on Further Strengthening the Building of the Multi-party Cooperation and Political Consultation System under the Leadership of the CPC, and Opinions on Strengthening the Work of the CPPCC -- to further standardize and institutionalize the multi-party cooperation system.

Since the founding of New China, the multi-party cooperation system has been continuously developing and consolidated, and is playing a significant role in the state's political and social life.

The political history and practice of modern and contemporary China prove that the construction of democratic politics in China must proceed from the country's basic conditions, and blind emulation of the political or party systems of any other country will never succeed; and that dictatorship will also end in failure, as it is against the law of historical development and the people's will. The formation and development of China's multi-party cooperation system was a logical choice of its modern and contemporary history, a product of the combination of Marxism-Leninism and China's own situation, and a crystallization of the wisdom of the CPC and other democratic parties.

This system is well suited to China's conditions, the reality of China's revolution, construction and reform, and the essential demands of socialist democracy. It reflects the fine cultural tradition of the Chinese nation, which features all embracing and harmony while reserving differences. With splendid Chinese features, this system both accords with the trend of the times and embodies the inherent requirements of China's social development.[21]

South Africa: Political Parties

South Africa is a federal parliamentary representative democratic republic, wherein the President of South Africa, elected by parliament, is the head of

[21] White paper on China's political party system, Alibaba Com Published: 26 Jul 2010

government, and of a multi-party system. The government exercises the executive power. Legislative power is vested in both in government and the two chambers of Parliament, the Council of Provinces and the National Assembly. The Judiciary is independent of the executive and the legislature. Government is three-tiered, with representatives being elected at the national, provincial and local levels. South African Political Parties had until the 2 March 2009 to submit their candidates for the South African 2009 Elections.

Altogether 42 political parties submitted candidates' lists of the 117 parties that are registered nationally.

General Elections 2009: African Christian Democratic Party: African Christian Democratic Party, ACDP, As a fast growing party in the country, the ACDP offers a fresh start based on Christian and family values. We are determined to address issues such as education, unemployment, health care, security and poverty, based on proven successful policies. We aim to rebuild the foundation of the nation by protecting families from the destructive effects of gambling, prostitutions etc.

African National Congress (ANC): The aims and objectives of the African National Congress, ANC are to:

(a) Unite all the people of South Africa, Africans in particular, for the complete liberation of the country from all forms of discrimination and national oppression.
(b) End apartheid in all its forms and transform South Africa as rapidly as possible into a united, non-racial, non-sexist and democratic country based on the principles of the Freedom Charter and in pursuit of the national democratic revolution.

(c) Defend the democratic gains of the people and to advance towards a society in which the government is freely chosen by the people according to the principles of universal suffrage on a common voters' role.
(d) Fight for social justice and to eliminate the vast inequalities created by apartheid and the system of national oppression.
(e) Build a South African nation with a common patriotism and loyalty in which the cultural, linguistic and religious diversity of the people is recognized.
(f) Promote economic development for the benefit of all.
(g) Support and advance the cause of women's emancipation.
(h) Support and advance the cause of national liberation, development, world peace, disarmament and environmentally sustainable development.
(i) Support and promote the struggle for the rights of children and the disabled.

Congress of the People: The Congress of the People (COPE) is a South African political party formed in 2008 by former members of the African National Congress (ANC).[1] The party was founded by ex-ANC members Mosiuoa Lekota, Mbhazima Shilowa and Mluleki George and will contest the 2009 general election. The party was announced following a national convention held in Sandton on 1 November 2008, and was founded at a congress held in Bloemfontein on 16 December 2008. The name echoes the 1955 Congress of the People at which the Freedom Charter was adopted by the ANC and other parties, a name strongly contested by the ANC in a legal move dismissed by the Pretoria High Court.

In an interview with The Sunday Times, Lekota stated that the ideology of the party will be one that embraces multiracial and multicultural participation in governance, promoting of the free market and removed from the Marxism that had long influenced the ANC's ideology since it first allied with the South African Communist Party in the 1950s during the anti-apartheid struggle.

Democratic Alliance: Democratic Alliance, DA, dreams of South Africa for an open opportunity society in which every person is free, secure and equal, where everyone has the opportunity to improve the quality of his life and pursue her dreams, and in which every language and culture has equal respect and recognition.

This is the dream they pledge to deliver – the South African dream of one nation, with one future, living together under the constitution in peace, security and prosperity, with opportunity and recognition for all the rainbow people.

The three components of the 'Open Opportunity Society for All' bring together three key concepts: –

(a) Individual freedom under the rule of law an open society;
(b) Opportunity with responsibility – an opportunity society; and
(c) Full equality for all.

In doing so, it creates a fourth concept that underpins our vision of the proper relationship between individuals, the state and society in South Africa today. Our vision is grounded in the idea that every human being has a right to dignity. Human dignity is the foundational concept that informs our values and vision.

Freedom Front plus FF+

(a)The Freedom Front Plus, FF, FF+, is closely associated with the Afrikaner settlement of Orania, whose long-term goal is to establish an independent state for Afrikaners.

(b)The Freedom Front Plus wishes to represent the voice of the Afrikaner in all spheres of government. As such, it cannot count on the attraction of large number of votes. Instead, it seeks to produce results for the Afrikaner in the way in which they approach the governing party.

(c)It is also looking at ways beyond normal parliamentarian politics to benefit Afrikaners. This forms part of their strategy of being "More than just opposition".

Independent Democrats ID: The Party believes that the most important problems facing the country are: Unemployment, Poverty, Crime, Corruption, Housing, HIV/AIDS, Education and Health. The ID aim to improve the lives of all South Africans.

Inkatha Freedom Party (I F P):

(a) Purpose, values & vision:
(b) Policy priorities and challenges
(c) Economic growth and job creation
(d) Combating poverty
(e) Law and Order
(f) Education
(g) Health
(h) Redressing the past
(i) Land reform
(j) The role of South Africa in the world
(k) The moral challenge

The United Democratic Movement (UDM) is a centre-left, social-democratic, South African political party, formed by a prominent former National Party leader, Roelf Meyer (who has since resigned from the UDM) former African National Congress and homeland leader, Bantu Holomisa and John Taylor former ANC

REC member in 1997. It has an anti-separatist, pro-diversity platform; and supports an individualist South Africa with a strong moral sense, in both social and economic senses.[22]

Europe's Democracy itself is at Stake

Amartya Sen[23] the Nobel laureate has analyzed the practice of democracy in Europe. It is therefore worrying that the dangers to democratic governance today, coming through the back door of financial priority, are not receiving the attention they should. There are profound issues to be faced about how Europe's democratic governance could be undermined by the hugely heightened role of financial institutions and rating agencies, which now lord it freely over parts of Europe's political terrain.

Two distinct issues need to be separated. The first concerns the place of democratic priorities, including what Walter Bagehot and John Stuart Mill saw as the need for "governance by discussion." Suppose we accept that the powerful financial bosses have a realistic understanding of what needs to be done. This would strengthen the case for paying attention to their voices in a democratic dialogue. But that is not the same thing as allowing the international financial institutions and rating agencies the unilateral power to command democratically elected governments.

Second, it is quite hard to see that the sacrifices that the financial commanders have been demanding from precarious countries would deliver the ultimate viability of these countries and guarantee the continuation of the euro within an unreformed pattern of financial amalgamation and an unchanged

---

[22] South African Political Parties and Election Results 2009

[23] Amartya sen (2011), "Europe's Democracy itself is at Stake", Guardian News Paper Limited, 2011 /

membership of the euro club. The diagnosis of economic problems by rating agencies is not the voice of verity that they pretend. It is worth remembering that the record of rating agencies in certifying financial and business institutions preceding the 2008 economic crisis was so abysmal that the U.S. Congress seriously debated whether they should be prosecuted.

Since much of Europe is now engaged in achieving quick reduction of public deficits through drastic reduction of public expenditure, it is crucial to scrutinize realistically what the likely impact of the chosen policies may be, both on people and the generating of public revenue through economic growth. The high morals of "sacrifice" do, of course, have an intoxicating effect. This is the philosophy of the "right" corset: "If madam is at all comfortable in it, then madam certainly needs a smaller size." However, if the demands of financial appropriateness are linked too mechanically to immediate cuts, the result could be the killing of the goose that lays the golden egg of economic growth.

This concern applies to a number of countries, from Britain to Greece. The commonality of the "blood, sweat and tears" strategy of deficit reduction gives some apparent plausibility to what is being imposed on more precarious countries like Greece or Portugal. It also makes it harder to have a united political voice in Europe that can stand up to the panic generated in the financial markets.

In addition to a bigger political vision, there is a need for clearer economic thinking. The tendency to ignore the importance of economic growth in generating public revenue should be a major item for scrutiny. The strong connection between growth and public revenue has been observed in many countries, from China and India to the U.S. and Brazil.

There are lessons from history here, too. The big public debts of many countries when the Second World War ended caused huge anxieties, but the burden diminished rapidly thanks to fast economic growth. Similarly, the huge deficits that President Clinton faced when he came to office in 1992 melted away during his presidency, greatly aided by speedy economic growth.

The fear of a threat to democracy does not, of course, apply to Britain, since a government empowered by democratic elections has chosen these policies. Even though the unfolding of a strategy that was not revealed at the time of election can be a reason for some pause, this is the kind of freedom that a democratic system does allow the electorally victorious. But that does not eliminate the need for more public discussion, even in Britain. There is also a need to recognize how the self-chosen restrictive policies in Britain seem to give plausibility to the even more drastic policies being imposed on Greece.

How did some of the Euro countries get into this mess? The oddity of going for a united currency without more political and economic integration has certainly played a part, even after taking note of financial transgressions that have undoubtedly been committed in the past by countries such as Greece or Portugal (and even after noting Mario Monti's important point that a culture of "excessive deference" in the EU has allowed these transgressions to go unchecked). It is to the huge credit of the Greek government — George Papandreou, the Prime Minister, in particular — that it is doing what it can despite political resistance, but the pained willingness of Athens to comply does not eliminate the European need to examine the wisdom of the requirements — and the timing — being imposed on Greece.

Worry about the Euro:

It is no consolation for me to recollect that I was firmly opposed to the euro, despite being very strongly in favour of European unity. My worry about the euro was partly connected with each country giving up the freedom of monetary policy and of exchange rate adjustments, which have greatly helped countries in difficulty in the past, and prevented the necessity of massive destabilization of human lives in frantic efforts to stabilize the financial markets. That monetary freedom could be given up when there is also political and fiscal integration (as the states in the U.S. have), but the halfway house of the euro zone has been a recipe for disaster. The wonderful political idea of a united democratic Europe has been made to incorporate a precarious programme of incoherent financial amalgamation. Rearranging the euro zone now would have many problems, but difficult issues have to be intelligently discussed, rather than allowing Europe to drift in financial winds fed by narrow-minded thinking with a terrible track record. The process has to begin with some immediate restraining of the unopposed power of rating agencies to issue unilateral commands.

These agencies are hard to discipline despite their abysmal record, but a well-reflected voice of legitimate governments can make a big difference to financial confidence while solutions are worked out, especially if the international financial institutions lend their support. Stopping the marginalisation of the democratic tradition of Europe has an urgency that is hard to exaggerate. European democracy is important for Europe — and for the world.

SRI LANKA

Tamil hopes and national unity

The sweeping victory of the Tamil National Alliance in local elections in Sri Lanka's North lends a fresh perspective to talks with the government that lie ahead.

More than two years ago the guns fell silent in Sri Lanka, ending a three decade-old civil war with the LTTE. But voices demanding an acceptable solution that accommodates Tamil aspirations are still strident. The country's leadership is seeking to meet these demands within a national unity framework. The expected landslide victory of the Tamil National Alliance (TNA) — the most popular political formation in the Northern Province, which before the war ended openly supported the armed secessionist movement — in the local body polls held in the Tamil-dominated Northern Province last Saturday has provided a platform from which the TNA can launch its renewed demand for an enduring long-term solution to the problem.

The elections have cleared the air once again on which party represented the Tamils of the North. President Mahinda Rajapaksa inaugurated a slew of schemes ahead of the elections. As many as 13 Ministers were in Jaffna and other parts of the Northern Province through the campaign. While the United People's Freedom Alliance (UPFA) made some gains in the North, the war-battered people still placed their faith in the TNA.

The elections affirmed that the lone Tamil Minister in the Sri Lankan Cabinet, Douglas Devananda, was a marginal player. His party, the EPDP, contested the polls as part of the UPFA. Some senior members of the EPDP contend that this was a mistake and ascribe the defeat to their being part of the UPFA. While the rest of the country preferred the UPFA (it won 250 out of the 335 local bodies in the country), the North was firmly with the TNA (30 local bodies).

With the local elections done, and the Northern Provincial Council election expected to be held in 2012, the TNA and the government have come back to the negotiating table. The TNA's victory lends a fresh perspective to the talks. It also gives the Tamil alliance a chance to exhibit its maturity while obliging the government to show better understanding and sensitivity.

Progress in the talks is imperative for the next step — a Select Committee of Parliament, which will consider the Tamil question, and come up with a proposed solution, including constitutional amendments, that will then go to Parliament. This move has been criticised by the TNA as yet another ploy to delay giving Tamils their rights. But in a country where any solution to the ethnic question is likely to be portrayed by chauvinist elements as a sell-out of national interests, the government clearly feels it is left with no choice but to involve all stakeholders in the process of finding a political solution.

Some commentators in the media have expressed scepticism about the parliamentary Select Committee route, citing examples from the past on the fate of such committees. Given the challenge of finding a worthwhile meeting ground between an exceptionally strong government and a hopelessly decimated opposition, the government has certainly given the impression that it appears to be in no hurry to push through a solution. It appears keen to create a perception that it would yield no ground to Tamils that even remotely hints at autonomy. In Sri Lanka, the words 'autonomy' and 'secession' have often been used interchangeably and Mr. Rajapaksa has made it clear that he will not allow anyone to divide the nation again.

The President had told *The Hindu* earlier that he had a solution to the Tamil problem in mind. In later interactions, he made it clear that he did not want to impose any solution. He wanted talks involving all stakeholders, but with the government and the TNA taking the lead, to map it out. His broad idea was to accord the maximum possible devolution without sacrificing the sovereignty of the country. The prospective political solution came to be known as '13th Amendment-plus,' with nobody apparently clear about the specifics.

The question that has been raised often is this: How much devolution is enough to run a Province in a small country without the central authority bearing down on it? There seem to be no ready answers.

As for democratic governance, for decades there has been no such institutional structure or framework for it in the North. The elimination of the LTTE as a military organisation in May 2009 gave rise to expectations that democratic elections would be held as early as feasible. Twenty six months after the war ended, eight out of the nine Sri Lankan provinces have elected Provincial Councils; the Northern Province is the only one without one. The powers of a Provincial Council might be limited, but an elected Northern Council would be a starting point for people to voice their grievances, opposition politicians feel.

While the LTTE's defeat weighs on the TNA, triumphalism and the need to cater to its Sinhala vote base have made it difficult for the government to concede the space required to make the Tamils, widely perceived as the vanquished, feel at ease. Opposition politicians, NGO activists, and some in the intelligentsia point to several moves in the North that could be misconstrued as the reason for the deep wedge between the minority Tamil and majority Sinhala communities.

For instance, there have been reports of lower level officials, who only know Sinhala, being posted to the North. Tamils in that region, unlike those in the plantations, hardly speak the Sinhala language. Opposition politicians have also expressed concern over the resettlement of ex-servicemen along the A-9 highway that leads to Jaffna from Colombo.

Apart from rehabilitation and livelihood issues, Sri Lanka will have to address the issue of missing persons. The chaotic last phase of the war, in which civilians were trapped between the Army's shells and the LTTE firepower, led to the loss of a large number of lives and many disappearances. Many persons are yet to be accounted for.

As Sri Lanka debates how best to integrate the northern Tamils into its evolving concept of Sri Lankan nationalism, individual players in the international community have been trying to apply pressure on the island nation. The Brussels-based think-tank, International Crisis Group, points out that all three communities — Sinhala, Tamil and Muslims — have suffered "immensely." It wants the major international partners in the region to "send a strong message against increasing authoritarianism and condition aid on transparency and restored civilian administration in the north and east."

A few recent developments have focussed attention on Sri Lanka since April 2011. One is the report of the United Nations Secretary General's Expert Panel on Accountability in Sri Lanka, which has held both the government and the LTTE responsible for the mass civilian casualties during the last stages of the war (There is also the U.S. State department report for 2010, the Human Rights Watch report on Sri Lanka and the International Crisis Group report). The second is a Channel 4 video that showed what it asserted were extra-judicial killings and other atrocities in Sri Lanka. The third item is a book *The Cage*, authored by an 'insider,' Gordon Weiss, former U.N. spokesperson in Sri Lanka, castigating Sri Lanka's handling of the final stages of the war and faulting the international community for doing little to limit civilian casualties. Although the Sri Lankan government has maintained that it carried out a humanitarian operation to rescue people from the LTTE's clutches, a U.N. Panel, which relied on, among other things, over 4,000 depositions and satellite images, came up with five findings against the Government of Sri Lanka and six against the LTTE.

Ever since the release of the United Nations report, Sri Lanka has been on a diplomatic offensive, seeking to win friends across the globe. China, Russia, and a few other countries have openly supported the Sri Lankan viewpoint — that the country was being unnecessarily victimised and that the U.N. Report did not help reconciliation in any manner. The release of the Channel 4 video and the Weiss book also saw Sri Lankan diplomats defend their country combatively across western capitals and even in Colombo.

India, one of Sri Lanka's staunchest allies, is somewhat impatient with the pace of rehabilitation and rebuilding in the Northern Province, for which India has offered wide-spectrum support, and with the pace of working out a 13th Amendment-plus political settlement in the post-conflict period. But there is also evidence of Indian tardiness in implementing the rebuilding work, especially the massive housing programme, Sri Lanka's big neighbour has undertaken in the North. From a distance, the brutal and bloody war against the LTTE seems to have been the easier campaign to win. Now Sri Lanka battles complex international and domestic pressures as it marches ahead to realise its dream of a bright and prosperous future for its people.[24]

Religious leaders denounce fanaticism

Religious leaders have joined with Pope Benedict XVI to denounce violence perpetrated in the name of their faiths, amid growing religious fanaticism across the world.

---

[24] Radhakrishnan R K (2011), " Sri Lanka: Tamil hopes and national unity", The Hindu, July 28, 2011

No more violence, no more war, no more terrorism! Never again! In the name of God, that every religion bring justice and peace, forgiveness and life and love to the world!
--- Pope at the Saint Francis basilica in Assisi, Italy.

The colourful crowd of religious representatives had taken a special train from Vatican City to Assisi, where Buddhist monks mixed with turbaned Sikhs, black-frocked patriarchs and Catholic cardinals in their red skullcaps.

The small group that waited under a leaden sky in the northern Italian city to meet them off the train was a far shout from the welcome crowd that greeted John Paul II at inter-religious councils in 1986 and 2002.

A frail-looking Benedict robed in white was the last to get off the train and walked slowly up to the basilica, greeting the delegation heads and members of the Franciscan order - founded by Saint Francis of Assisi - on his way.

More than 50 Islamic representatives were in attendance, alongside Jewish rabbis, Hindus, Buddhists, Jains, Sikhs, a Zoroastrian, a Bahai and delegates of Taoism, Confucianism and traditional religions from Africa and America.

In the vast basilica, which includes the tiny chapel where the animal-loving Francis died in 1226, dignitaries watched a film that looked back over the past 25 years to celebrate the anniversary of the first Assisi meeting.

The pallid 84-year-old Pope seemed much smaller and more fragile than his guests, sitting between Bartholomew I, the Archbishop of Constantinople, and Rabbi David Rosen, representing the Chief Rabbinate of Israel.

Addressing the delegates, the pontiff strongly denounced religious terrorism, describing it as "the antithesis of religion" which "contributes to its destruction".

He also expressed his shame for Christian acts of violence committed in the name of God in the past.

Mr. Kyai Haji Hasyim Muzadi, chairman of the International Conference of Islamic Scholars (ICIS), said that violence committed in the name of God included elements which "seem" religious but are "political, economical and cultural."

Professor Wande Abimbola, representing Africa's traditional faiths, called for them to be given the same respect as other religions and encouraged his fellow dignitaries not to underestimate the importance of nature.

"Until Mother Nature receives our attention, human beings will not be able to find the true peace and tranquility we all search for," he said, before launching into a Yoruba hymn.

The event had been criticized by Catholic fundamentalists, who are strongly against the idea of dialogue with other religions and accused the pontiff of "welcoming false religions".

In organizing the "journey of reflection, dialogue and prayer for peace and justice", the Vatican had been careful to avoid any moments of common prayer.

The delegates were treated to a frugal lunch of rice, salad and fruit before withdrawing to spend a solitary hour and a half in individual monk cells, praying and reflecting on the day's themes.

Bartholomew I, who sat with the Pope at lunch, expressed concerns over "the increased marginalisation of Christian communities in the Middle East"

"The only way to end the warmongering use of religion is to set ourselves up as mediators of the peace," he said.

That peace, according to Olav Fykse Tveit, general secretary of the World Council of Churches should be brokered as soon as possible in Jerusalem, a city that has fuelled other conflicts around the world, he said.

At the end of the day of talks, the main participants renewed their commitment to peace in the square in front of Saint Francis's Basilica.

French Cardinal Jean-Louis Tauran, the head of the Pontifical Council for Interreligious Dialogue, said he hoped each would "return home as a witness and a messenger" because "peace is possible, even today".[25]

Conclusion

A political party-in-power undertakes populist measures like cheap rice, subsidized petrol, cooking gas, free small houses, and free uniform to students and free blankets to senior citizens to attract the voters in democracy. Similarly, the poor peasants are awarded subsidized fertilizer, seeds, and pesticides by the government. The government also allows subsidized bank loan, tractor, pond digging and low cost houses to poor farmers. This attracts the vulnerable section of the society toward the political party in power. Because the intention of subsidy is to attract voters; and they give vote to that political

[25] David Smock (2011), "Religious leaders denounce fanaticism" USIP's Religion and Peacemaking Center of Innovation, November 16, 2011

party. But the political parties can not cheat the poor people for all time.

This happened in the United States of America in 1890s. The farmers observed the visible demons – land monopolists, railroad owners, wholesale merchants, speculators, bankers and politicians – who had taken a lot more than legitimate profit in their dealings with the rural masses. The initial grumblings slowly grew into a frenzied movement with which other underprivileged groups joined and all of them staked their hopes on political action. Soon enough, politicians emerged to take advantage of this discontent. Thus was born the **People's Party** which was the lynch pin of the popular movement. The Blacks and women joined the movement. This combination succeeded in the electoral battle despite fraudulent voting, violence, political murders and so on indulged by their opponents. This populist movement collapsed in 1896. Hence, the government should not take steps that harm the people in the long run.

1. The political party must include or hire or take the help of economists, planners and social workers in the party to assist and guide in formulating the 'election manifesto' and annual plans for the best uses of resources for the benefits of the people and country.

2. The regional parties behave as adopted sons of the country, which speak against the central government to hide their own mistakes and corruption. So, all political parties must be national political parties. If a political party cannot get 5 percent polled votes in the general election, the political party stands de-recognized by the Election Commission.

3. Each country needs good and cultured people to be elected to the Parliament, Senate or Assembly to

make laws for the benefit of all. Let the august house do justice to the nation.

4. Let percentage of votes polled by each party has the same percentage of elected members in the Parliament or Assembly. So only the presidents of all political parties should contest for the nation and party candidates would be only shadow candidates for each constituency. This would reduce political nuisance and vote capturing expenses.

5. Each political party should invite corporate houses, editors of news papers, farmer organizations and hungry people to know their suggestions for the future plans separately.

6. There could be only national political parties in each country and it should be limited to 10 political parties. A number of regional parties could be united and be designated as a national party. Only party candidates can contest in General Elections.

7. The aim of each political party should be for the welfare of the people and country. It can not be personified. A great man, who is no more, cannot be the property of his son or relatives as he worked for the nation. A party with a proper name must be disallowed by the Election Commission.

8. Each political party must respect the Constitution and law of the land and assure justice to all without ifs and buts. So reservation or positive discrimination must be avoided by law. The political party in power must see that all scheduled tribe and scheduled caste students be awarded **'full assistance in education'** till completion of graduate studies because they were the real sufferers for centuries.

9. There should not be reservations in elections, constituencies, government services, and cadre promotions for any religion, caste, creed or sex or for

any special cause because all are equal with others as per the Constitution.

10. The Presidents of political parties should hold the post for a period of 4 years only. He / she should not hold a government post during this period. A person can hold the political post for two terms only.

11. The posts of the President of a country / Governor of a state should be for 4 years and they could be reappointed for the second term too. But they cannot be evicted before the term ends.

12. The term of MPs or MLAs or Senators should be 4 years only. They can be the Members for the Parliament or Assembly for two terms in life.

13. There should not be 'Quota System or Reservation System' in election to the Senate, Parliament, or Assembly elections. There should not be bye-election after the sad demise of an elected leader; his/her spouse should be allowed to the august house by simply speaker's notification.

14. We can achieve WORLD PEACE provided the United Nations makes an attempt to achieve it by making international laws through mutual cooperation and implementation of the laws. And, it is possible.

+++++

Chapter – III

POLITICAL PROBLEMS IN COUNTRIES

I have just three things to teach: simplicity, patience, and compassion. These three are your greatest treasures. Simple in actions and thoughts, you return to the source of your being. Patience with both friends and enemies, you accord with the way things are. Compassionate toward yourself, you reconcile all beings in the world. -----Tao Te Ching: 1967

Politics is associated with power, prestige, money, corruption, false promises, garlands, reception, publicity and achievement. Politics can add misfortune, unemployment, family trouble, political rallies, political jail and poverty through out life. In broader prospective, politics can make a change in the society by an individual, a group of like-minded youths.

Political problems arise when there is a tussle between revolutionaries and the corrupt government.

A corrupt political party has corrupt leaders and corrupt workers. They want to earn maximum possible wealth within the shortest period.

Poor governance of corrupt government adds problems to the citizens of the country. It creates problems through out the country and the country faces price rise, shortage of food grains, rape and murder issues, women atrocities, war between neighbour countries and political turmoil in the government.

In this chapter, political problems in Africa, Myanmar, and south Arabia, Chile, Middle East, India, Nepal and other countries have been included to study the nature of political problems and these could be solved to award peace to all people in the world.

AFRICA
Understanding Conflict and Peace

Key Concepts in Conflict and Peace:

The Greater Horn of Africa suffers from ongoing conflicts and tensions. The degree of conflict varies from country to country: dealing with conflict in the Greater Horn ranges from stopping active wars to protecting and strengthening peace so that violence is not triggered. In areas currently in violent conflict, the main challenge is to contain the conflict, alleviate suffering, and if possible, reduce the violence—for instance, in the Sudan and Burundi.

Where conflicts have abated but tensions remain high, principal tasks are reconstruction, social reconciliation and healing so that social and economic progress can be made and future conflicts avoided—in Rwanda, for example.

Where conflicts have recently ended and basic political order has been restored (Eritrea, Ethiopia) and in areas that have been at peace for some years (Uganda, Kenya, Tanzania), the main tasks are to further political and social reconciliation while protecting and advancing the social and economic progress that has been made. This means resolving tensions over ethnic relations, human rights, and political representation to ensure that further violence does not destroy or thwart larger achievements.

Conflict prevention can aim to end violence or to keep violence from occurring. Dealing with conflict can also mean pursuing positive goals of preserving, strengthening and building on good things where they exist or are coming into being. Reducing or preventing violent conflict and building peace are parts of a single whole.

This Guide builds on certain basic concepts:

(a) Conflict and peace are not random, unexplainable phenomena. Both are created, and both can be influenced.
(b) Conflict and peace are not static. They are dynamic, connected processes that evolve over time.
(c) Not all conflict is violent; some conflicts are settled peacefully.
(d) Preventing violent conflicts requires understanding the dynamics of conflict—peaceful and violent—and understanding the ingredients of peace.
(e) Effective conflict prevention and mitigation requires an understanding of the particular conflict's causes and applying different policies, programs and techniques according to the particular type and stage of conflict.
(f) It is possible to develop a framework to analyze conflicts and choose policy options to prevent or mitigate conflict.

To provide this analytic framework, this section will:

(a) Examine the nature and ingredients of violent conflict as compared to peace, and look at the gradations between these differing states within societies and in the relations between nations.
(b) Discuss the structural, proximate and immediate factors that determine whether a particular place is in peace or in violent conflict.
(c) Illustrate the life cycle of a typical conflict, showing gradations from peace to initial conflict to war, then back to peace.

Subsequent sections in this Guide will profile and evaluate policy tools used in conflict intervention, with illustrations from around the world; offer preliminary conclusions about how and why various tools were successful in keeping incipient conflicts from escalating or in reducing outbreaks of violence; and examine the main policy and implementation tasks facing policy-makers and field personnel to be more effective in preventing and mitigating violent conflicts.

Levels of Conflict and Peace:

Situations do not fall into the simple categories of war and peace, where peace is the opposite of war. Instead, there are degrees of conflict, and conflicts vary in the level of hostility between parties. Whatever the issues, weapons, parties and geographic scale, the intensity of hostility between the parties is a useful way to assess a conflict. This level of hostility can be measured through the attitudes and behaviors the parties exhibit towards each other.

What is Conflict?

Conflict is present when two or more parties perceive that their interests are incompatible, express hostile attitudes, or take pursue their interests through actions that damage the other parties. These parties may be individuals, small or large groups, and countries. Interests can diverge in many ways over:

(a) **Resources:** territory, money, energy sources, food—and how they should be distributed.
(b) **Power:** how control and participation in political decision-making are allocated.
(c) **Identity:** concerning the cultural, social and political communities to which people feel tied.
(d) **Status:** whether people believe they are treated with respect and dignity and whether their traditions and social position are respected.
(e) **Values:** particularly those embodied in systems of government, religion, or ideology

Incompatibilities can be seen in changes in **objective** circumstances—a lowered standard of living; demographic changes or population movements; technological changes that alter communications, material capacities, weaponry and relative power.

Subjective changes can also generate conflict through, for instance, newly felt social resentments or a rising new nationalist ideology; these subjectively felt changes can arise whether or not objective changes have occurred. The parties' emotional states and mental outlooks influence conflict. Time is a factor as well: observers note that with time, a conflict's subjective content gains importance as its objective basis is obscured. A group or nation's objective circumstances do not themselves cause violent conflicts. Conflicts only arise when it is perceived that some other party threatens interests.

Latent conflict: Sometimes an observer may believe that parties' interests are incompatible but the respective parties are not aware of these incompatibilities. This may be caused by self-delusion, rationalization, lack of knowledge, or suppressed information. We call such unacknowledged or barely recognized conflicts of interests' latent. Conflicts become **manifest** when these unacknowledged contrary interests become conscious and voiced.

Violent Conflict: Conflicting interests can be pursued without violence or coercion: not all conflicts are violent. Conflicts handled peacefully and non-coercively can be positive events. Societies can progress when parties' changing needs are identified and accommodated, as happens when minorities are recognized and better served.

Peaceful conflicts are handled according to regulated mechanisms to pursue competing interests.

Various factors regulate conflict: national constitutions and laws, family and clan structures, court systems, Robert's Rules of Order, the Law of the Sea, religious codes, and habits of decorum, debate and discourse, among other mechanisms. These can be informal and tacit—social mores and customs. They can also be highly formal and institutionalized, as in a nation's written statutes. Elections are a classic way that conflicts can be addressed peacefully. Recent research shows that violent conflicts—rebellion, inter-communal violence, civil war—account for less than one percent of potential conflicts in regions such as sub-Saharan Africa and the former republics of the Soviet Union.

Peaceful conflict resolution mechanisms can be traditional or modern, local, national, or international. Such mechanisms operate effectively in the regions and communities around the world called "zones of peace," generally keeping these areas' social and international conflicts from becoming destructive and violent.

Violent conflicts can become violent when parties go beyond seeking to attain their goals peacefully, and try to dominate or destroy the opposing parties' ability to pursue their own interests.

With so much violence around the world, we might assume that violent conflict and coercion are the natural order of things: human beings are inherently aggressive, and wars and violent conflicts are inevitable. Yet violence does not always occur, even when interests differ: violence is not inevitable. Violence is contingent upon the presence or absence of certain conditions.

Different dimensions distinguish violent conflicts:

(a) The main **substantive issues** in contention or interests at stake — natural resource competition, government control, territorial control, governing ideologies.
(b) The **parties' involved** — ethnic, religious or regional communities, states, political factions.
(c) The types of **force or coercion** used — nuclear war, conventional war, terrorism, coups, repression, genocide, gross human rights violations, ethnic cleansing.
(d) The geographic **scope** or arena for killing and destruction—international conflicts, inter-communal conflicts, state-sponsored terrorism

These dimensions are essential to understanding and comparing particular conflicts. But conflicts have many dimensions and exhibit several variations simultaneously; feature may fluctuate in importance over the course of a conflict. For these reasons, policy-makers and practitioners should exercise caution in using any single dimension to label a conflict: such simplification can obscure a conflict's many facets and cause policy errors.

3. The Continuum from Harmony to War

Different levels of conflict vary in the degree of cooperation or hostility. Some conflicts may be handled amicably without coercion or violence. Others rise to high levels of confrontation or involve repression and sustained physical violence.

These levels of interaction in conflicts can be arranged along a continuum from cooperative to hostile relations—from total harmony of interests to sustained all-out war. This continuum shows that there is overlap between peace and war.

The overlap is reflected in graduated terms such as hot war, cold war, co-existence, rivalry, detente, alliance, special relationship, confederation, and so on.

The gradations from harmony to all-out war defined below are a kind of barometer of peace and conflict. The figure shows terms for important turning points such as the shift from latent to manifest conflict and from non-violent conflict to violence.

Harmony can be defined as a relationship between communities and nations in which there are virtually no conflicts of interests or values. An example might be the feeling of solidarity and bonding those members of groups and occasionally a nation's citizens feel when they share a common cause.

Durable peace, "lasting," "positive" or "just peace" involves a high level of cooperation at the same time as awareness and pursuit of conflicting interests. Parties value their overall relationship more than specific self-interests. Separate interests are pursued within peaceful, institutionalized dispute settlement mechanisms; parties feel no need for military force to safeguard security against others. Cooperative, regulated conflict hinges on shared values and goals, accommodating political institutions, outlets for political expression and access to decision-making. Violent conflict or repression is virtually impossible. Examples are a democratic nation's policy debates, US/Canada relations or reunified Germany.

Stable peace or "cold peace" is a relationship of limited communication and cooperation within a context of basic order, mutual respect and general absence of violence. Value or goal differences remain; groups or nations may compete in various ways, but competition follows accepted rules, and disputes are generally worked out in non-violent, more or less predictable ways. Violent conflicts are possible but unlikely. Examples are US/Soviet détente in the late 1960s, the Israel/PLO accommodation until late 1996, US/Russian relations and US/China relations in the early 1990s. Domestic illustrations include national political compacts among competing, sometimes hostile political factions as in South Africa (1994-1995) or Nicaragua (1991-1994).

Unstable peace or "cold war" involves palpable tension and suspicion among parties, possibly with sporadic overt violence—for instance, US/Iran. A "negative peace" prevails: there is little physical violence but no friendship. The parties do not value their relationship enough to guarantee not to use coercion or violence to gain particular objectives. Peace is tenuous; levels of tensions rise and fall, and parties maintain armed forces as a deterrent.

There are few or no explicit mutual agreements.

When one party is much weaker than the other, order and absence of violence derive largely from the powerful party's suppression of the weaker party's efforts to assert or achieve its interests. Crisis or war is not unlikely. Government repression of groups is a domestic variety of this type of conflict, as in Burma. Some analysts refer to states of peace with political and economic injustice but no physical violence as "structural violence."

Crisis is a level of conflict with tense confrontation between mobilized armed forces. These forces may engage in threats and occasional skirmishes but have not exerted significant amounts of force—relations between US and the Soviet Union in the late 1950s, or, at times, Taiwan-PRC or North-South Korea. The probability of war is high—as in the 1962 Cuban missile crisis. In national contexts, this condition involves imminent civil war or a general breakdown of law and order—at times, Peru or Colombia.

War is all-out, sustained fighting between organized armed forces. It may include low-intensity local conflict such as gang wars, low-intensity guerilla wars, national anarchy—Somalia, Algeria, current Burundi—or "hot" civil and inter-state wars—World War II, Vietnam, Sudan.

In actual situations, these different conditions are not sharply demarcated but are matters of degree, which shade gradually from one to another. Situations may exhibit several levels of conflict. Yet distinguishing these gradations has several practical implications for policy-makers and practitioners. The gradations suggest that conflicts and peace rarely, if ever, arise suddenly, shift quickly from one status to another, or end suddenly. Relations do not move from total peace to total war without going through intermediate states—even the "Cold War" evolved through periods of direct confrontation, détente, and renewed hostility.

Numerous factors can cause a shift from one gradation to another:

(a) The intensity and number of grievances
(b) Parties' awareness of their differences; perceptions and attitudes towards each other.

(c) The intensity of emotion and psychological investment in the parties' positions and views of the world.
(d) The amount of direct interaction and communication the parties have with one another.
(e) The level of political mobilization and organization behind the parties' positions
(f) Cohesion between the respective parties' leaders and constituencies
(g) The amount of hostile behavior
(h) The extent that parties use or threaten to use arms.
(i) The number of parties supportive of each side

These factors can be analyzed as a first step to determining ways to stop a conflict from worsening.

Determinants of Violent Conflict or Peace

Regions vary widely in how peaceful they are and what kinds of conflict they experience. Policy-makers and practitioners in conflict prevention need to know what factors promote and sustain social peace in each society, and what region- or country-specific variables make conflict more or less likely.

Violent conflicts stem from multiple interconnected causes. Yet there are key factors or variables that are likely to determine whether political disputes evolve into violence or are settled peacefully. These variables can be causes of violence or causes of peace; analysts can examine conflict settings to assess these factors' relative influence.

Determinants of conflict can be systemic (structural), proximate (enabling) or immediate (triggering). These factors can be internal or external to the area in conflict. These types of causes overlap and interrelate.

(a) Systemic Causes: Structural Conditions

Systemic determinants cause objective changes in parties' material circumstances; environmental deterioration, population growth, resource scarcity and competition, the colonial or Cold War legacy, breakdowns of values and traditions, poverty, the poverty of pastoralists, and ethnicity are all examples of systemic causes of conflict. A study of 113 instances of failed states, civil wars, and related national crises from 1955 to 1994 tested 75 political, leadership, demographic, social, economic and environmental factors and found that three factors—a nation's infant mortality rate, the extent of a nation's trade, and the extent of democracy—were the most strongly associated with the crises and were linked with other factors that affect the risks of crisis, even though they did not directly cause the crises themselves. The first two variables are systemic.

Systemic sources of conflict are pervasive and affect large numbers of people. Their influence on the probability of conflict operates slowly. Measures like international programs or government policies that seek to prevent or reduce conflicts by treating their systemic sources often show results over the long term.

(b) Proximate Causes: Political and Institutional Factors

Proximate sources are problems in the social, political, and communications processes and institutions that mediate the effect of systemic conditions on peoples' lives and behavior. Proximate factors are crucial influences on whether systemic conditions give rise to violent reactions or to more peaceful ways of dealing with conflicting interests. The linkage between proximate determinants and manifestations of violent conflict are easier to discern and their effect is more direct. Government policies, social organization, economic reform programs, the problems of political liberalization, strengthening the military and external military aid can all be proximate sources of conflict.

(c) Immediate Causes: Acts and Events

The most immediate and direct causes of violent conflict are found in actions and events that trigger violent actions—for instance, a government cracks down on an oppressed group, which prompts a rebellion. Because they are more visible, these factors may be relatively easier to influence.

(d) External and Internal Factors

The source of the cause of conflict is another major dimension influencing a country's position on the spectrum from conflict to peace. Domestic and regional factors can encourage or help to head off violent approaches to resolving tensions, as can exogenous factors carried out by third parties. Internal and external determinants of conflict can be systemic, proximate or immediate.

(e) Sample Causal Analysis

An analysis of the causes of conflict in the Greater Horn of Africa is as follows:

Internal causes

Ethnic group imbalance: Is the society composed of one majority and one minority ethnic group, or is it more heterogeneous, with three or more active and sizeable groups competing for political space through shifting coalitions? Societies composed of one single majority and minority group hold higher potential for violent conflict than societies with three or more groups: mutual hostility between two groups is likely to be more focussed, and when groups with similar power compete for the same political space, the zero-sum nature of the game can cause hostilities to build. Macedonia illustrates this tendency, and the Greater Horn offers numerous examples of ethnic preponderance as a basic cause of violence when combined with other proximate and immediate causes: the Amhara /Tigrayan split in Ethiopia, the Northern Arab-Islamic Sudanese /Dinka conflict in Sudan, Tutsi/Hutu hostility in Burundi and Rwanda, and the many ethnic splits in the various regions of Somalia.

Ethnical political parties: Are the most important national political parties organized around ethnic groups, or do parties organize around shared non-ethnic interests such as political ideologies? Where ethnic parties predominate, elections are in effect ethnic censuses where parties reflect the numerical power of the groups they represent. Without alternatively based parties, political instability can increase when winning groups use state power to dominate others. In anticipation, minority groups may subvert the elections process or take up arms after losing to protect themselves or to take control of national politics. The 1990 Yugoslav elections are a case in point; Burundi and Ethiopia are examples within the Greater Horn.

Leadership extremism: Do conflicting parties' leaders show moderation in their words and actions and seek bilateral or multilateral negotiations to resolve disputes, or do they engage in demagogic rhetoric, provocative acts or coercion to achieve their objectives? Studies show that individual leaders' behavior can shape the political atmosphere and promote or discourage conflict. Coercive actions provoke like reactions, escalating conflicts into vicious cycles of increasing violence and moving parties further from mutual agreements. Conciliatory behavior, moderate declarations of intent and enacting institutional reforms and policies can enhance the likelihood of non-violent outcomes to disputes. These accommodative actions help to preempt extreme demands and can foster a "virtuous circle" of increasing cooperation. Burundi, Rwanda, Yugoslavia and Moldova are notable examples of inflammatory rhetoric feeding conflict; Tanzanian president Julius Nyerere's ethnicity policy illustrates accommodation's leadership.

External Causes

Global and regional isolation: Does the state enjoy political, commercial and trade relations with neighboring countries and with countries outside the region? Does the state participate in regular meetings and forums or is the state politically or economically isolated? A common variable associated with "state failure" is the extent of economies' isolation from trade and commercial relations with other economies. Global and regional organizations have procedures that encourage regular contacts and active dispute mediation between governments and internal groups, including regular forums for discussing common issues, special envoys, confidence-building measures, and negotiations. Sudan is an example where a fundamentalist Islamic regime is largely isolated from political and economic organizations and has been highly resistant to outsider attempts to resolve its war against non-Islamic peoples in Southern Sudan.

Cross-conflict spillover: Are conflicts crossing borders to increase levels of conflict in neighboring countries, or are leaders taking steps to avoid the conflict outcomes they observed in nearby countries or regions with similar group conflicts? Leaders may be repelled by external conflicts, constraining them from violent escalation and encouraging them to undertake measures to keep domestic angers from destabilizing their own states. Burundi's leadership struggled to reduce tensions after the Rwandan genocide, and Rwanda's leaders vowed not to allow their country to follow Burundi's path once Burundi's conflict escalated. Greece-Macedonia (1992 on), the Czech and Slovak Republics (1992-1993) and Hungary/Slovakia (1992-1994) conflicts have all been informed and mitigated by the carnage of the Yugoslav wars.

Absence of third party engagement: Have third parties become engaged early in a dispute or is the international community standing by to await developments in a local conflict? Early third party engagement increases the chances that conflicting parties will talk rather than fight. Early third party engagement means positive or negative inducements for peaceful resolution of a conflict, with sufficient political or military pressures on disputants to bring them to work toward a mutual solution. The impact of these pressures will be reduced if they occur once a party has made gains and perceive it as winning the conflict. The Greater Horn unfortunately abounds with examples of disputes escalating into violence when third parties intervenes late (Somalia, Sudan) or even after the conflict (Rwanda). Moldova and Chechnya are recent European examples of conflict escalation without early intervention.

Ethnic Conflicts: Ethnicity, the identity felt by people as a language group, tribe, clan, religion, or region is seen as a factor that drives many current conflicts. There are two general positions about ethnic identity's influence on conflicts. The "primordial" explanation sees the main source of conflict in a deep sense of identity: ethnic conflicts arise when ancient hatreds are unleashed because certain authoritarian controls were removed. The theory attributes conflicts to systemic causes outside the control group leaders and thus of third parties as well.

The other view, "instrumentalism," sees such conflicts arising from policies pursued by groups who use group identity as a tool to mobilize people in pursuit of specific gains. Conflict may be fomented by elites who manipulate the symbols dear to their group and can stir resentment against other groups. They invoke hatred through propaganda, or they take covert actions to provoke violent reactions from their followers. This implies that group emotion does not usually combust spontaneously: it must be whipped up. From this perspective, ethnic conflicts are less subject to unalterable forces and more contingents on the action of elites and individual leaders.

A reasonable position to take in this debate is not to accept either extreme. We can acknowledge that some societies' history and physical circumstances may have fostered a much stronger sense of identity in some groups than in others. If ethnic identities are deeper in some people and societies and shallower in others, the amount of "pull" a particular identity has on behavior can be affected by economic interest, history, political persuasion, and other factors. Thus, many analysts prefer to call conflicts with ethnic overtones "ethno-political," suggesting that willful activity may cause feelings of identity to become linked to political causes.

Violent Conflicts: Emergence and Cessation

Conflicts change over time; hostilities emerge, grow and abate. Hostilities rise and fall.

1. Dynamics of Escalation

Dynamic and interactive processes in individual and collective behavior explain whether hostile attitudes and behavior escalate or not.

Escalation may be **vertical** — hostile behavior becomes more intense — or **horizontal** — hostile behavior of the same intensity spreads over a larger area. Escalation can take both forms. Escalation can be caused by the parties themselves or by actions that third parties take.

Spiraling conflicts are fueled by a set of social-psychological phenomena within each party's collective mind and behavior. People get more committed to a struggle as they become more involved. A sense of urgency takes over; time pressures to make decisions narrow options to little more than existing courses of action. The psychological investment that conflict requires shapes each side's perceptions of the other: one's own cause is seen as just, the other sides as evil. Stereotyping and dehumanizing the opposition feed parties' positions; acts of brutality are seen as completely justified.

Leaders may become more committed to their positions once they are announced publicly: it becomes harder to back down, and if there is competition for leadership positions, rivals can appeal to the broader constituency by questioning the leadership's determination and ability to conduct the struggle. Moderates may quit or be driven out; leadership is left to militants. Commitment to fight increases; once conflict is being waged, specialists in using force gain influence over the governments or organization's leadership and policies. Fighting may widen the discussion: additional issues and grievances are raised, adding more reasons to pursue the struggle.

Escalation proceeds: harmed parties feel justified in striking back, and vice versa. Coercion and violence discourage communication between the parties, limiting opportunities for addressing issues through compromise. Even lack of retaliation may be perceived as weakness and lead the attacking party to persevere in the conflict.

The escalated conflict may affect third parties who feel that intervention would help their own interests. Other parties entering the conflict may prompt additional parties to take sides.

2. Early Warning

Truly preventive action requires early intervention to avoid being caught by surprise when conflicts erupt. Policy-makers must know how to recognize signs of impending conflict in order to make decisions based on informed analysis and Marshall the resources required to head off incipient violence. Anticipating possible conflicts is not a matter of precisely predicting specific events and their timing since this level of exactitude is not possible. Early warning informs the probability of certain events, which would lead to violence or other crises. This requires reliable information on a range of possible common events—border crises, disintegrating regimes, civil wars, genocide, human rights abuses, refugee flows—and estimating where these are most likely to emerge.

Threats to security and national order emerge subtly out of social, political, economic and cultural, international, national and local conditions and events. These indicators are as diverse as price fluctuations, demonstrations, government policies, social movements, political infighting, leaders' attitudes, and arms flows. At the same time, change, tension and political turmoil can be positive as well as negative in transitions between economic and political systems. Monitoring and information gathering must reach deeply into a country's social fabric and grassroots politics to identify possible sources of conflict. Table 2-2 below draws on recent research into developing reliable early warning systems to illustrate some of the proximate and immediate warning signs analysts have posited as the antecedents of possible civil wars, genocides, secessionist wars, or failed states. In short, the causes and factors of conflicts are as follows:

Proximate Factors

(a) Governing elites express exclusionary ideologies (beliefs that elevate some ethnic group or class to a position of superiority over other groups).
(b) Competition occurs among governing elites in a context in which the state security apparatus has few constraints.
(c) A charismatic leadership emerges that attracts a mass following through abstract appeals to a group's destiny.
(d) Severe economic hardship or differential treatment occurs for certain ethnic or other groups. Scapegoats are sought.
(e) Provision and distribution of public services decline.
(f) Government responds to threats by enacting emergency measures or suspending rule of law.
(g) Paramilitary organizations and militias grow or conduct training exercises.
(h) Arms flows increase.
(i) Politically active communities are increasingly polarized.
(j) The state's perceived legitimacy appears to erode.

Triggering Factors

(a) A regime enacts new discriminatory or restrictive policies such as abuses of human rights.
(b) Clashes occur between regime supporters and targeted groups.
(c) Politically active groups receive external material or rhetorical support.

(d) Sudden economic events such as price drops affect large numbers of people.
(e) Political leaders call openly to overthrow the government or expel certain groups.[26]

Myanmar:
Challenges and Way Forward

As a neighbour of immense relevance to our nation, Myanmar deserves constant attention. Elections held last November, followed by the release of Daw Aung San Suu Kyi from house arrest, triggered extensive media coverage. In recent months, however, attention has dipped due to paucity of information on the emerging change in Myanmar.[27]

In the above context came an invitation to participate in an international seminar, 'Myanmar and the International Community — the Way Forward,' the first of its kind in Yangon after the formation of the new government, in March. Hosted in end June by Myanmar's Ministry of Foreign Affairs in collaboration with the German foundation, FES, the event proved worthwhile. Myanmar's internal politics — the launch of the new Constitution, swearing in of a new President and the Cabinet, convening of Parliament and regional Assemblies, and the assumption of office by Chief Ministers in provinces — was discussed more on the sidelines. The condemnation of elections as "neither free nor fair" by a powerful and vocal section of the international community divided analysts into two broad camps — those who believed that 'nothing has changed' and those who argued that 'much has changed.' But gradually, a more credible approach emerged favouring the view that 'something has changed.'

---

[26] Creative Associates International Com
[27] Rajiv Bhatia (2011), "Myanmar: Challenges and Way forward", The Hindu, July 5, 2011

Strategists of the Tatmadaw (military), who conceived the seven-point roadmap to democracy in 2003, planned to introduce a guided form of democracy. The regime's spokesmen made it clear that elections would be conducted, keeping in view past mistakes. They were determined not to let 1990 be repeated when free elections resulted in a landslide victory for the National League for Democracy (NLD). Limited democracy is what has now been ushered in. By misreading the regime's intentions and actions, sections of the international media created the impression that real democracy was on its way. Expectedly enough, when this did not come about, they began denigrating Myanmar's rulers for their failure to deliver what they had never promised. Many in Myanmar believe that political change, however imperfect, is better than direct military rule.

But what about the political forces which have been excluded from the process of change: pro-democracy movement led by Ms Suu Kyi, her party NLD, its Myanmar supporters living abroad and their powerful allies in the West? This coalition has fundamental objections to the new Constitution and its manifest pro-military bias. It has demanded a broader dialogue involving ethnic minorities, and the immediate release of all political prisoners.

No one I spoke to in Yangon doubted the popularity and charisma of 'The Lady' — she is stuck with that phrase even now — but few believed that she wanted confrontation or could obtain political power through dialogue. Many regretted that Myanmar was missing another historic opportunity to secure a national reconciliation through a decisive move towards inclusive governance.

President Thein Sein's reform agenda includes national reconciliation but his plate is full of pressing challenges. He is likely to focus on the economy and re-connecting with the world. Therefore, Myanmar is likely to move on, with the two principal protagonists watching closely from the sidelines: the previous regime's 'strong man' Senior General Than Shwe is not quite out yet, and the heroine residing in people's hearts, Ms Suu Kyi, is clearly not in.

The participants broadly agreed that the top priority now was the economy. The previous SPDC government's publicity machine spent much energy convincing people that 'development' was its major achievement but participants recalled, with amazement, how a recent seminar under official patronage had focussed on poverty alleviation, conceding the critics' view that the country suffered from widespread poverty and deprivation.

'Market economy' is the new mantra in Myanmar but, as a former top official argued, there was little clarity or consensus about the scope and sequencing of reforms relating to the budget, monetary policy, exchange rate unification and financial sector. Another former official presented a hard-hitting diagnosis of what ailed the agriculture sector.

The seminar also explored the possibilities of a change in the country's external relations. Foreign Minister Wunna Maung Lwin stressed in his inaugural statement that Myanmar had turned "a new chapter in its history." The country, he asserted, was set to move towards realising the agenda of reforms spelt out in the March 30 speech of President Thein Sein. The government planned to introduce market economy and conduct a foreign policy based on Five Principles of Peaceful Co-existence.

Myanmar's foreign policy framework has been anchored on three pillars: Asia, European Union and the United States. Much of the substantive relationship has been with Asians — Asean, China and India. Surprisingly, the fourth Asian partner, Japan, was conspicuous by its absence at the seminar; nevertheless, it reflected Asian primacy.

Presenting the ASEAN perspective, a Singapore academic leader noted: "Change has occurred, though in the eyes of some it might seem glacial." He highlighted the importance of forming provincial assemblies designed to give representation to the ethnic minorities, but this was "a first step in a thousand miles journey." He made three other significant points.

First, Asean was committed to non-interference in the internal affairs of member-states, but this did not prevent the association from expressing "concerns, reservations or even criticism when necessary, using quiet diplomacy" on the internal situation, including in Myanmar. Second, he referred to the controversy on Myanmar's bid to chair the 2014 Asean Summit, suggesting that an Asean member-state should be allowed to assume the Chairmanship "if it feels that it has the political will and organisational capacity to undertake that responsibility." Third, he advocated "a regional initiative" to help Myanmar build capacities for change and pointed to Asean's ability to assist in re-structuring the economy, education, rural development, and in strengthening institutions.

The presentation on China-Myanmar relations was along predictable lines. The two countries enjoyed a "fraternal" relationship. It had been transformed into "a comprehensive strategic cooperative partnership," following the visit to China by President Thein Sein — his first to a foreign country — in May. The two countries agreed to enhance cooperation in border management and secure greater coordination in dealing with the U.N. and Asean. Thein Sein called the equation with China "the closest and most important diplomatic relationship."

While delineating the profile of India-Myanmar relations, I briefly referred to their rich history from the ancient times through the colonial period to the post-independence era. A mention was made of India's endeavours to balance its commitment to democratic values with the need to protect its national interests. I stressed on two critical points. India's Myanmar policy has been facing criticism from the idealists' camp which blames New Delhi for abandoning the cause of democracy as well as from others who express a rising concern about Myanmar's growing dependence on China. Therefore, our relations are bound to be affected by what the new Myanmar government does in future.

In the presentation on Myanmar's relations with China and India, a senior Myanmar official emphasised that her country needed cooperative relations with both neighbours, for its security in the border regions and its national development.

Myanmar's relations with the EU and the U.S. were under severe stress in the past two decades as sanctions were imposed in the light of the crushing of the pro-democracy movement, violation of human rights and imprisonment of Ms Suu Kyi. The EU's policy could change now. European panelists, both serving officials, conveyed this subtle signal. They suggested that the new government consider releasing political prisoners, which would have a dramatic impact. The Myanmar panelist stressed the need for lifting the sanctions and observed that it would be in mutual interest to strengthen the Myanmar-EU relations, allowing Myanmar access to European capital and technology.

As for the U.S., although the Obama administration undertook a policy review and opened a dialogue with the previous regime, it is very cautious. U.S. scholars at the seminar voiced their opposition to sanctions but explained that the President would have to spend huge political capital to ensure their withdrawal as Ms Suu Kyi enjoyed immense support in Congress. One of them said she had been 'mentioned' 1598 times in Congressional records.

In the final session, a well-known British expert called on the international community to recognise that change was on its way in Myanmar, which needed suitable response.

A young Myanmar scholar, known both for his impressive academic attainments and lineage, underlined that Myanmar faced "multiple watersheds." He expressed the hope that a pragmatic and flexible approach would be adopted by all concerned. On this would depend where Myanmar — the region's "black swan" — would be in 2050.

I returned with a clear impression that Myanmar is passing through a complex transition: the old era of the State Peace and Development Council rule has ended and the new era of 'civilian' rule, with all its imperfections, has begun.

Political Instability Index

Vulnerability to Social and Political Unrest

Our index draws on recent insights of the political science literature that seeks to identify and quantify the main social, economic and political factors and traits that are causally associated with, or that can predict, political instability. In particular, it draws on the work of the so-called Political Instability Task Force (PITF) based at George Mason University in the US. The PITF has created a simple model that has a rate of success of over 80% in identifying, ex post, outbreaks of serious instability for a data set that stretches back to 1955.

These attempts to predict the occurrence of unrest on the basis of quantitative models was borne of a dissatisfaction with the experience of traditional, qualitative analysis and assessments, which have had a poor record in predicting outbreaks of social and political turmoil. Some recent analyses have pointed to the need to combine quantitative models with traditional qualitative assessment by country experts. Although quantitative models have greater predictive success, they can miss out possibly pertinent specific features in countries that are not captured by the general model and the data that the model uses may also contain errors or may not always be up to date.

The final PITF model that had the greatest predictive power is a simple model that is based on only four factors: the level of development as measured by the infant mortality rate; extreme cases of economic or political discrimination against minorities (according to assessments and coding by the Minorities at Risk Project); "a bad neighbourhood" (if a country has at least four neighbours that suffered violent conflicts); and regime type (intermediate regimes that are neither consolidated democracies nor autocratic regimes combined with the existence in these regimes of intense factionalism in domestic politics, as coded by the Polity Project on democracy). Although over 80% of outbreaks of instability could be predicted (a very high "hit rate"), the model cannot predict the intensity or duration of the instability, or its exact timing.

We also look and measure other factors associated with instability that have been identified in the literature, such as inequality, a prior history of instability, ethnic fragmentation, poor governance, a proclivity to labour unrest, the level of provision of public services and state strength.

Economic distress and dislocation tend to be associated causally with instability that is they precede, not only accompany, instability. Indeed, of the 50 cases of instability (instances of "adverse regime change") identified since 1980 by the PITF (about one-half of these were in Africa), in the vast majority of cases (46) the country that had an outbreak of instability had suffered a decline in GDP per head in at least one of the two years prior to the occurrence of instability.

Economic distress appears to be almost a necessary condition for serious instability, but it is not a sufficient one. There are many instances of declines in GDP per head that have not been followed by political instability. It is only when economic distress is accompanied by other, underlying or structural features of vulnerability that there is a high vulnerability to or risk of serious outbreaks of political and social unrest.

Defining political unrest

We define social and political unrest or upheaval as those events or developments that pose a serious extra-parliamentary or extra-institutional threat to governments or the existing political order. The events will almost invariably be accompanied by some violence as well as public disorder. These need not necessarily be successful in the sense that they end up toppling a government or regime. Even unsuccessful episodes result in turmoil and serious disruption. The assessment of what constitutes a "serious threat" still requires judgment and can be arbitrary, but this is a step forward from having no definition at all.

Political Instability Index

The overall index on a scale of 0 (no vulnerability) to 10 (highest vulnerability) has two component indexes—an index of underlying vulnerability and an economic distress index. The overall index is a simple average of the two component indexes. There are 15 indicators in all—12 for the underlying and 3 for the economic distress index.

The Underlying vulnerability can be measured by the following causes. These are:

Inequality, State history, corruption, Ethnic fragmentation, Trust in institutions, Status of minorities and history of political instability, Proclivity to labour unrest, Level of social provision, Country's neighborhoods - Regime type - Region type and Factionalism

Moreover, growth in incomes, unemployment, level of income per head, controls economic distress and ultimately the political unrest.

The most **political instability countries** are:

Zimbabwe, Chad, Congo (Democratic Republic), Cambodia, Sudan, Iraq, Cote d' Ivories, Haiti, Pakistan, Zambia, Afghanistan, Central African Republic, North Korea, Bolivia, Equator, Angola, Dominican Republic, Bangladesh, Guinea, Kenya, Moldova, Senegal, Guinea Bissau, Nepal, Niger and Bosnia and Herzegovina.

It is reported that out of 165 countries studied as many as 94 countries were in danger zone.

Similarly, the least political turmoil or social unrest countries are: Norway, Denmark, Canada, Sweden, Finland, Switzerland, Mauritius, Costa Rica, News land and Luxembourg.[28]

In short, 57 percent of countries are affected with more political turmoil and social unrest that need the attention of political pundits,

[28] View Wire, Economist Intelligence Unit, March 19, 2009

world leaders and more particularly the United Nations Organization.

It suggests that democracy is in peril in most of the countries. The communist countries, military-ruled countries, family-ruled countries and corrupt politicians-ruled countries are posing threats and harassing the peace loving people in this world. It is time to search for suitable policies for clean governance and fair election process.

The world has witnessed two most dangerous World Wars; hence the twenty-first century must search for a political system that can award WORLD PEACE politically.

All wars are caused by the governments, and carried out by the soldiers. And the end result is that the innocent people suffer and the country spends trillions of dollars annually that could have been utilized for the hungry, diseased and squalors. A warmonger government should be penalized for waging wars and for production of atom bombs, military investments and causing terror.

South Arabia

Its concern relating to Arab springs, foreign policy and Iran

It was a very discreet meeting deep in the English countryside. The main speaker was Prince Turki al-Faisal, one of Saudi Arabia's best-known and best-connected royals. The audience was composed of senior American and British military officials. The location was RAF Molesworth, one of three bases used by American forces in the U.K. since the Second World War. Now a Nato intelligence centre focused on the Mediterranean and the Middle East, the sprawling compound amid green fields was an ideal venue for the sensitive topics that Turki, former head of Saudi Arabian intelligence, wanted to raise.

After an anecdote about how Franklin D. Roosevelt was told by Winston Churchill that nothing between them or their countries should be hidden, Turki warmed to his theme: "A Saudi national security doctrine for the next decade." For the next half an hour, the diplomat, a former ambassador to Washington and tipped to be the next foreign minister in Riyadh, entertained his audience to a sweeping survey of his country's concerns in a region seized by momentous changes. Like Churchill, Turki said, the kingdom "had nothing to hide."

Even if they wanted to, the leaders of the desert kingdom would have difficulty concealing their concern at the stunning developments across the Arab world. Few — excepting the vast revenues pouring in from oil selling at around $100 a barrel for much of the year — have brought much relief to Riyadh.

Stability:

Chief among the challenges, from the perspective of the Saudi royal rulers, are the difficulties of preserving stability in the region when autocracies that have lasted for decades are falling one after another; of preserving security when the resultant chaos provides opportunities to all kinds of groups deemed enemies; of maintaining good relations with the west; and, perhaps most importantly of all, of ensuring that Iran, the bigger but poorer historic regional and religious rival just across the Gulf from Saudi Arabia's eastern provinces, does not emerge as the winner as the upheavals of the Arab spring continue into the summer.

"The [Saudi king], crown prince and government cannot ignore the Arab situations, we live the Arab situation and hope stability returns," the *al-Sharq al-Awsat* newspaper quoted Prince Nayef, the second in line to the throne and Minister of the Interior, as saying in Riyadh last week.

Iran, a majority Shia state committed to a rigorous and highly politicised Islamist ideology, remains at the heart of such fears in Saudi Arabia, a predominantly Sunni state ruled by the al-Saud family since its foundation in 1932. Recent moves such as the Saudi-inspired invitation to Morocco and Jordan, both Sunni monarchies, to join the Gulf Cooperation Council (GCC), a group of Sunni autocratic states, are seen by analysts as part of Riyadh's effort to bolster defences against Tehran. So too is the deployment of Saudi troops under the umbrella of the GCC to Bahrain, where largely Shia demonstrators took to the streets to demand greater democratic rights from the Sunni rulers.

One fear in Riyadh is that the 15 per cent or so of Saudi citizens who are Shia — and who largely live in the oil-rich eastern province — might mobilise in response to an Iranian call to arms.

"It is a kind of ideological struggle," said a Ministry of Interior official. Describing Iran as a "paper tiger" because of its "dysfunctional government ... whose hold on power is only possible if it is able, as it barely is now, to maintain a level of economic prosperity that is just enough to pacify its people," Turki, according to a copy of his speech at RAF Molesworth, said the rival state still had "steel claws", which were "effective tools ... to interfere in other countries."

This Tehran did with "destructive" consequences in countries with very large Shia communities such as Iraq, which Turki said was taking a "sectarian, Iranian-influenced direction", as well as states with smaller ones such as Kuwait and Lebanon. Until Iraq changed course, the former intelligence chief warned, Riyadh would not write off Baghdad's $20bn debts or send an ambassador.

More worryingly for western diplomats was Turki's implicit threat that if Iran looked close to obtaining nuclear weapons, Saudi Arabia would follow suit. "Iran [developing] a nuclear weapon would compel Saudi Arabia ... to pursue policies which could lead to untold and possibly dramatic consequences," Turki said.

A senior adviser said it was "inconceivable that there would be a day when Iran had a nuclear weapon and Saudi Arabia did not". "If they successfully pursue a military programme, we will have to follow suit," he said. For the moment, however, the prince told his audience, "sanctions [against Iran] are working" and military strikes would be "counterproductive."

One alternative, Turki told his audience, would be to "squeeze" Iran by undermining its profits from oil, explaining that this was something the Saudis, with new spare pumping capacity and deep pockets were ideally positioned to do.

Money:

Money has long been a key foreign policy tool for Saudi Arabia. Turki's speech reveals the extent to which the kingdom is relying on its wealth to buy goodwill and support allies. In Lebanon, to counter Syrian influence and the Shia Hezbollah movement, the kingdom has spent $2.5bn since 2006.

The aim of such expenditure — only a fraction of the state's $550bn reserves — is to minimise any potential ill-will towards Saudi Arabia among populations who have deposed rulers backed previously by Riyadh.

King Abdullah, who has ruled Saudi Arabia since 2005, initially backed long-term ally Hosni Mubarak, reportedly personally interceding on his behalf with President Barack Obama.

"The calculation in Riyadh is very simple: you cannot stop the Arab spring so the question is how to accommodate the new reality on the ground. So far there is no hostility to the Saudis in Tunisia, Egypt or elsewhere, popular or political," said Dr. Mustafa Alani, from the Gulf Research Centre, Dubai.

One difficult issue is that of the "unwanted house guests." Saudi Arabia has a long tradition of offering a comfortable retirement home to ex-dictators, and two of the deposed leaders — Zine al-Abidine Ben Ali of Tunisia and Ali Abdullah Saleh of Yemen — are now in the kingdom. Ben Ali is reported to have been housed in a villa on the Red Sea coast. Saleh is in a luxury hospital receiving treatment for wounds caused by the bomb that forced his flight from the country he ruled for 21 years as president, and is now under pressure from his hosts to retire permanently. Other regional rulers are being gently pressured to ease crackdowns, in part in response to western outcry over human-rights abuses, one official said.

Yemen, however, remains a major security concern to the Saudis, who worry about the presence of Islamic militants and Shia rebels who, again, they view as proxies of Iran. "It is very important to make sure Yemen is stable and secure and without any internal struggle," said one Interior Ministry official. In his speech in the U.K., Turki worried that Yemen's more remote areas had become a safe haven for terrorism comparable to Pakistan's tribal areas.[29]

Chile: **Does political instability affect economic growth?**

Ari Aisen and Francisco José Veiga of Central bank of Chile have studied on political instability that affects

---

[29] Jason Burke (2011), "South Arabia's Three Worries", Guardian Newspapers Limited, 2011

economic growth. They have attempted to empirically determine the effects of political instability on economic growth. Using the system-GMM estimator for linear dynamic panel data models on a sample covering 169 countries, and 5-year periods from 1960 to 2004, they found that **higher degrees of political instability were associated with lower growth rates of GDP per capita**. Regarding the channels of transmission, they found that political instability adversely affected growth by slowing productivity growth and, to a smaller degree, physical and human capital accumulation. Finally, economic freedom and ethnic homogeneity were beneficial to growth, while democracy might had a slight negative effect.

Their observations are as follows:

Political instability is regarded by economists as a serious malaise harmful to economic performance. Political instability is likely to shorten policymakers' horizons leading to sub-optimal short term macroeconomic policies. It may also lead to a more frequent switch of policies, creating volatility and thus, negatively affecting macroeconomic performance. Considering its damaging repercussions on economic performance the extent at which political instability is pervasive across countries and time is quite surprising.

Measuring political instability by Cabinet Changes, that is, the numbers of times in a year in which a new premier is named and/or 50 percent or more of the cabinet posts are occupied by new ministers, figures speak for themselves. In Africa, for instance, there was on average a cabinet change once every two years in the period 2000-2003. Though extremely high, this number is a major improvement relative to previous years when there were, on average, two cabinet changes every three years. While Africa is the most politically unstable region of the world, it is by no means alone; as similar trends are observed in other regions.

A frequent change in the cabinet supposes political instability in the government and in the country. The widespread phenomenon of political (and policy) instability in several countries across time and its negative effects on their economic performance has arisen the interest of several economists. As such, the profession produced an ample literature documenting the negative effects of political instability on a wide range of macroeconomic variables including, among others, GDP growth, private investment, and inflation. Alesina et al. (1996) use data on 113 countries from 1950 to 1982 to show that GDP growth is significantly lower in countries and time periods with a high propensity of government collapse. In a more recent paper, Jong-a-Pin (2009) also finds that higher degrees of political instability lead to lower economic growth.

As regards to private investment, Alesina and Perotti (1996) show that socio- political instability generates an uncertain politico-economic environment, raising risks and reducing investment. Political instability also leads to higher inflation as shown in Aisen and Veiga (2006). Quite interestingly, the mechanisms at work to explain inflation in their paper resemble those affecting economic growth; namely that political instability shortens the horizons of governments, disrupting long term economic policies conducive to a better economic performance.

Another interesting thing is the channel via which political instability works:

In this section, we study the channels through which political instability affects economic growth. Since political instability is associated with greater uncertainty regarding future economic policy, it is likely to adversely affect investment and, consequently, physical capital accumulation. In fact, several studies have identified a negative relation between political instability and investment (Alesina and Perotti, 1996; Mauro, 1985; Özler and Rodrik, 1992; Perotti, 1996). Instead of estimating an investment equation, we will construct the series on the stock of physical capital, using the perpetual inventory method, and estimate equations for the growth of the capital stock. That is, we will analyze the effects of political instability and institutions on physical capital accumulation.

It is also possible that political instability adversely affects productivity. By increasing uncertainty about the future, it may lead to less efficient resource allocation. Additionally, it may reduce research and development efforts by firms and governments, leading to slower technological progress. Violence, civil unrest, and strikes, can also interfere with the normal operation of firms and markets, reduce hours worked, and even lead to the destruction of some installed productive capacity.

Thus, we hypothesize that higher political instability is associated with lower productivity growth. Finally, human capital accumulation may also be adversely affected by political instability because uncertainty about the future may induce people to invest less in education. And what do authors find? Political instability impacts total factor productivity and not much of human and physical capital accumulation. This is surprising actually.[30]

Our results suggest that governments in politically fragmented countries with high degrees of political

---

[30] Amol Agrawal (2010), "Does political instability affect economic growth?" Mostly Economics, Academic Research and Research papers, Central Bank/ Monetary Policy quoted from Ari Aisen and Francisco José Veiga of Central bank of Chile

instability need to address its root causes and try to mitigate its effects on the design and implementation of economic policies. Only then, countries could have durable economic policies that may engender higher economic growth.

Political Turmoil Spurs:
Divergence in Arab Economies

The Arab nations facing political turmoil are likely to see their economies shrink this year. But many of their larger oil-exporting neighbors will experience strong growth and higher revenues as oil prices rise partly due to the regional political upheaval, the **Institute of International Finance** said in a report on May 3, 2011.

The IIF, a global banking trade group, said Arab oil importers as a group — Egypt, Jordan, Lebanon, Morocco, Tunisia, and Syria — will see "a collapse in growth" in 2011 (declining 0.5 percent in 2011 after 4.4 percent growth in 2010) but a strong rebound in 2012 if the regional unrest ends in the coming months. The economies of Egypt, Tunisia and Syria are projected to shrink by 1 percent to 3 percent, while the other nations in the group show modest growth.

The oil importers face considerable downside risks to growth. Not only is the political reform process unlikely to be smooth and could drag on beyond 2011, further delaying investment decisions and slowing any economic recovery, but also investigations into political corruption are adding to business uncertainties. Those nations need rapid development of credible economic programs that recognize the legitimate expectations of the citizens of these countries. Meanwhile, most Arab oil exporters (except for Libya and Yemen) are expected to see significant growth and higher revenues from rising oil prices. Iraq's economy grew by 0.9 percent last year but should see growth of 11 percent or more in 2011 and 2012.

The leading Persian Gulf economies overall — Saudi Arabia, the UAE, Kuwait, Qatar, Oman, and Bahrain — are projected to experience 2011 growth of 6.5 percent, up from 5.1 percent in 2010 as oil prices rise and government spending increases. The exception is Bahrain, which is facing political turmoil, leading growth to slow to 3 percent this year from 4.5 percent in 2010. The trade group estimates average oil prices at $115 a barrel in 2011 and $110 in 2012, up from $80 in 2010.[31]

Political Unrest in the Middle East

For decades the Middle East has been ruled by totalitarian regimes. The United States' foreign policy toward these regimes has been determined largely by two factors: The oil reserves in these countries and/or their policy toward Israel. Indeed, until Saddam Hussein invaded oil-rich Kuwait he was not considered a threat. After all he was a sworn enemy of Iran.

Many times the United States has found itself on the wrong side of principle by supporting regimes with terrible human rights records and not a shred of democracy. But this is the way of international relations. For decades democratic India was more closely allied with communist USSR while the United States was a closer friend of non-democratic Pakistan. The situation changed only about a decade ago.

It is difficult to make too strong a moral judgment about U.S. policy toward the Middle East given not only the importance (to the United States) of the two factors mentioned above but also the fact that regime

---

[31] The Wall Street Journal, May 3, 2011

change in the Middle East has some important political and security ramifications. When the Shah of Iran – who brutalized his political opponents and was fully supported by the United States – was replaced by an Islamic regime, the United States gained a determined and well-entrenched enemy.

One form of tyranny replaces another

The focus now is on Egypt, a country that is not a large oil producer. A popular uprising without any clear leader or figurehead has taken the country by storm, challenging the three decade-old regime of Hosni Mubarak. Mohamed El-Baradei – the ex-chairman of the International Atomic Energy Agency – has entered the fray flying from Vienna to Cairo on Thursday, January 27. The next few days in Egypt promise to be interesting. The United States for its part has now officially called for political, social and economic reform in Egypt. Three decades late it seems.

The common thread throughout the Middle East is that most countries are ruled by repressive regimes. It is also true that in most countries there exist diverse dissident movements that yearn to break the shackles of the current regimes.

Middle East and North Africa countries are classified by degree of Freedom. Here only Israel is free from unrest. But countries like Morocco, Lebanon and Kuwait are partly free. . And countries such as Western Sahara, Algeria, Tunisia, Libya, Egypt, Iraq, Jordan, Israel Occupied Territories, Palestinian Territories, Syria, Saudi Arabia, Yemen, Oman, Qatar, UAE, Bahrain and Iran are not free from Political unrest as per freedom house report.

In country after country, the dissident movements are led not necessarily by democrats, but in many cases Islamist movements hostile toward the United

States. Many of the regimes are secular like the overthrown Ba'ath party of Iraq and the ruling Ba'ath government in Syria. While Saddam Hussein was embraced by the United States for his enmity toward Iran, at least up until the invasion of Kuwait, the Syrian regime has been at odds with the United States and Israel. Syria is also not an oil-rich country. Other secular regimes are those in Algeria and Morocco.

Countries like Saudi Arabia are run according to a strict interpretation of Islam. Yemen is a prime example of the complexities of Middle Eastern politics because no one is really sure whether Al Qaeda is truly a grave threat or whether the threat has been manufactured by the ruling regime as an excuse to crush opposition and to gain U.S. financial aid.

The Middle East is a complex region of many intellectual, social and political currents. In many countries the ruling establishment is far removed from the existential realities of the majority. All of a sudden now, we see protests in countries as far flung as Yemen, Egypt and Tunisia. There is the possibility of new uprisings in Algeria. Could this be a new phase in the political and social development of the Middle East? Might the unthinkable happen in Iran?

Any drastic changes in Middle Eastern political arrangements have broad implications for the rest of the world. Nowhere would the consequences of radical political change be felt more than in energy markets, at least in the immediate aftermath. What are the possible scenarios and what would be their effects?

Scenario 1: The uprisings in Egypt and Tunisia are contained either through concessions and/or brutal measures by the government. It seems unlikely, however, that either government will be able to get away with too much brutality. Given that none of these countries are oil-rich the effect on oil prices should be negligible.

Scenario 2: It seems most likely that the regimes in both countries are on their way out. The pressure will now be on both governments to make concessions to their people and make amends for the appalling economic performance and widespread kleptocracies that have robbed their people of material wealth for decades. The change may not occur overnight, but the process is clearly underway toward the exit of the existing regimes in both countries.

Scenario 3: The events in Tunisia, Egypt and possibly Yemen electrify the populations of countries in the Middle East, spurring popular uprisings across the region. Governments throughout the region give way to new leaders and systems of government and the ensuing uncertainty results in runaway oil prices. It is highly unlikely.

While it is unlikely that the unrest and protests will spread rapidly across the Middle East, I believe the seeds of change have been sown in some of the countries in the region. Over the next few years the effects of change in a few countries will spread to more countries in the region. In the immediate future it is unlikely that there will be radical political change in any of the countries of the Middle East. I, however, remain hopeful about Iran.

Most probably the politics of the region will not have much of an effect on oil prices. This is especially true because the countries making the news right now are not large oil producers.[32]

---

[32] Kumar Belle (2011), " Political Unrest in the Middle East", Seeking Alpha, January 28, 2011

Indian Democracy and Maoists

Arundhati Roy speaks that Indian democracy faces generic problem of capitalism. She has published two books on 'Walking with the Comrades' and 'Broken Republic' through Penguin India as publisher. She explains the character of Indian democracy as follows:

When you have 800 C. R. P. F. (Central Reserve Police Force, a paramilitary force deployed to fight country's internal insurgencies) marching three days into the forest; surrounding a forest village and burning it and raping women, what are the poor supposed to do?

- **(a) Can the hungry go on a hunger strike?**
- **(b) Can people who have no money boycott goods?**
- **(c) What sort of civil disobedience we are asking them to adhere to?**

But at the same time what goes on in the forest in terms of resistance cannot go on outside the forest.

Ms. Roy recounts the time she spent in 2010 in the forest with the banned Maoist insurgents, who are active in large swathes of central and eastern India.

Today, it's true that usurping of land, the colonization of the land of the poor is at the heart of the unfolding civil war in our country.

If you look at the map of India today, the forests, the tribal people, the natural resources, the Maoists and the civil war, they are all stacked one on top of another. You have to be blind not to be able to notice the vertical connection between them all. Anti-capitalism was the reining tone of capitalism's linguistic tactics.

When you call something like bauxite (a raw mineral from which aluminum is extracted), which is in the mountain, a resource you are automatically falling into the language of **extractive capitalism**. Because for the tribal people, the bauxite outside the mountain is worthless, the bauxite inside the mountain is the source of life, is the source of faith, and is the source of everything. You take the bauxite out of the mountain, and then give it to some corporations' worth of **four trillion dollars.**

Ms. Roy said that state governments have signed hundreds of memorandums of understanding with the mining companies for the mining of the tribal land. She said many of those have not been actualized because of "the stubbornness and the resilience of the battle that the poorest people are waging against the richest corporations. But these mining corporations historically are used to winning their battles. So they are just waiting like lazy predators. If it's not the Salwa Judum (a state-supported vigilante group fighting Maoists in the central state of Chhattisgarh), it will be the army.

We are at the moment facing the prospect of a militarized democracy, if that isn't an oxymoron. It is a generic problem of capitalism.

Ms. Roy also criticized the country's middle and upper classes of society. We are living in a country where simultaneously we are trying to make the discourse of democracy sophisticated while we are colonizing ourselves.

The most successful secessionist struggle in India is the secession of the middle and upper classes into outer space from where they look down and say 'what's our bauxite doing in their mountains, what's our water doing in their rivers, what's our timber doing in their forests.

India continues to be a charade of democracy where you have all the rituals; you have all the institutions of democracy that appear to be functioning. "You have these institutions—the courts, the media, the parliament—all of these being hollowed out and then shells being put in place.

Ms. Roy explained why she sees Indian democracy as being reduced to a ritual. I say what if any poor man or woman, any tribal person living in the forest—What if they were to turn around and say to us tell me one democratic institution in this country where I can appeal and where I can get a hearing? I can guarantee you there are no answers to that question today in India. There is absolutely no answer to that question. They cannot go to the courts. If they vote, it's like voting for this washing soap or that washing soap both owned by the same holding company.

I stand on the other side of the line with the "bandwidth of resistance movements. From there I turn around and ask our comrades the question, which is: Will we leave the bauxite in the mountain?' And that I think is the real question facing all of us.[33]

INDIA
India must revisit Tibet policy

The international community treats Jammu & Kashmir as a *de facto* — but not *de jure* — part of India. Similarly, it treats Pakistan-occupied Kashmir and Gilgit - Baltistan as a *de facto* — but not *de jure* — part of Pakistan. In pursuance of this policy, other countries honour the Indian passports held by the residents of Jammu & Kashmir and issue them normal visas on those passports when they want to travel. Similarly, they honour the Pakistani passports held by

[33] Krishna Pokharel (2011), Arundhati Roy on Indian democracy and Maoists, Indian Real Time, May 24, 2011

the residents of Pakistan-occupied Kashmir and Gilgit - Baltistan and issue them visas on those passports.

The modifications in the Chinese policy have the following implications.

Firstly, China has started treating Pakistan-occupied Kashmir and Gilgit - Baltistan as *de facto* and *de jure* parts of Pakistan. It does not recognize Indian claims to these territories.

Secondly, it has diluted its past acceptance of Jammu & Kashmir as a *de facto* part of India. This would give satisfaction to Pakistan, which projects Jammu & Kashmir as Pakistani territory under the illegal occupation of India. This would also lend support to the Pakistani contention that it has a political, diplomatic and moral right to support the so-called freedom struggle in Jammu & Kashmir.

Thirdly, by questioning the legitimacy of India's sovereignty over Jammu & Kashmir, the Chinese may be creating a future option for themselves of questioning India's *locus standi* to negotiate with them on the future of Indian Territory in the Ladakh area occupied by them in the past. They could use this option in future if their relations with India deteriorate.

As a starter in the reexamination of our Tibet policy, we should make evident how seriously we are unhappy with Beijing on this issue by immediately including His Holiness the Dalai Lama in the project for revival of the Nalanda University.

The Indian government's response to the ongoing protests in Tibet has been to merely state its "distress" about the situation and reaffirm its position that Tibet is an "internal" affair of China. New Delhi has assured Beijing that its position on the Tibet issue is "clear and consistent" and that this "would not change in the future." The Indian position is based on its traditional opposition to separatist movements and to foreign intervention in support of such movements. Also, given the present dynamics of India-China relations with greater synergy as the goal, New Delhi does not favour supporting the Tibetan cause. However, protests by Tibetans have implications for India as the Tibet issue is entangled with the India-China border dispute.

The Tibet issue is rooted in the histories of the three countries – India, China and Tibet. Tibet has existed throughout history as a distinct civilization with rich culture, language, religion, polity and identity. Through the centuries India and Tibet have maintained strong religious and trade ties, and have shared a peaceful border. But the advent of British power in the Indian sub-continent altered the nature of this relationship.

The British Raj's policy towards Tibet was shaped by the Great Game and the need to prevent Russia from posing a threat to India. It was against this backdrop that the Raj called for the tripartite Simla conference in October 1913, which was attended by representatives from British India (Henry McMahon), Republican China (Chen Yifan) and Tibet (Lonchen Shatra). The goal was to settle the boundary between British India and Tibet on the one hand and between Tibet and China on the other. The result was the Simla Agreement of 1914, which the Chinese representative initialled but only under British pressure. The Agreement divided Tibet into Inner and Outer Tibet. China was given sovereignty over Inner Tibet but only suzerain control over Outer Tibet. And the boundary between India and Tibet was demarcated, with the Raj retaining trading and extra-territorial rights in Outer Tibet.

Independent India inherited this arrangement, which boiled down to sustaining Tibet as a buffer zone with de facto independent status under Chinese suzerainty. In the post-1949 period, when the People's Republic of China came into being, India urged China to let Tibet continue as an autonomous region in line with its historical status, religious, cultural and political identity. However, the entry of 20,000 PLA troops in 1950-51 into Tibet ended its independent status and eventually brought to the fore the India-China border issue.

During his 1954 visit to China, Jawaharlal Nehru had raised the issue of inaccurate border alignment as depicted in some Chinese maps. Premier Chou Enlai responded that these maps were reproductions of old Kuomintang maps and that his government has had no time to revise them. However, Nehru's December 14, 1958 letter, in which he had once again raised the issue of Chinese maps depicting the border alignment inaccurately, elicited a different response from Chou. The Chinese Premier wrote back on January 23, 1959 stating that the Sino-Indian border was never delimited and that China has never recognised the McMahon Line.

After the 1962 India-China war, China began to claim some **90,000 square kilometres** of Indian Territory in the eastern sector and **38,000 square kilometres** in the Aksai Chin area. These claims flow directly from China's control over Tibet and its felt need to consolidate its rule over this rebellious territory.

Between 1947 and 1954, India's position on Tibet was based on recognising it as an independent nation. Tibet represented itself as an independent country at the Asian Relations Conference held in New Delhi in March-April 1947. But India subsequently gave up this position on April 29, 1954, when it signed an agreement with China on trade and intercourse between India and Tibet. Under the terms of the agreement, India gave up all extra-territorial rights and privileges that it had inherited from the British Raj and recognised Tibet as part of China. This, in effect, was a unilateral concession without the Indian government gaining anything in return.

In subsequent decades, New Delhi has repeatedly reiterated that Tibet is a part of China, in spite of the latter's encroachment into and extravagant claims over Indian Territory, the border war it imposed on India in 1962, and the unresolved border dispute at the centre of which lies Tibet. In effect, such reiteration has meant the dilution of a bargaining card in the border negotiations. In 2003, the Vajpayee government went further than any other government before by stating that the "Tibetan Autonomous Region of China is part of the territory of China." This has two critical implications for Indian security. First, it excluded Inner Tibet (present day Sichuan, Yunnan and Qinghai provinces) from the geographical notion of Tibet, thus recognising Inner Tibet as Chinese land. Second, it provided China a greater opening to advance its claims on Arunachal Pradesh. For, Outer Tibet or the Tibetan Autonomous Region (TAR), according to the Chinese definition, includes Arunachal Pradesh, which it refers to as its 'southern state'.

India has consistently failed to understand nuances in Chinese diplomatic practice and negotiating tactics. China is tackling the Tibet problem at two levels. One, it is involving the Dalai Lama's representatives in fruitless talks, while also disparaging him as a 'splittist' who aims to disintegrate China. Two, it is arm-twisting India by repeatedly claiming that Arunachal Pradesh is part of China. Here, it is worth noting that at the sixth round of talks with Tibetan representatives Chinese negotiators had conveyed that the Dalai Lama should accept Arunachal Pradesh as part of China, which the Dalai Lama has refused to accept. China is not seriously considering a resolution to the Tibet issue or the border dispute with India. It is simply buying time till the Dalai Lama passes away, after which, it hopes, the Tibetan movement would fizzle out. This would also further weaken India's bargaining position on the border negotiations while at the same time gaining for itself greater manoeuvrability.

The presence of the Dalai Lama in India along with 120,000 Tibetan refugees spread across 35 settlements is leverage for India. But India has so far steadfastly avoided using the Tibetan card. Given the intricate linkage between the Tibet issue and the border dispute, India needs to revise its policy on Tibet. Its present policy of appeasement and unilateral concessions has not stopped China from claiming Indian Territory. Chinese maps continue to show Arunachal Pradesh as part of China, and Jammu and Kashmir as falling outside India. Some Chinese maps still do not represent Beijing's revised position on Sikkim.[34]

The latest unrest among Tibetans provides an opportunity for India to revisit and revise its Tibet policy. First, India should make it clear to the Chinese government that developments in Tibet are a concern for India and that it cannot remain unaffected by developments there. Second, on the border issue, instead of merely restating that all of Arunachal Pradesh is an integral part of its territory, India should make it very clear that these are non-negotiable. Third, upholding its democratic principles as well as its cultural affinity with the Tibetans, India should impress upon the Chinese that while it does not support political activity by Tibetans in its soil, it also cannot suppress peaceful demonstrations by them. Fourth, India should move away from its 'over-

---

[34] Abanti Bhattacharya (2008), "India Should Revisit its Tibet Policy", Institute of defense studies and analysis, April 4, 2008 and B Raman (2010), " India must revisit Tibet policy", the Pioneer, August 30, 2010

cautious' and diffident policy on Tibet and adopt a more independent stand that takes into account its national interests.

The poverty of politics

LIFE is coming full circle for the itinerant economists of our age. They were, after all, elevated by a largely uneducated public discourse promoted primarily by a mildly illiterate mass media to the position of soothsayers in the 20th century. Perfectly appropriate false prophets for modern, post-industrial societies that have internalized the politics of blame, a culture of entitlement, and have developed a penchant for solutions sans the human factor.

Before you go running away with the idea that this just another rant, though, let me make a terribly old-fashioned and not cutting-edge at all but still valid distinction between economics and econometrics given that the practitioners of the latter were raised, in the last few decades of the previous century, from the level of being glorified clerks or the mechanics of the field of study to be considered on a par with those doing seminal work under the social sciences rubric on economic theory using the inter-linkages the discipline provides with sociology, philosophy, history and, yes, even statistics.

Examine, then, in the above context, the uproar over and debate about the figures released by the Planning Commission on its estimates of poverty, wherein valid question have been raised, including in this newspaper, about the absurdity, in the absence of a marked change in the situation between September 2011 and March 2012, of bringing down the poverty line benchmark from 32 INR a day in urban areas to 28.56 INR and from 26 INR a day to 22.43 INR (Indian rupees). And, I say, whether you give the statisticians collating the data the benefit of doubt or not, it doesn't matter. The scandal is elsewhere — are we as a nation saying that a monthly income ranging between Rs 600-odd and just under INR 1,000, to take the broadest possible range, in an economy that the Prime Minister described as among the pack of countries leading the growth race, is the starvation/ subsistence/ poverty—take your pick — line?

Despite the sneer some of you may have detected in my categorization of the economists and statisticians putting out the figures and the skullduggery alleged in their latest output, they are, at the end of the day, looking at objective parameters ranging from calorific intake and the rate of food inflation to the consumer price index among other factors. The latest bout of outrage is focused on the discrepancy in the figures between September and March and the lack of anybody standing up to set the record straight, and that's perfectly justifiable. It is time, however, a 65-year-old nation-state questions the political consensus that once the economists and statisticians have come up with the data we argue on the quantum of social sector, food security and pro-life (in the literal and not anti-abortionist sense) spending that's valid and/or affordable.

I suggest we do it the other way around. Those politicians, i.e. the duly elected representatives we have freely chosen to govern us despite the very serious flaws in those processes, set, a priori, the poverty line figure. Only set, please understand, and nothing more, the amount they think their worst off fellow citizens can manage on. Government economists will continue to collect and put out the data and be expected to answer the questions that are asked of them when, like in the current instance, the discrepancies in their figures are glaring. But this is not about statistics, damn statistics — on the contrary, without an accurate data base, the scientifically proven and statistically sound procedure that is the basis for any targeting of welfare and/or security schemes, we will be reduced to a dependence on arbitrariness and whim. Also, the reality of the scale of poverty — and relative affluence — is to be found in these cold, hard numbers and not anecdotal or even lived evidence.

But what we as a nation define as the poverty line has to be a political decision in which the input of these government servants and experts is certainly of vital importance, not an end in itself; that would be tantamount to letting those elected to govern us evading their responsibility, and that is precisely what has been encouraged till today. Let the government of the day, say in its Budget each year, announce where it has pegged the poverty line for the coming year as an aspiration target, at the very least. But decouple it from the figures produced by the Planning Commission delineating who is surviving on just how much and how much is needed to survive, as long as it is all based on expert and empirical evidence. These statistics will continue to be released, apace, as an exercise in data dissemination and as input for policy formulation but the government of the day has to be held accountable to the poverty line it has enunciated, and credible figures will do just that.

Perhaps we can then finally stop fooling ourselves and governments will have to take the decisions necessary to the raise the resources to ensure that those living at subsistence levels by their own benchmark in any quality-of-life sense are taken care of. And that would mean, realistically, cash transfers, partnership with the private sector and the non-profit sector with strong regulatory mechanisms in place, a strong anti-graft institutional framework, rightsizing of government, bureaucratic accountability and performance-related incentives. (Gotcha, if you thought I was some Left-wing loony suggesting profligate spending by Big Brother to deepen dependence on the state that will bankrupt my country, make my poorest fellow citizens beggars, whilst getting irresponsible populists re-elected as long as elections are "allowed"...)

So, 5,000 INR a month for urban citizens and 4,000 INR a month for their rural counterparts is fair, in my view, as a poverty line benchmark. Then, we can examine, apart from questioning when needed, Planning Commission figures to see just how woefully short Indians are of human dignity because our leaders would rather hand out sops and produce excuses for non-performance than take the decisions needed to alleviate their condition.[35]

NEPAL
The country is on the brink again

With only three months left before the Constituent Assembly runs out of time, a Constitution for 'New' Nepal still remains a distant dream as politicians bicker.

Nepal has hit a new crisis, this time not over the extension of the Constituent Assembly, which is 28 days away, but over the continuation of the five-month-old Government led by Prime Minister Jhala Nath Khanal and supported by the Maoists. Nepali politics has dug itself deeper into a hole. The threat by Maoist leader Pushpa Kamal Dahal, better known as Prachanda, of withdrawing support made Mr. Khanal hurriedly fall in line, accepting Maoist diktat in defiance of his party high command and the five-point agreement. He has bought time and, as the logjam following former Prime Minister Madhav Kumar Nepal's resignation shows, finding a new Prime Minister is a divine challenge for the Constituent Assembly.

---

[35] Ishan Joshi (2012), "The poverty f politics". The Sunday Statesman, March 25, 2012

'Old' Nepal's transformation to 'New' Nepal has hit a pause button. But the transformation of erstwhile Maoist guerrillas who see themselves as the flag-bearers of this change into a democratic political entity has made some progress. Out of power since May 2009, fresh churning of the party has thrown up new challenges and opportunities. The appetite for power and the lure of loaves and fishes of office have driven both the behaviour of the Maoists and the pace of the peace process. Despite the constitutional timeline of two years plus plus, there is little urgency over growing concerns of political instability which has fuelled the economic downturn and frustration among the people awaiting the Maoist miracle of a 'New' Nepal.

As key drivers of the peace process, Maoists have only last month resolved— rather, patched up— inner contradictions in the strategic methodology of securing power and their perceived prerogative to shape the contours of 'New' Nepal. They enjoy pre-eminence in the peace process by virtue of being the single largest party in the Constituent Assembly and the need for their political and military organisations to be mainstreamed.

Maoists have been fixated on leading the Government to drive their agenda after their rule ended prematurely when un-constitutional means were employed to establish civilian supremacy over the Army. The latest ploy of the Maoists to wriggle back into Government and capture its leadership through a seven-point secret agreement with Mr. Khanal was foiled by the unimplemented five-point agreement, which allowed the three-month extension of the Constituent Assembly beyond May 28 this year. The Maoists secured Ministerial berths but Prachanda ordered Monday's reshuffle of the pack in order to please different factions of his party according to a new power-sharing arrangement within the high command.

While Prachanda remains chairman of the party (and retains parliamentary party leadership) he has been forced to delegate his other powers to the three vice-chairmen—Mr. Mohan Baidya (organisation and discipline), Mr. Baburam Bhattarai (prime ministerial candidate), Mr. Narayan Kaji Shreshtha (leader of the new Ministerial team in the Khanal Cabinet) and general secretary Ram Bahadur Thapa, head of the PLA. This is the first exercise in decentralisation of power and more democracy in the party as a *quid pro quo* for the hardliners shelving 'revolt' and accepting the democratic political line for continuing the peace process. This is a Band-Aid on the peace process.

With just 28 days left for the third deadline for integration and drafting the Constitution to expire, Prachanda has said it is impossible to complete the peace process by August 31. At best, an agreement on modality and specific numbers of PLA to be integrated is feasible. Separating Maoists from its parallel army will be a positive step. A *status quo* on the peace process is not surprising. Each of the four major parties — Maoists, Nepali Congress, United Marxist-Leninist and Madhesis — is deeply divided; yet the ruling Left-alliance looks strong, though addressing the peace process is not a priority issue.

Mr. Khanal acted in self-interest. While the Nepali Congress and members of his own party asked him to resign in deference to the five-point agreement to facilitating a national unity Government, Prachanda demanded the reshuffle to accommodate Mr. Narayan Kaji Shreshtha's team. A signatory to the five-point agreement, Prachanda is looking both ways: But he does not want Mr. Babu Ram Bhattarai to become the Prime Minister of a future national unity Government.

Mr. Khanal is doing what his predecessor; Mr. Madhav Kumar Nepal did — echoing that he will step down as soon as a national unity Government is ready. This will shelve the peace process further. The next 28 days will be spent protecting the Government against the wrath of the divided Nepali Congress.

Nepal has tried all combinations of coalition Governments except one with the two political adversaries, Maoists and the Nepali Congress, together. For long it was known that only a national unity Government has any chance of bringing to fruition the unfinished peace process. Mr. Bhattarai has been articulating the need for a national unity Government to achieve a consensus on sticky constitutional issues.

Legal difficulties persist about extending the term of the Constituent Assembly any further. Last time, the Supreme Court served a show cause notice to President Ram Baran Yadav for extending the Constituent Assembly's tenure after the deadline had expired. The Supreme Court has overturned a verdict of November 4, 2010 that approved the one-year extension and the enabling Eighth Amendment. It argued that the interim Constitution had not thought of extension beyond two years: Except six months in an emergency. The doctrine of necessity allows extension of only six months of which three months will have been utilized by the end of this month. That leaves just three months to complete the peace process.

Surprisingly India-bashing is on the decline. No one is blaming New Delhi directly for the current political tensions, which are the outcome of political formations being fractured irreparably. The Nepalese are happy that a new Indian team — Foreign Secretary, Joint Secretary and Ambassador — is taking the crease. The last two — Ambassador Jayant Prasad and Joint Secretary Akhilesh Mishra — are both Biharis and the latter has served in the Katmandu mission.

Home Minister P Chidambaram told visiting Nepali

editors that lack of a stable Government had impeded the peace process and enhanced security challenges for India, especially of terrorism and fake currency. He ruled out closing the 1,800 km border and instead called for its better joint management.

Only a national unity Government has a chance of reviving the peace process and restoring political stability, both imperatives for closure of the peace process and ushering in a 'New' Nepal with former Maoist guerrillas transformed into responsible citizens, soldiers and politicians. For this the collective blessings of the presiding deities of Swargadwari, Manakamana and Pashupatinath will be necessary. It too depends upon Prachanda's good sense. [36]

The urge for democracy is universal

When the Arabs start overthrowing their rulers in non-violent revolutions that are just about democracy, not about Islam or Israel, there is astonishment and disbelief. It's time we deconstructed the conventional image of Arabs.

One of the incidental pleasures of the past few weeks has been watching the western media struggling to come to terms with the notion of Arab democracy. The Arabs themselves seem clear enough on the concept of a democratic revolution, but elsewhere there is much hand wringing about whether Arabs can really build democratic states. After all, they have no previous experience of democracy, and it's basically a Western invention, isn't it? The Arabs don't even have Athens and the Roman republic up their family tree.

Sure the revolutions are brave, and they're exhilarating to watch from afar, but in the end the

---

[36] Ashok K Mehta (2011), " Nepal on the brink again", The Pioneer, August 3, 2011

military will take over, or the Islamists will take over, or they'll mess it up some other way. This is the assumption -- sometimes implied, sometimes flatly stated that still underpins much of the outside comment and analysis on the Arab revolutions.

The current rationale for this arrogant and ignorant assumption is the "clash of civilisations" tripe that Sam Huntington and his pals have been peddling around the official circuit in Washington for almost two decades now. The Arabs just belong to the wrong civilization, and so they can't get it right.

If this sounds vaguely familiar, that's because it's really the centuries-old justification for European imperial rule over the rest of the planet, re-cycled for modern use. Europe once ruled the lesser breeds with a firm hand, but it can no longer do that directly. Instead it backs tough local rulers who promise to provide "stability" -- and coincidentally protect the West's interests in the area.

So when the Arabs start overthrowing their rulers in non-violent revolutions that are just about democracy, not about Islam or Israel, there is astonishment and disbelief in the western media. It is time for a little deconstruction. What makes the Arabs suitable candidates for democracy is their heritage as human beings, not their specific cultural or historical antecedents. Democracy didn't need to be invented; just resurrected.

The default mode for human beings is equality. Every pre-civilized society we know about operated on the assumption that its members were equals. Nobody had the right to give orders to anybody else.

What drove this was not idealism but pragmatism. In hunting-and- gathering groups, nobody can own more than they can carry, so there is no way to accumulate wealth. If you want meat, then you'll have to cooperate in the hunt. These were societies where nobody could control anybody else, and so they had to make their decisions democratically.

They were all very little societies: Rarely more than 50 adults (who had all known one another all their lives). On the rare occasions when they had to make a major decision, they would actually sit around and debate it until they reached a consensus. Direct democracy is possible if you like.

People have been running their affairs that way ever since we developed language, which was almost certainly before we were even anatomically modern human beings. So 99.9 per cent of our history says. That is who we are, and how we prefer to behave unless some enormous obstacle gets in our way.

The enormous obstacle was civilization. All hunting-and-gathering societies were essentially egalitarian. The mass societies that we call civilisations arose less than ten thousand years ago, thanks to the invention of agriculture. Until very recently, all of them, without exception, were tyrannies, pyramids of power and privilege in which the few decided and the many obeyed. What happened?

A mass society, thousands, then millions strong, confers immense advantages on its members. Within a few thousand the little hunting- and-gathering groups were pushed out of the good lands everywhere. By the time the first anthropologists appeared to study them, they were on their last legs, and none now survive in their original form. But we know why the societies that replaced them were all tyrannies.

The mass societies had many more decisions to make, and no way of making them in the old, egalitarian way. Their huge numbers made any attempt at discussing the question as equals impossible, so the only ones that survived and flourished were the ones that became brutal hierarchies. Tyranny was the solution to what was essentially a communications problem.

Fast-forward ten thousand years, and give these societies mass communications. You don't have to wait for Face book; just invent the printing press. Wait a couple of hundred years while literacy spreads, and presto! We can all talk to one another again, after a fashion, and the democratic revolutions begin. We didn't invent the principle of equality among human beings; we just reclaimed it.

Modern democracy first appeared in the West only because the West was the first part of the world to develop mass communications. It was a technological advantage, not a cultural one -- and as literacy and the technology of mass communications have spread around the world, all the other mass societies have begun to reclaim their heritage too. The Arabs need no instruction in democracy from anybody else. They own it too.[37]

Global Political Problems

Mr. Sergey Lavrov, Foreign Minister of Russia told: **Moscow deems it inadmissible that the international community solves political problems by force; rather they should attempt to solve the existing political problems through discussions.**

Lavrov said at a press conference following a meeting of foreign ministers of CIS countries that took place in the Ukrainian capital on Friday. Lavrov added that the unsettling events in the Middle East and North Africa underline his point. The Russian Foreign Minister also noted that these same events demonstrate that the

---

[37] Gwynne Dyer (2011), "The urge for democracy is universal", The Pioneer, Wednesday, March 2, 2011

authorities of foreign governments should not waste time introducing necessary reforms that would assist their normal development.

Lavrov's counterpart from Tajikistan, Khamrokhon Zarifi, said that he was sure that the Middle East crisis would not spread to other countries, in particular in Central Asia. "Every region has its specifics and therefore we cannot connect the influence of one region on another in a mathematical way," Khamrokhon Zarifi said. "I believe that there are no prerequisites for such an effect on Central Asia."

Lavrov mentioned that Moscow was concerned about the fate of several Russian journalists reportedly detained by the opposition forces in Libya near the city of Benghazi. The foreign minister said that the Russian authorities might address governments that are rumored to have special troops in Libya with a request to assist in freeing the Russian citizens.

Lavrov also touched upon the issue of foreign trade in his statements, acknowledging that Russia, like Ukraine, will seek the introduction of a free-trade zone with the European Union. The Russian official added that the membership in the Customs Union (the economic organization of Russia, Belarus and Kazakhstan) would not prevent any country from entering the World Trade Organization (WTO). Lavrov reminded the press conference that Russia is actively seeking membership in the WTO.[38]

Conclusion:

World Peace would create cooperation, compassion and justice to all. It would bid farewell to war, hatred, hunger, and rivalry.

---

[38] Sergey Lavrov (2011), "Global Political problems must not be solved by force", Russia Politics", April 8, 2011

All voters should exercise franchise in elections. If a voter does not find a suitable candidate in the fray, he should exercise the 'None of the above' (NOTA) option in the EVM.

A group of people can make a political party with certain primary commitments but it must be a national party.

There should not be local, regional or state level political parties in a democracy. Small political parties create turbid and hostile activities that cause political instability and road shows for media coverage. They speak against the Central government in order to hide their own mistakes.

There are about 1760 political parties in India. Most of the political parties are sleeping political parties or road show political parties. These political parties are purely on–record political parties that are used to collect donations. The Election Commission of India (ECI) must **de-recognize these political parties** as they have neither contested in elections nor secured more than 5 percent of votes in the elections.

The Election Commission of India should maintain records of cleanness, purity in thought and need of the party for people of the country. A number of new political parties might be formed with amalgamation of all sleeping or state-level political parties. But there should be only a maximum of seven political parties in a country with different ideology and purpose.

There could be political alliance after the election to form the government. But political alliance before the election should not be entertained as it confuses the voters. The Comptroller and Auditor General must audit the political account of all political parties each year. But details should not be publicized in press or electronic media.

Foreign funding, corruption and educated unemployment have demoralized people, political parties and democracies. There should not be bye-election after sad demise of the elected leader. The party should nominate his/her spouse, or eldest offspring as substitute.

There should be a General Election in a single day for the entire country through Internet and free-registered postal ballot for Parliament and Assemblies. There is no necessity of polling stations or police force to maintain law and order. Bribing the voters by a political party would be treated as a disqualification. Only the party president should contest for the entire country. The MP, MLA, Senator would be proxy candidates for the constituencies.

In case, internet facilities are not available, voters should vote the preferred party in Election booths. This would be sufficient to choose MLA or MP for the state and country. Percentage of votes to a party would indicate percentage berths in Assembly and Parliament.

As individuals would not be candidates in the General Election, money distribution would be minimized or stopped. And political rivalry would be changed to friendship among different groups.

Persons engaged in adultery, suspended or dismissed from services, with double nationality, with disproportionate assets and found guilty by a court in corruption, money laundering, theft, vulgarly, murder or dacoit should not be allowed to enter into Parliament as honored Member.

+++++

Chapter –IV

POLITICS AS BUSINESS

Happiness is when what you think, what you say, and what you do are in harmony.

Mahatma M. K. Gandhi

Political leaders should possess human characters like higher equanimity, humanity, and selflessness. They should be ideal persons to represent the masses. They should take care of the people, which have accepted their leadership. But politicians of most of the developing countries are wedded to selfishness, greedy and possess duplicate characters to cheat the people whom they represent.

Inge Amundsen has illustrated the definitions and concepts of corruption. The researcher says that political corruption is more dangerous than other forms of corruption. Corruption has recently been the subject of substantial theorizing and empirical research, and this has produced a bewildering array of alternative approaches, explanations, typologies and remedies. Corruption is understood as everything from the paying of bribes to civil servants and the simple theft of public purses, to a wide range of dubious economic and political practices in which business people, politicians and bureaucrats enrich themselves.[39]

The issue of corruption is an old one, which has re-entered the current political and economic debate from the new interest in the role of the state in the developing world, and from the assumption that the state is an indispensable instrument for economic development, redistribution and welfare. In contrast to the largely rejected "State-dominated" and "state-less" development models, there is now much consensus on the need for an efficient medium-sized state apparatus with a political will and adequate economic policies to ensure economic development. Corruption is seen as counter-productive to the needed economic and political reforms, accountability, transparency, and good governance.

Political corruption can be classified for analytical and practical purposes. First, different forms of corruption will be outlined. Secondly, corruption will be defined as a particular state-society relationship, and the distinction made between political corruption and bureaucratic corruption. Then two more distinctions will be added, namely between "individual" and "collective" forms of corruption, and corruption as a mechanism of either "upward extraction" or "downward redistribution". This will sum up to the basic argument that the fight against corruption will have to be placed within a broader agenda of democratization.

---

[39] Inge Amundsen (2000), " Corruption: Definitions and Concepts", Draft, Chr. Michelsen Institute Development Studies and Human Rights, 17 January 2000

Forms of corruption

The main forms of corruption are bribery, embezzlement, fraud and extortion. Even when these concepts are partly overlapping and at times interchangeable with other concepts, some of the basic characteristics of corruption can be identified through these concepts.

Bribery is the payment (in money or kind) that is given or taken in a corrupt relationship. To pay or receive a bribe is corruption *per se*, and should be understood as the essence of corruption. A bribe is a fixed sum, a certain percentage of a contract, or any other favour in money of kind, usually paid to a state official that can make contracts on behalf of the state or otherwise distribute benefits to companies or individuals, businessmen and clients.

There are many equivalent terms to bribery, like kickbacks, gratuities, baksheesh, sweeteners, pay-offs, speed money and grease money, which are all notions of corruption as perceived from the public.

These are payments needed or demanded to make things pass swifter, smoother or more favourably through the state bureaucracy. By "greasing palms" corporations and business interests can buy for instance political favours and escape the full burden of taxation and environmental regulations, or buy protected markets and monopolies, import/export licenses, etc. Bribery, however, can also be a form of "informal" taxation, when public officials charge additional under-the-table payments or expect "gifts" from clients. It is an extractive form of bribery when for instance a government minister or party boss goes on a promotion tour, and is able to fill the luggage compartment of his car with "donations" and "gifts" from his "devoted followers".

Embezzlement is theft of public resources by public officials, which is another form of misappropriation of public funds. Embezzlement is when a state official steals from the public institution in which he his employed, and from resources he is supposed to administer on behalf of the state and the public. However, disloyal employees in private firms can also embezzle money and other resources from their employers.

Embezzlement is *not* considered as corruption from a strict legal point of view. In legal terms, corruption is a transaction between two individuals, one state agent and one "civilian", where the state agent goes beyond the limits of the law and regulations in order to secure himself a personal benefit in the form of a bribe.

Embezzlement is regarded as theft because it does not involve the "civilian" side directly. The general public is deprived when public funds are embezzled, but no individual property is stolen, and thus individual citizens will have no legal right to present themselves as forfeited.

This point refers to one of the dangers of embezzlement. There will have to be a political will as well as an independent judiciary and a legal capacity in order to clamp down on embezzlement. Embezzlement is one of the forms of corruption and power abuse that can develop in closed institutional and moral spheres, independently of the public moral and with few possibilities of public sanctions. In many corrupt countries, embezzlement is one of the most important modes of economic accumulation. It can be a fundamental part of the resource extractive capacity of ruling elite, and it can be even more important than extraction through bribes.

To be considered, as another form of embezzlement is the fact that some power-holders systematically use their political office to enter into, secure and expand their private business interests. In some countries the political elite has nationalized foreign businesses, property and monopoly rights, and redistributed these to the members of the ruling families. Large numbers of former state enterprises and parastatals have been handed over to friends and family of ministers and presidents, for symbolic sums of money and in the name of "privatization". In Zimbabwe, ruling party bosses now own large formerly white farms. In the Côte d'Ivoire, the president's family holds the largest coffee and cocoa plantations. In Cameroon and other African countries the president and his family own the biggest breweries, sugar refineries, transport and other companies.

Fraud is an economic crime that involves some kind of trickery, swindle or deceit. It is a broader legal and popular term that covers more than bribery and embezzlement. It is fraud for instance when state agencies and state representatives are engaged in illegal trade networks, counterfeit and racketing, and when forgery, smuggling and other organized economic crime is propped up by "official" sanction and involvement. It is fraud when ministers and top bureaucrats take a share for closing their eyes on this; it is serious fraud when they have an active role in it.

Dirty tricks politics: The fraudulent ways of money extraction of certain African rulers have been called"dirty tricks politics"**.** Dirty tricks politics include "import" of toxic and atomic waste from Western countries, presidents who print large amounts of national bank notes to pay civil servants and military men (who force these upon local traders; at gunpoint in the case of Zaïre), and the many state or parastatal institutions that have persuaded private firms to give them loans, assistance and services that will never be paid back.

Besides, members of the ruling elites in Nigeria and Kenya are presumably involved in the international drug trade, money laundering is done through African state banks and parastatals, and public agencies are issuing falsified certificates of country of origin and of brand names, enabling faked goods from Taiwan and Hong Kong to reach international markets. What is widespread and even increasing, according to this book, is the role of certain African states as active mediators, facilitators and partners in fraudulent and criminal business activities, in international organised crime.

Extortion is money and other resources extracted by the use of coercion, violence or the threats to use force. "Protection" or "security" money can be extorted in the classical, infamous mafia style. By creating an atmosphere of insecurity where individual citizens, private businesses and public officials are harassed and intimidated, a mafia and other criminals can blackmail and extort money in return for their kind of peace. Only those who pay the protection money will be exempted from further harassment. Blackmailing and extortion is basically a corrupt transaction, but the money is more violently extracted and the returns are meagre. The exchange of benefits is highly unequal: in return for millions in protection money, the blackmailed may get no more than a negative freedom, a lax promise of impunity.

Corruption in the form of extortion is usually understood as a form of extraction "from below". It is for instance when real mafias, like in Russia and Italy, are able to impose their influence upon individual state officials and entire state agencies through threats, intimidation and targeted assassinations. What they obtain in return may be preferential business opportunities and privileges, and freedom from taxation, regulations, and legal prosecution.

Corrupt practices of this kind can also be "from above", when the state itself is the biggest mafia of them all. This is known for instance where the state, and in particular its security services and paramilitary groups, extorts money from individuals and groups to protect them from further harassment. With more or less concealed threats, rulers can extract resources from private sector businesses. These businesses rarely take the chance of refusing state or ruling party officials what they demand, when exaggeratedly strict taxation, overtly delayed licenses, repeated and brutal police inspections or other harassment are to be expected. Presidential reelection campaigns are for instance frequently "irrigated" by private companies.

Also extortion made by military and police units in their many roadblocks can be understood as "informal" taxation or extraction. Roadblocks are widespread over most of Africa, from Tunisia in the north to South Africa. When you leave or enter a town, there is a checkpoint where a small fee is expected for making the passage smooth. In some cases, these checkpoints are used to restrict the movement of dissenters, but usually governments tolerate them as income for underpaid divisions.

Favouritism is mechanism of power abuse implying "privatization" and a highly biased distribution of state resources, no matter how these resources have been accumulated in the first place. Favouritism is the natural human proclivity to favour friends, family and anybody close and trusted. Favouritism is related to corruption insofar as it implies a corrupted distribution of resources, whereas corruption strictly defined is about the accumulation of resources.

In the political sphere, favoritism is the penchant of state officials and politicians, who have access to state resources and the power to decide upon the distribution of these, to give preferential treatment to certain people. Favouritism or cronyism is for instance to grant an office to a friend or a relative, regardless of merit.

Favouritism is a basic political mechanism in many authoritarian and semi democratic countries. In most non-democratic systems, the president has for instance the constitutional right to appoint all high-ranking positions, a legal or customary right that extends exceedingly the possibilities for favouritism. It easily adds up to several hundred positions within the ministries, the military and security apparatus, in the parastatal and public companies, in the diplomatic corps and in the ruling party.

Nepotism is a special form of favouritism, in which an office holder (ruler) prefers his proper kinfolk and family members (wife, brothers and sisters, children, nephews, cousins, in-laws etc.). Many unrestricted presidents have tried to secure their (precarious) power position by nominating family members to key political, economic and military/security positions in the state apparatus.

Other kinds of favouritism are for instance when certain people are commissioned to buy privatised public property (cheaply), or given preferences, state guaranteed or subvention loans, or selected as entrepreneurs for public works, nominated to represent corporate interests in various public councils and committees, and given other privileges through selected economic policies. Through such mechanisms, many politicians and bureaucrats have been able to move from public position into private business, to transfer public power into private wealth.

Favouritism is not only a legal and procedural problem, but also a problem of flawed qualifications, lacking skills and inefficiency. Furthermore, where public position is strongly correlated to possibilities of corrupt and extractive practices, favouritism can secure substantial prerogatives and profits for certain families, clans or some social sub-groups.[40]

The state is usually involved

The decisive role of the state is reflected in most definitions of corruption. Corruption is conventionally understood, and referred to, as the private wealth-seeking behaviour of someone who represents the state and the public authority. It is the misuse of public goods by public officials, for private gains. The working definition of the World Bank is that corruption is the abuse of public power for private benefit. Another widely used description is that corruption is a transaction between private and public sector actors through which collective goods are illegitimately converted into private regarding payoffs.

Most definitions of corruption will underline corruption as a particular (and, one could say, perverted) state-society relation. Corruption is usually understood as involving some "corrupted" politicians and public administrators. Corruption is when a civil servant, official, bureaucrat or politician (anyone elected or appointed to a position of public authority, with power to allocate (scarce) public resources in the name of the state or the government) is abusing this official position for personal or group gain. The corrupt act is when this person demands or accepts money or some other form of reward, for himself or for his family, friends and allies.

The genesis of corruption is found within the international, the national institutional and the national societal levels. At the international level, the globalization of markets, finances, and numerous other transactions have expanded the opportunity of

---

[40] Bayart, Jean-François et al "*La criminalisation de l'État en Afrique*", Paris, 1997,

collusive and concealed transactions between various players in the global game and a "host" government and its representatives. Multinationals are for instance buying concessions, preferences and monopolies. Kickbacks are offered on tenders, loans and contracts, and development projects are sometimes eased through by including travels, computers and other fringe benefits for officials. Foreign sponsored corruption is held by many observers in Third World countries to be the most significant contributing factor to corruption.

At the national institutional level, corruption takes place between the government (the executive) and the administrative and bureaucratic institutions (the civil service, judiciary, legislature, parastatals and local authorities). This relationship can be corrupted because of overlapping and conflicting authority, political power struggles over access to scarce resources, and personal relationships of dependence and loyalty. Other contributing factors are a weak separation between civil service and partisan politics, a weak professional of the bureaucracy, a lack of administrative accountability and transparency, and deficient political control and auditing. The more discretion officials have through abundant, complex and nontransparent regulations, the more corruption becomes likely.

At the national societal level, the corrupt relationship is between the state and various non-state actors. On the one side is the corrupt state official (at any level), on the other side is the corrupter, the supplier of bribes. There is a range of possible counterparts to a corrupt official. It can be the general public, any non-governmental and non-public individual, corporate and organizational, domestic and external. Many theories and conceptualizations of corruption will call attention to these "corrupters", those who offer the bribes in the first place, and the advantages they gain.

Corruption, however, also exists within and between private businesses and within non-governmental organisations, without any state agency or state official being involved. There is corruption in terms of bribing, swindling, and mafia-methods in businesses, and there are treacherous individuals and disloyal employees in many private firms, organisations and associations. Besides, corruption also exists as a moral and cultural problem in society, among individuals in their personal dealings.

For instance do accepted and expected practices of gift-giving, tipping and patronage exist in most societies, even when such habits may be illegal, impose hidden costs on public services and/or confuse the distinction between public and private? The level of "private" corruption can be very symptomatic for the general economic and political development of a society. Besides, all forms of "private" corruption can be destructive to the public morale and undermine the general trust and confidence in rules and regulations. However, by focusing on private sector corruption *only*, a core element in corruption is lost. Most definitions of corruption will emphasize corruption as a state-society relationship because public sector corruption is believed to be a more fundamental problem than private sector corruption, and because controlling public sector corruption is a prerequisite for controlling private sector corruption.

Political corruption and bureaucratic corruption

Political or grand corruption takes place at the highest levels of political authority. It is when the politicians and political decision-makers, who are entitled to formulate, establish and implement the laws in the name of the people, as they are corrupt.

Political corruption is when political decision-makers use the political power they are armed with, to sustain their power, status and wealth. It is when policy formulation and legislation is tailored to benefit politicians and legislators.

Political corruption can thus be distinguished from bureaucratic or *petty* corruption, which is corruption in the public administration, at the implementation end of politics. Petty corruption has also been called "low level" and "street level" to name the kind of corruption that citizens will experience daily, at times, in their encounter with public administration and services like hospitals, schools, local licensing authorities, police, taxing authorities and so on. 3

The distinction between political and bureaucratic corruption is rather ambiguous. It depends on the separation of politics from administration, a particularly unclear delineation in Third World countries. The distinction is nevertheless important. Political corruption is namely something *more* than a deviation from formal and written legal norms, from professional codes of ethics and court rulings.

Political corruption is when the rulers abuse the laws and regulations, sidestepped, ignored, or even tailored to fit their interests. It is when the legal bases, against which corrupt practices are usually evaluated and judged, are weak and furthermore subject to downright encroachment by the rulers.

The consequences of bureaucratic or petty corruption are severe. Bureaucratic corruption is a predicament to private businesses as well as to any citizen's everyday dealings with state officials. It excludes many people from public services and increases their cost, it obstructs, impedes and skews public spending, it makes markets irrational, and it makes the public administration and the entire political system illegitimate in the eyes of the population.

Political corruption has even more substantial political repercussions, because it affects the manner in which decisions are made. Political corruption implies the manipulation of political institutions and the rules of procedure, and it consequently distorts the institutions of government. Political corruption is a deviation from the rational-legal values and principles of the modern state, and leads to institutional decay. The basic problem of political corruption is the lack of political will to encounter the problem: the power-holders do not wish to change a system of which they are the main profiteers.

In some cases, political corruption might take place in higher places without the general public coming across it in their daily life, or ever knowing about it.

Political corruption might be incidental, controlled or concealed, as in most consolidated liberal democracies. Likewise, bureaucratic corruption might take place at the implementation end of public administration without necessarily being a part of 3. The distinction between bureaucratic and political corruption is sometimes seen as similar to "corruption of need" versus "corruption of greed". The latter distinction emphasizes the point that lower level officials sometimes cannot escape the pressures from a corrupt system, like low, late and unpaid wages, intimidating "offers" from corrupters and enforced returns to superiors. Such an emphasis, however, tends to excuse "low level" corruption regardless of its devastating effects, and it tends to ignore the fact that a political and economic system may also push high-level officials and power-holders into corruption. Furthermore, an expressed disapproval of "greediness" is irrelevant to an understanding of the structural factors behind corruption and the economic and political reforms required changing a corrupt system. the political system or having political repercussions. This happens in particular when a clean and strong government has been able to purify the corridors of power, but not every inch of the public service so that certain services or bureaucracy are (still) polluted.

However, widespread and systematic bureaucratic corruption and political corruption tends to go along and to be mutually reinforcing. Political corruption is usually supported by widespread bureaucratic or *petty* corruption, in a pyramid of upward extraction. And corruption in high places is contagious to lower level officials, as these will follow the predatory examples of, or even take instructions from, their principals. This is why a strict definition of corruption as a deviation from formal rules, and a particular focus on bureaucratic corruption alone, can be misleading.

Widespread and systematic political corruption may be a basic mode of operation of certain regimes. Actually, with the exception of a few cases of strong authoritarian regimes with a strict political and economic control (also on corruption), corruption is widespread in most non-democratic and neo-patrimonial countries. Here, corruption is one of the mechanisms through which the authoritarian power-holders enrich themselves. It is not a disease that the responsible politicians are eager to avoid, but it is a deliberately applied practice.

Bureaucratic corruption can by large be controlled and restricted when there is a political will and ability to implement the necessary regulations. A number of experiences demonstrate that bureaucratic corruption can be dealt with through auditing, legislation, and institutional arrangements. In most liberal democratic countries, where the problem of political corruption is of an incidental and occasional nature, this can be dealt with within the existing political system: by reforming, strengthening and vitalizing the existing political, judicial and administrative institutions.

In countries with systemic political and administrative corruption, the formal legal framework of the state is insufficient as terms of reference to assess and judge the problem of corruption. Thus, the degenerative effects of political corruption cannot be counteracted by a legalistic or administrative approach alone. Moral, normative, ethical, and indeed political benchmarks will have to be brought in.

Endemic corruption calls for radical political reforms - a system of checks, balances and democratization.

Private and collective corruption

The money or benefits collected through corruption is "privatized" to various degrees. It may be extracted for the benefit of an individual who will share nothing or very little with his equals, or it may be extracted for the benefit of a particular group with some coherence and unity. This has led to a second analytically important classification of corruption, namely between *private* and *collective* forms of corruption.

The "private", the individual and intimate nature of corruption is repeatedly underlined in the literature because of the illegal and surreptitious nature of any corrupt transaction. The ban and stigma on corruption necessitates collusion or conspiracy between individuals, or at least a certain closeness and confidentiality.

Such definitions tend to individualize a societal phenomenon. Corruption is also "collective" because it has a substantial economic effect in aggregate terms, and because it may in itself be a deliberate way of resource extraction for the benefit of a larger group. Some definitions of corruption therefore accentuate the point that the rulers can act as a group or a class (or an institution or organisation), in misusing their powers to extract resources for the benefit of the group as such. Many well-known and well-documented cases of grand corruption have involved political parties (ruling parties and also prospective ruling parties), entire administrative bureaucracy and national governments.

Corruption has indeed a strong inclination for "collectivization". A conspiracy between individuals is easily extended into a larger practice involving colleagues, partners, assistants, patrons and superiors. Instances of petty corruption may therefore develop into larger networks, cliques and medium-sized brother-hoods, and finally into large-scale institutionalized corruption if unchecked, whenever there is "room for maneuver".

An understanding of corruption includes the possibility that it might be "collective", institutionalized and organized in the interest of the ruling elite. Hence, it is vital to analyse the causes and logics of grand scale systemic corruption. In most cases the vested interests for most corruption cases are confined to the political/institutional levels. Hence, the anti-corruption organization should look into political and bureaucratic persons involved in the deals.

Redistribute and extractive corruption

The question "who benefits from corruption" could, however, be taken one step further. Most definitions of corruption maintain that corruption is a particular state society relationship based on a mutual exchange of benefits, from which both the state agent and the non-state actor will draw some immediate and private benefit. In other cases, businesses and other interest groups may be very successful in getting tax exemptions and other privileges from corrupt officials in weak states. In extreme situations, the state may be held hostage to and torn apart by forceful groups in society.

Rose-Ackerman[41] has suggested analyzing the bargaining power of government officials versus private actors in terms of the number and organisation (coherence) of each party. She argues that the nature of corruption depends on the organisation of government as well as the organisation of private actors. The Philippines has been given as one example of a weak state dealing with a powerful oligarchy of private business interests. Other examples are Bangladesh with a weak state and strong client list networks, and Russia with a collapsing state and emerging business and mafia dominance. It is because either party has monopoly power in dealing with the other.

In what can be called the theory of redistributive corruption, the state is the weaker part in the state-society relationship. The briber is viewed as the "active" party and the public official as the "passive". Here, various social and economic groups, interests or individuals are organised and powerful enough to draw more benefit from the corrupt practices with the state as a counterpart, than is the state and the ruling elite. The main beneficiaries of the resources extracted, privatised and consumed are not the political and state-based elite, but various groups and interests in society. State resources are consequently depleted and distributed to according to the relative bargaining power of each of these groups.

Analysts tend to have weak states in mind when they are focusing on the "subversive" groups and their "state destructive" capacity, i.e. the degenerative effects of corruption on the state institutions and the national economy. They will for instance analyse the politically strong and organised groups and the challenge they pose to state authority through bribery

---

[41] Rose-Ackerman, Susan: "Corruption and Government Causes, Consequences, and Reform". Cambridge, 1999, Cambridge University Press

and deception. Through corruption, alliances will be forced with functionaries who will deliver state services and goods. Politicians will be bought to tailor rights and regulations that will benefit those who pay for it, and political influence will be bought or extorted. The survival of certain weak regimes may depend on political support from particular groups. Who, in society, will benefit the most from this kind of corruption depends on the local distribution of forces. It can be powerful ethnic or regional groups or clans strong enough to extract much more from the state than their fair part (in terms of public investments, development projects, international aid, regional autonomy and representation in national institutions etc.). It can be foreign or local corporate interests who are able to buy resources, concessions and other advantages. It can be politically well-connected and influential individuals who are able to buy benefits like tax exemptions, subsidies, pensions and unemployment insurance, or to get preferential access to privileged schools, medical care, housing, real estate or ownership stakes in enterprises being privatised.

The loser in this game is the state and its regulating capacity. When private citizens, commercial businesses (local and international) and various interest groups (formal and informal, modern and traditional) are able to buy national and public resources cheaply, to buy exceptions, privileges, immunity and impunity through the use of kickbacks and mafia methods vis-à-vis public officials, the state will be undermined. The effect of "redistributive" corruption is that the state is rendered incapacitated and politically impotent. The capacity of the state to extract taxes and render public services erodes, as well as its ability to implement coherent policies.

Besides, it is destructive to the state's ability to transform the society and the economy according to political priorities, and to execute rational development policies. In the alternative view, in what can be called the theory of extractive corruption, the state is the stronger and more active part in the corrupted state-society relationship. According to this theory, the corrupted (the state or some state agent) benefits the most from corruption and the corrupters are more or less passive players.

The ruling elite is the strongest force in society, and this elite or class uses the state apparatus as its instrument to extract resources from society, and it does so for their 5 Therefore, the notion of "redistribution". However, this notion does not imply any equal or fair allocation of resources. The distribution of the gains will always follow the distribution of power in society own benefit. This theory is partly based on the operation of authoritarian countries in general, and on the experience of the neo-patrimonial states in particular.

Authoritarian regimes have always been understood and portrayed in terms of some ruling elite or class that uses and misuses the powers of the state primarily to safeguard their own corporate or class interests. And they inevitably do so at the detriment of –and usually in conflict with– other groups and interests in society. In political terms, the means available for authoritarian rulers range from charisma and persuasion to the overt use of violence. In order to restrict participation and power sharing them may use sophisticated institutional arrangements like presidential and/or single party systems, and expedient off-hand methods like the co-optation of rivals.

They will use censorship and electoral fraud, establish unjust laws and disrespect their own legislation, and they may turn to human rights violations, intimidation, imprisonment and torture. In economic terms, corruption, and in particular political corruption, will inevitably be one of the many modes of economic accumulation and private appropriation applied by authoritarian rulers.

The theory of extractive corruption is derived from the relatively stable and flexible neo-patrimonial political systems found in most of Africa and in a few Latin American and Asian countries. In neo-patrimonial systems, public office and position is seen as a personal asset and a personal right, and it is treated as a private resource.

The entire political system is therefore characterised by a deep and thorough privatisation and usurpation of public resources. Politics is to a large extent about distributing resources in the form of jobs, contracts, scholarships, gifts and other public resources to one's relatives, friends and political allies. That is, the rulers use public authority to extract resources from the ruled and from the nation's riches. Public office is used to enforce the collection of rents and "gifts" of all sorts from the dependent clients. Corruption, embezzlement, theft and extortion are used to make private fortunes, and political power is used by power-holders to enter into profitable businesses (and to establish monopoly rights, tax exemptions and other advantages for these).

The theory of extractive corruption mainly applies where the state in addition to being the strongest force in society is furthermore ruled by elite that has developed into a dominant and ruling class, who is in control of the powers of the state. In most neo-patrimonial countries, long lasting clienteles' practices have established what has been called hegemonic elites, or ruling state-classes. These are composed of rather small elite of politically and economically dominating families.

Studies have shown that the countries like for instance the Côte d'Ivoire and Cameroon is ruled and dominated by an elite composed of some 50 families or approximately 1000 individuals who are controlling most of the public as well as the private sector.

The direction the aggregated flow of resources will take, and thus the effect of the corrupted state-society relationship, is not given *a priori*. Only historical and empirical research in given countries can reveal whether corruption should be understood as "extractive" or "redistributive". The role of corruption as a particular state-society relationship is, however, usually understood –implicitly, and in aggregate terms– as either benefiting certain sectors of the society (like business interests, emerging capitalist classes, or traditional rulers and local strongmen) or certain state elites (like juntas and single-party nomenclatures).[42]

In short, corruption is a deviation from the formal rules that regulate the behaviour of public officials and it can be handy when the problem is limited. But because narrow (legal) definitions may ignore vital parts of the problem, like the lack of political will to curb corruption in certain regimes, broader and more open-ended definitions, like corruption in terms of power abuse, will have to be applied to address the situations of pervasive and massive corruption. Even when the effect of democratization in curtailing corruption is still much debated and not very strong according to available statistics, one basic and practical argument is that democratizing the state can only reverse corruption. Economic and political competition, transparency and accountability, coupled with the democratic principles of checks and balances, are the necessary instruments to restrict corruption and power abuse.

---

[42] Amundsen, Inge: "In Search of a counter-hegemony State and civil society in the struggle for democracy in Africa", Unpublished Ph.D.-thesis, Institute of political science, University of Tromsø, 1997.

Election allows corrupt people to rule

Svetlana Babaeva has opined that election as a tool for the democratization of the world has become a trap that often allows ambiguous figures to rule indefinitely.

Elections have become a crucial tool in attempts to achieve broader democratization of the world. The fall of the Berlin Wall and collapse of the Soviet Union stirred up drastic changes around the world, among them the appearance of new actors and coalitions seeking a democratic future. Inspired by the crash of the 'authoritarian beacon,' the Western community, in turn, attempted to pull itself out from the 'son of a bitch, but he's our son of a bitch' approach to propping up foreign allies, and began helping emancipated states achieve a better life as the West perceived it. In this drive, elections have become the basis, the criterion, the tool and often the end in itself of a political process.

Westerners accustomed to elections as an indispensable feature of their life, tend to overlook other crucial components of democracy such as strong civil groundwork and a responsible government. But some foreign regimes that are unaccustomed to political competition have quickly grasped the inversion of this. By conducting recurrent elections in name only, they are recognized as legitimate by the Western community while maintaining the political configuration they want to preserve. Westerners assume that elections are the only crucial ingredient for a democratic 'startup,' yet elections by themselves mean little. This has been proven even in American history.

Though the Founding Fathers had carefully conceived the balance of power, fears of the President stifling the other branches of Government arose nonetheless, particularly during the times of Andrew Jackson, and both Roosevelt's, not to mention Richard Nixon and, most recently, George Bush. If such concerns arose in the United States with its mighty legislative and judicial 'checks and balances,' what distortion must other countries experience whose institutions are much flimsier?

This civic weakness points to another crucial aspect of democratic existence, namely whether the people of a country have a chance to influence their Governors in the interim between voting. This is taken for granted by Westerners with their formidable free media, strong non-governmental organisations and grassroots activists. That is not so with other nations with no extensive societal structure and, thus, no tools to maintain accountability of the Government, resulting in a lack of public influence between elections.

Prominent American thinkers, for instance Samuel Huntington and Immanuel Waller stein, have warned since the mid-1970s of elections with no influence. Waller stein wrote about "the important difference between formal and substantive democracy". The scholar wrote: "The liberal concern with procedures lends itself towards a formal analysis of democracy where procedures and institutions exist in order to make democratic processes theoretically possible, while in practice inequalities of social power render them largely empty processes." Another aspect of election is the rotation of ruling elites and its impact on a nation.

For Americans who never faced the menace of a figure 'growing into the throne,' it's hard to realize that in a great number of countries elections are conducted not to facilitate the replacement of political leaders but to prevent this. Elections for the sake of voting helps increase the legitimacy of a Governor or a clan, giving them an additional argument to remain in power 'till deaths do us part'.

The absence of a strong Opposition can give a Governor additional argument to stay on for another term. He throws up his hands and utters that were he given the opportunity to quit, he would gladly do so, but until someone more reliable shows up, he must reign over the nation.[43]

CHINA

CPC Will Carry Political Reforms to tackle corruption

Chinese President Hu Jintao on July 1, 2011 said economic development and ensuring social stability would remain the priorities of the Communist Party of China (CPC), even as he warned its leadership that tackling widespread corruption within the party was key to "ensuring its very survival" as it marked its 90th anniversary.

Addressing a grand celebration at Beijing's Great Hall of the People on Friday morning, Mr. Hu said:

The CPC would "actively yet prudently" carry out political reforms, but stressed that any reforms would be carried out under the "core" leadership of the party. We must see to it that all state powers belong to the people... and ensure that the people can participate in democratic elections, decision making, administration and oversight in accordance with the law. However, the biggest priority for the party would be to uphold stability a critically important task. Without stability, nothing could be done, and even the achievements already made could be lost.

On its 90th anniversary, Mr. Hu said the CPC had won the support of the Chinese people for its role in securing national independence and for the development the country had achieved in the three decades since the reform and opening up. But

---

[43] Svetlana Babaeva (2011), "Election do not always mean democracy" State Times, June 17, 2011, Friday,

retaining that support is no guarantee, cautioning that the party's "survival" rests on tackling rising corruption.

If not effectively curbed, corruption will cost the Party the trust and support of the people. Fighting corruption o would require a complicated and arduous battle. Leading officials at all levels must bear in mind that our power is entrusted to us by the people and can only be used in their interests. Mr. Hu, who is also the CPC's General Secretary, is the head of its powerful Central Committee.

Achievements

In the days leading up to July 1, the CPC has grandly celebrated its 90th anniversary, with events and performances being held in every city and province to mark its founding. On Friday, Beijing's streets and parks were turned into a sea of red, with hundreds of banners celebrating the party's achievements and red flags lining the city's main avenue. Events were held in the city's parks to commemorate the Communist revolution, with the singing of Red songs and enactments of Mao Zedong's Long March.

The party has highlighted China's economic progress over the past three decades, underscoring the message by unveiling landmark infrastructure projects this week.

On June 28, 2011, the government opened a $33 billion high-speed rail link between Beijing and Shanghai, as well as inaugurated the world's longest sea-bridge, which connects the port of Qingdao and Huangdao.

On its anniversary, the party has presented its legacy carefully, focusing on its role in securing national independence and on the economic development that has spurred China's revival. Mr. Hu on July 1, 2011 hinted at the troubled first three decades of the party's rule, saying the party would learn from the positive and negative lessons from its past.

He said the biggest risk the party faced today is: alienation from the people. Therefore, we must always place the people's interests before everything else. It has thus become even more important and urgent than ever before for the Party to police itself and impose strict discipline on its members.[44]

INDIA

Stopping road is the only road.

Electricity, road, water is a distant memory for fatalist India has given up hoping for better infrastructure and none seems agitated over the appalling condition of our roads

A few years ago, B-S-P became a catchphrase in Indian electioneering. It was not about Ms Mayawati's Bahujan Samaj Party, but the abbreviation fitted nicely for three popular aspirations, especially in rural India, namely, Bijli (power), Sadak (roads) and Pani (water). Acutely aware that, decades after independence, successive Governments had failed to deliver these essentials, the NDA regime under Mr. Atal Bihari Vajpayee drew up ambitious plans for them. He initiated a gigantic highway development plan centred round two projects — the Golden Quadrilateral to link all four major metros and the North-South-East-West Highways to connect Silchar in Assam with Porbandar in Gujarat and Srinagar in Kashmir to Kanya Kumari, India's southernmost tip. Additionally, the NDA Government launched the Pradhan Mantri Gram Sadak Yojana, a Centrally-funded programme to link every habitation with a

---

[44] Anantha Krishnan (2011), "Tackle corruption, Hu tells party leaders", The Hindu, July 2, 2011

population of 1,000 (500 in the case of hill regions) to the nearest highway with an all-weather road.

The early part of the 21st Century was an era of abundant hope. While the road projects took off, transforming the face of rural India wherever construction began, Mr. Vajpayee's humongous River-Linking Plan to connect all major national rivers through canals seemed to be the answer to the farmers' need for water to quench the thirst of his fertile land. It was hoped that the project would help multiply agricultural productivity and ensure that surplus water from Himalayan and eastern India's rivers would flow seamlessly into rain-starved central and southern India.

The NDA Government also initiated a series of mega-power projects all across the country, keeping in mind the need to generate 100,000 megawatts of additional electricity by 2020. Although the Enron project ended in a fiasco, other projects were sanctioned rapidly and it appeared that by 2010, at least half the target of additional power generation would be achieved. Sadly, all three ambitious programmes subsequently slowed down or, as in the case of river-linking, got abandoned altogether. The dream of India Shining came crashing down when the NDA was voted out of power in 2004.

The Congress-led Governments have since shifted the focus from development of infrastructure to redistribution of wealth or, to put it more cynically, redistribution of poverty. With populist schemes like MNREGA, waiving of agricultural loans and now the proposed Food Security Act, Central resources have been diverted to a dole-based economic model, which must factor in colossal wastage and siphoning off of funds. No money is available anymore for B-S-P.

Based on my own regular experience, I wish to focus only on roads to underline the tragedy that has befallen India since the UPA Government first came to power in 2004. Perhaps the DMK Minister entrusted with the Surface Transport portfolio in UPA1 realized it was a most lucrative ATM (Any Time Money) Ministry. There is no evidence that the massive funds allocated to road building were transported away to private pockets or party coffers, but the fact that even the GQ could not be completed till 2009 (it was to be ready in 2003), is adequate circumstantial proof that kickbacks determined disbursement of funds by the Ministry.

For example, the Delhi-Moradabad stretch of NH 24, which links the Capital to Lucknow and goes further on to Guwahati, languished for full five years. It is a road down which I travel at least six times every year to reach my hillside home near Nainital in Uttarakhand. It used to take me nearly six hours on an average to cover the paltry distance of 150 km to Moradabad, with incomplete flyovers and abandoned four-laning material blocking much of the road. To Mr. Kamal Nath's credit, he restarted the work in 2009. Now Delhi-Moradabad takes less than three hours, with all flyovers ready and four- laning almost complete except for the second bridge on Ganga at Brijghat near Garh Mukteshwar. This just shows that when the Government makes up its mind, things can fall in place rapidly.

But once you descend from the Moradabad bypass, it is a nightmare getting to Rampur barely 20 km away. With a railway over bridge taking over a decade to complete, traffic jams compounded by unruly drivers breaking all rules of the road can get you stuck for three hours on any given day. Recently when I was caught in such a jam my entreaties to a fellow driver to move his vehicle sufficiently to allow me passage, met with a stoic but typically fatalist Indian response. "Brother, there isn't any point in your hurry. It routinely takes four-five hours to get past this point!" he nonchalantly declared. The problem often is not the intent, but the delivery. A flyover in the middle of nowhere, which should not take more than two years at the most to build, ends up taking 10 to 15 years! Imagine the loss in terms of wasted man hours, fuel burnt unnecessarily by idling engines and so on.

Not wanting to get entangled in a similar situation on my return journey, I chose another route from Nainital to a place called Bajpur and onto Moradabad down State Highway 65. To call it a highway is an insult to the term. Forget highway, it is no longer even a road. No vehicle can afford to travel at a speed of more than 10 km per hour; every bone in the body creaks and a car's suspension as well as wheel alignment goes for a toss, costing a pile to fix. Buses and trucks that brave the journey - lurch precariously from side to side as they negotiate craters of lunar proportion.

Incidentally, five years ago, this road was in a similar condition. I spoke to Rampur MP Jaya Prada in whose constituency this 42-km stretch is located. She took the initiative and three years ago, SH 65 became a shining, smooth highway that took barely an hour to traverse. But contractors had obviously made a killing repairing it. By last year, it began to deteriorate and now it is quite impassable.

Such is the stoic indifference and sheepish acceptance of these pathetic conditions that local residents never seem to protest. I met a person at the just-concluded BJP National Executive meeting who introduced himself as a party office bearer in one of the units along this road. I asked him why they had not thought of organizing a Road Stoppage to force the Government to act.

He scratched his head in some bewilderment, wondering if he would get the support of people on an issue which, he frankly admitted, locals had been resigned to.

Marching With The Times

In the most lucid explanation of the term, a bandh[45] implies that the community or political party declares it and expects that the general public should stay in their homes and do not use roads and attend government offices.

It must be noted that in a rather laconic ruling, the Supreme Court of India had banned strikes in 1998. Nearly a decade later, in 2007, the Supreme Court in another ruling had clarified that strikes, bandhs or complete shutdowns were illegal but strikes and hartals were not.

"You don't seem to understand the difference between strikes bandhs and strikes. strikes Bandhs are illegal [but] not strikes, which are only a way of raising objections," the court had maintained, dismissing the petition of a Chennai resident who had sought action against political parties that had called a "general strike" across Tamil Nadu on February 4, 2007 to press for a ceasefire in Sri Lanka.

Acknowledging the distinction between strikes and bandhs, it would be logical to deduce that some of the biggest Indian revolutions of the last century Gandhi's non-cooperation movement, the salt strike and Quit India movements were strikes and not bandhs. The 1974 railway strike in India which went on for 20 days and had 17 million workers participate in it, was clearly a strikes and thus illegal according to the SC ruling which came into effect later. Around the same time in 1974, J P Narayan led the students' movement in Bihar which gradually developed into a popular people's movement known as the Bihar movement. It was during this movement that JP gave a call for peaceful Total Revolution. JP's crusade against the "imperialistic" Indira Gandhi, which was

[45]Note: Bandh is 'no work and no vehicular movement'

to lead to Emergency and subsequently the formation of the first non-Congress government in India, employed a mix of strikes and bandhs. The most interesting feature about the JP movement was that here was a Gandhian who had participated in at least two of Gandhi's biggest mass movements against the British now trying to replicate a similar mass movement against a Congress government in independent India.

Thirty-five years later, the concept of strikes needs to be revisited. There is disenchantment, at least among the poor, on the issue of price rise. Yet there is no trust in remedial protests/strikes. By default, thus, the situation remains unaddressed.

The success of any mass protest/movement broadly depends upon two factors: one, the credibility of the leadership leading the movement and, two, people's support for the cause and the leadership. In case either is found wanting, the movement, in order to prove its non-failure, invariably turns coercive, often turning detrimental to the cause. This, unfortunately, was the anti-climax that met the recent Bharat strikes of July 5.

Political parties need to realize that what worked in the 1970s will not work now. There are a host of political and social reasons for this. Politically, the unrestricted growth and avarice of regional parties has led to a whole new gamut of permutations and combinations wherein a party may or may not support a cause for entirely selfish reasons. Reasoning for their decisions is subsequently doctored conveniently. That the clout of regional parties has grown to an extent wherein both the national parties are critically dependent upon their support makes the situation that much more difficult. Hence, the strike, even if it is eventually supported by most non-Congress parties, is largely disorganized.

Socially, there has been a sea change in the attitudes of people given our consumerist lifestyles post the early 1990s. Except in Bengal which still witnesses more than three dozen strikes on an average each year, the rest of India seems to have developed a healthy aversion towards it. How can then a bandh for a just cause like price rise have its desired impact today?

Broadly, there are two ways. Any successful mass movement needs a face to drive it. Pre-independence, we had Gandhi. The Emergency had JP. The rail strike had George Fernandes. Do we still have that one face that will inspire the trust of the masses? One needs to take into account that this is the age of living-room politicians people who are very good on television but have little support on the streets. Can this age still produce a 'street-side' politician and have the whole of India support him? More importantly, can this person bring the entire opposition together, at least on an issue that is critically important for the poor?

The other equally important factor is that bandhs need a makeover to keep pace with changing times. Things need to happen faster in order to register their impact in an age where everybody has a limited attention span. An effective bandh could thus mean a voluntary coercive defeats the purpose halt of work for, say, two hours wherein people in offices switch off their computers and cell phones, bus drivers stop their buses in the middle of roads and students and professors unanimously walk out of their classes. This would be more in sync with the way Gandhi, if he were alive today, would have liked to protest.

Till such time as the opposition gets a unanimous face and that face reinvents protests that would make them workable in the present day, bandhs in modern India will continue to grapple with the increasing disparity between the issue and response it generates.[46]

Corruption rules politics

Corruption in India is now a major concern because of the gigantic and mind-boggling amounts illegally appropriated in the Satyam, IPL, CWG, and 2G Spectrum scams. By all objective criteria, India today has by far one of the most corrupt governance. The 2G Spectrum Scam (title of my new book released on June 11) is the most shocking rip-off of all.

It was first fired by the fraud and forgery that became apparent in the sudden divestment of equity stake in Swan Capital Company by Anil Dhirubhai Ambani, the owner of ADAG who strategically controlled Swan, in favour of the Shahid Balwas-run DB Realty Company, and reportedly on then Telecom Minister A Raja's behest. DB Realty then sold the controlling shares of Swan to Etisalat.

This latter company was considered in a Home Ministry report to be a front for ISI and Dawood Ibrahim. Shahid Balwas was held by the Ministry to be an undesirable person. Yet, Etisalat was allowed by the Union Home Minister P Chidambaram to buy out the Swan Telecom at eight times the price paid by Swan for the 2G-spectrum license. National security was seriously compromised for greed of money.

The opening batsman, who repeatedly brought out the extent of corruption in India, is Dr. subramanian Swamy. He wrote a letter to the Prime Minister dated November 29, 2008, for sanction under Section 19 of

---

[46] Tuhin A. Sinha (2010), "Marching with the Times", the Times of India, Bhubaneswar Jul 12, 2010 / Note: Bandh means: paralyzing the government, transport system and business establishments for a demand from the government.

the Prevention of Corruption Act (1988) to prosecute Telecom Minister A. Raja by filing a private complaint before the Designated Sessions Court. Thus began his venture into the 2G-spectrum scam.

Dr. Swamy opines: The PM's procrastination led me to the Supreme Court. Thereafter, a Bench of Justices Singhvi and Ganguli, by their meticulous reading of the briefs and documents filed and by their crisp orders and directions have changed the national public mood from despair and despondency to hope and expectation. This judicial intervention came none too soon. An international watchdog committee conducted a study on the illicit flight of money from India, perhaps the first ever attempt at shedding light on a subject steeped in secrecy, and concluded that India has been drained of $462 billion (over Twenty Trillion Indian Rupees) between 1948 and 2008. The amount represents nearly 40 per cent of India's gross domestic product.

The unanimous view throughout the world today is that corruption is no more the inevitable grease or speed money to be tolerated in any system, but a cancer that could cause the death of a society by continuous debilitation — unless it is cured at an early stage.

The Indian financial system also suffers from a hangover of cronyism and corruption that have brought the government budgets on the verge of bankruptcy. This too needs fixing. India's infrastructure requires about $ 150 billion making it world class, and the education system needs 6 per cent of GDP instead of 2.8 per cent today. But an open competitive market system can find these resources provided the quality of governance and accountability is improved. Obviously a second generation of reforms is necessary for all this.

One of the worst problems with corruption in India is

the creation of "black money"— money that is used in such transactions and is obviously unreported, hence is neither taxed nor is spent openly. It travels to secret bank accounts abroad, or, worse, is used by the corrupt to indulge in gross luxurious consumption and bribery. Such black money stock also creates inflation by enabling easy finance for hoarding of supplies even as the GDP growth rate accelerates.

Corruption impacts on economic development of a nation in five dimensions:

1. Decisions taken for corrupt motive sub-optimize the allocation of scarce national resources and hence in the long run lower the rate of growth in GDP. It also encourages buccaneers instead of innovative entrepreneurs.

2. By the use of bribe money which escapes the tax net and is mostly stashed away in banks abroad or in trunks in safe houses, is deployed in luxury goods purchase, ostentatious life, splurging in five star hotels, real estate, and on partying. This raises demand for luxury production and services, and in turn distorts investment priorities. In India, 70 per cent of the investment goes directly or indirectly to sustain the luxury sector.

3. Unaccounted bribe money is lent to hoarders and speculators who then cause artificial shortages and thus inflation and property bubbles.

4. Since the most in corrupt activities would be in public office, they enact laws to not only to safeguard the booty by lax criminal investigations and prosecutions, but to enable earning interest or return on the bribe money. The invention of Participatory Notes (PNs) and the Mauritius Tax & Capital Gains exemption treaties is aimed at that sordid objective.

5. Corruption enables beneficiaries to involve foreign governments seeking influence and criminal gangs' resident abroad to launder money and provide protection.

The view of Integral Humanism as propounded by Deen Dayal Upadhaya or what we have for centuries have called, as Hinduism is that a society is healthy only if there is a harmonization of material pursuits and spiritual advancement in a human being. The social structure called caste (Varna), till it degenerated into a birth-based social cartel, was designed to downgrade wealth as the indicator of status and elevate sacrifice and simplicity as a desirable value. But now greed is driving all of us as it has become in the globalization process. Materialistic progress alone however does not guarantee national security of a nation. What is essential is the character and integrity of its citizens. Hence, besides the objective of acquiring knowledge and getting employment that require cognitive intelligence, the youth must be motivated in other dimensions of intelligence that of emotional, moral and social.

In the United States, as Business Week has recently reported, these concepts have become highly popular in the corporate world, and have been incorporated in the best-selling books written by Daniel Goleman, Deepak Chopra, Anthony Robbins, among others.

In brief, out National Policy for integrating spiritual values and organisation leadership can be achieved by measures by which we can create a modern mindset in the youth of India, not only to motivate the youth to acquire technical competence, but to develop emotional, moral social and spiritual values that will make that person a self-reliant individual of high character, patriotic, and possessing a social conscience.

Our goal has to be thus the efficient use of resources, human and physical, hardware and software by an able and human spiritually guided and ethically organizational leadership in a framework of competitive market economies.

Hence, concisely stated, for a corruption free society to be achieved on a long-term basis the Indian economy should be founded on a harmonization of efficient organizational leadership and abiding spiritual values, which we call as Sanatana Dharma. That can be nurtured only bottom up i.e., educate our growth accordingly — to synthesize material pursuits with spiritual values, which lauds simplicity and eschews greed.[47]

Ultimately it will also be decided by how we vote in elections. But we need a new ideology to combat the cancer of corruption in our system. For this we need a new breed of Indian leaders-educated, courageous, and rational risk takers. That we can get only if the ethos of our people changes from the purely individualist pursuit of material pleasures and goals, to an integral outlook. Corruption is the cancer today in our society but Hinduism imbibed character is the cure.

Mining a Loophole in Orissa State

Of the 341 mines existing in Orissa, only 126 operate on the basis of a valid lease. A paragraph in the 53-year-old Mines and Minerals Development and Regulation Act has proved to be the State's bane and the mining companies' boon: It is allowing illegal operators to plunder Orissa to the tune of **3 Trillion INR** (Indian Rupees).

Mineral-rich Orissa has become a paradise for illegal mining in the last one decade. To earn big bucks,

---

[47] Subramanian Swamy (2011), "Why fighting corruption is important", The Pioneer, June 11,

smugglers are making a beeline for the State with the sole aim of plundering its precious minerals. Legal lacunae make illegal mining easy. A sizeable number of mines in the State have been operating years after their leases have expired. The miners use a legal clause involving extension of their leases as an excuse to continue their activity.

Out of 341 mines existing in Orissa, only 126 operate on a valid lease. Of the 215 mines that existed illegally, the leases of 15 expired more than 20 years ago, those of 17 expired 15 to 20 years ago. The lease period of 38 mines ended 10 to 15 years ago and that of another 65 mines ended 10 years ago. The remaining 80 mines have been operating five years after their leases lapsed. This was brought to light by the interim report of the Supreme Court-appointed Central Empowered Committee (CEC).

In November 2009, a 150-page petition filed by Mr. Rabi Das, senior journalist and president of Orissa People's Conference (Orissa Jana Sammilani), brought the mining scam to the notice of the Supreme Court. In response to the petition, the apex court had entrusted the CEC with the task of investigating the scam. The CEC had asked the State Government to furnish all details related to it. The findings of the interim report are based on the submissions made by the Orissa Government and the petitioner.

The 85-page report has laid bare rampant illegal mining making use of lacunae in the Mines and Minerals (Development and Regulation) Act, 1957. As per the 'deemed extension' clause under Rule 24A(6) of Mineral Concession Rules 1960, if a lease holder applies for the renewal of mining lease within a stipulated period, the lease is automatically 'deemed' to have been extended till the State Government actually deals with the applications.

"A large number of mines are operating in Orissa even after the expiry of the mining lease period. This is being done under the provision of 'deemed extension' of mining leases provided under Rule 24A(6) of Mineral Concession Rules and is happening because the applications filed for the renewal of the mining leases remain undecided for a considerable period of time after the expiry of the mining lease period," the report said, adding: "The deemed extension clause is primarily meant to deal with contingency situations and to ensure that the mining operations do not come to an abrupt end because of administrative delays in deciding renewal applications."

But the rule has been misused to allow the expired leases to exist for years. Why the lease is not cancelled automatically? The lease owner cannot avail the benefits indefinitely. Moreover, continuing mining over a long period of time without renewal of the mining lease becomes a potential source for serious illegalities and irregularities.

Scores of mine owners have excavated iron ore, chromites, manganese and other minerals much beyond the stipulated limit. "The mining activities also exceeded the production limit as approved under the mining plans," the report said. In Orissa, a good number of mines co-exist with the forestland or reserve forest areas. According to an estimate, as much as 80 per cent of the State's mineral-rich forestland is being exploited. While carrying out illegal mining, the miners shamelessly flout the Forest Conservation Act and environmental norms.

"Mining activities were going on in a large number of mines in Orissa without requisite approvals under the Forest (Conservation) Act, 1980, environmental clearances, and Air and Water Acts," the CEC report said, adding, "There was lack of effective coordination and common understanding between the officials of the Mines Department and the Forest Department resulting in ineffective enforcement of statutory provisions.

The report has suggested a set of recommendations aimed at curbing illegal mining. The CEC has asked the State Government to dispose of the mining lease renewal applications pending for years expeditiously and in a time-bound manner. Deemed extension clauses should only be used in contingency situations and cannot be availed of indefinitely, the CEC said. It also further said that mining in non-forest areas can be allowed only after obtaining environmental and other statutory clearances by the lease-holder. The CEC has decided to charge all illegal miners a one-time fine on a land cost valuation formula. For both renewal of mining lease and mining lease, the lessees would have to pay the net present value of the forests for the entire lease area as per a 2002 Supreme Court directive, the report stated. The fine amount is expected to run into 20 billion of INR. But the Orissa mining scam is estimated at 3 Trillion of INR. The figures tell their own story. The CEC formula does not take into account the millions of tonnes of illegal minerals.

Ever since media coverage of the scam, the BJD Government has been in the dock. Well aware of the large-scale pillage, it turned a blind eye - indeed, let the red-tape allow illegal mining and smuggling, thereby providing covert help to the *jholawallah* brigade in siphoning off Orissa's minerals. The image of the Naveen Patnaik-led Orissa Government has been dented. The Orissa Government is trying hard to underplay the scam and sweep it under the carpet. It is reluctant to go for a CBI inquiry into the matter. An indifferent Orissa Government, sitting on the renewal of mining lease applications for years now, is saying it is not at fault as the miners are to blame for not submitting documents, forcing authorities to keep the files on hold.

The Green Bench of the Supreme Court has directed the Orissa Government to implement the recommendations of the Central Empowered Committee with immediate effect. It is now up to the Orissa Government to follow the directive.[48]

Relentless plunder:

Crack down on crime of illegal mining

The news of a Mumbai-based mining company extracting at least 10 times more bauxite ore than it is allowed to from a village in Ratnagiri in Maharashtra and causing the State a revenue loss of billions of rupees by not paying the royalty has once again brought to the fore the issue of rampant illegal mining across India. What is shocking is that the State Government has been caught napping — or did it elect to look the other way? — While the company continued with the plunder long after its lease expired in November 2009.

This is not a case in isolation. Scores of mine-owners have excavated iron ore, chromites, bauxite, manganese and other minerals much beyond the stipulated limit in Jharkhand, Odisha, Karnataka, Maharashtra and other mineral-rich States. In Odisha, out of 341 mines, only 126 have been found to have a valid lease. Since most mines have been operating years after their leases have expired by using a loophole in the Mines and Minerals (Development and Regulation) Act, we can arrive at only one conclusion: There is a nexus between politicians, bureaucrats and mining companies. How else can one explain the misuse of the deemed extension clause that is meant to ensure that mining operations do not come to an abrupt halt due to administrative delays in deciding renewal applications?

---

[48] Saswat Panigrahy (2010), " Mining a Loophole", The Pioneer, July 7, 2010

The UPA's hyperactive Minister for Environment and Forests, Mr. Jairam Ramesh, has been selective in acting against the mining companies that are looting India's wealth. He prefers to use different standards. As a result, companies indulging in illegal mining are also flouting the Forest Conservation Act and damaging the fragile ecosystem as a good number of mines co-exist with reserve forest areas. The bureaucrats, well aware of the large-scale pillage, turn a blind eye as long as their nests are feathered. This casts serious doubt on the Congress's assertions that it would uphold green laws and not sacrifice environmental sustainability. Worse, there is growing evidence that the revenue from illegal mining in tribal areas is going towards funding insurgent activities of Maoist outfits.

Mr. Ramesh's failure to crack down heavily on illegal operators is in essence allowing law-shirking plunderers to line the pockets of anti-nationals covertly. Now that the Supreme Court-appointed Central Empowered Committee has submitted its detailed report, what is needed is an expeditious implementation of CEC's recommendations without any bias and better coordination between officials of the Mining Ministry and the Environment & Forest Ministry to effectively enforce statutory provisions.

Further, exemplary actions must be taken against *babus* whose deliberate delay in disposing of mining renewal applications results in a revenue loss of billions of rupees. This is the least that Mr. Ramesh can do to stop the loot and save the country's precious mineral resources.[49]

Corruption reaches mythical levels

Never before has any great mass of people so thoroughly obsessed itself with corruption — and

---

[49] Editorial The Pioneer, January 8, 2011

that's because in India today it has reached mythical levels.

What can one say about corruption in India or around the globe that has not already been said before? How many more people does it take to cry their hearts out in disgust, pain, and horror before we can see any perceptible change in the vulgar acts of hoarding, thieving, manipulating, and marauding that the rich and the powerful indulge in, not ignoring of course the daily acts of petty perfidy of the lowly police constable, the office peon, and the "junior engineer" in charge of supervising some "public works" or the other? Is this the tail end of *Kali Yuga* when, we are told, the crooked prevail and the righteous wilt away?

Anna Hazare's 97-hour fast was too quickly given up and too poorly executed, and his coterie of "civil society" leaders too gullible and fractious making it easy for the manipulative ruling politicians and their "dirty tricks" henchmen to de-fang the Gandhian and his not-so Gandhian lieutenants. Even before we could spell "Lokpal Bill" the ungainly dance of the civil society leaders and government ministers is grinding to a halt. It is now the turn of yoga guru Baba Ramdev to go on a planned fast but he may even more quickly get his public persona disrobed by the crafty Digvijay as hired by the "ruling family". Meanwhile, some of the smug and cynical editors of new-fangled magazines and crusty old newspapers speak from both sides of their mouth — bemoaning corruption and belittling those who seek to do something about it.

Prime Minister Man Mohan Singh, the titular head of a corrupt government, cannot do more than mouth platitudes and promise some vague, future action. "This (corruption) is a scourge that confronts all of us. The government intends to introduce the Lokpal Bill in parliament during the monsoon session," he said when Hazare ended his fast. "The fact that civil society and government have joined hands to evolve a consensus to move this historic legislation augurs well for our democracy. I am pleased that Anna Hazare has agreed to give up his fast," the good cop's office messaged to the world, while the bad cops had already launched their plans of devious dissimulation. Hazare therefore is now a spent force, and his lieutenants are bitter losers in the battle against the crooks, the criminals, and the new-age "saviors" who rule the Delhi administration.

In Transparency International's Corruption Perception Index (CPI) for 2010, India ranked 87 among 178 nations. There was a decline in India's integrity score to 3.3 in 2010, from 3.5 in 2007, and 3.4 in 2008 and 2009. These figures are on a scale of zero to 10 — zero indicating high corruption and 10 indicating low levels of corruption. India's ranking has dipped since 2006 when it was ranked 70 among 163 countries, indicating that under UPA-I and UPA-II, with Man Mohan Singh and Sonia Gandhi at the helm, India has got on to the fast track towards catching up with the most corrupt in the world — the Somalia, the Afghanistan, and the Myanmar.

There is an old Kannada adage: He is clever who eats at the mad widow's wedding. What it means is that those who take advantage of chaotic conditions to benefit themselves are clever. The UPA governance can be likened to a mad widow's wedding. The people who ate at the wedding — the Rajas, the Kanimozhis, the Kalmadis, and the less known politicians, bureaucrats, and business leaders — looted trillions of rupees and were the clever ones.

In this regard, and as an aside, when will Indians discard the unwieldy and provincial terms "millions" and "billions" and adopt modern number terminology to effectively gauge and identify the level of spending and looting? For example, the Central Vigilance Commission estimated that some 80 billion of Indian rupees (INR) was "misappropriated" in the hosting of the Commonwealth Games. That translates to about US$ 1.75 billion, roughly calculated. The Comptroller and Auditor General estimated that in the 2G scam some 1,767 billion INR or about US $40 billion.

And then there is the staggering amount of black money stashed away in Swiss bank accounts, which is about $1.5 trillion dollars according to some estimates, making Indians the number one users of the **"don't ask, don't tell" Swiss banking rules.** In fact, according to the group constituted by LK Advani, some $5.7 trillion is stashed away by Indians in foreign banks. And India, according to Global Financial Integrity, a programme of the Center for International Policy, is one of the world's largest exporters of black money with an outflow of $104 billion between 2000 and 2008. In June 2014, the Swiss Bank reported that Indians have deposited **140 billion of INR (Indian rupees)** or 1.95 billion Swiss francs directly by depositors and another 77.3 million Swiss francs through fiduciaries and wealth managers till the end of 2013.

An intrepid blogger calculates that the $1.5 trillion is "enough to relieve the debt of all farmers and landless workers in India, build world-class roads all over the country, take electricity to every rural home, provide drinking water in all villages and towns, construct good homes for 100 million families, and allocate Rs 40 million to every village — to build a school, a health centre, a veterinary clinic, a playground with gymnasium, and more in every village".

Alas, India is a land of maya (attachment, illusion, magic, phenomenal), and one can never really get a handle on even simple truths; forget about the more complex and large scale matters. Who stole how much, when, and stashed it away where is therefore mostly guesswork, and the present government will not lift a finger to find out what even foreign governments are willing to share. We keep reading newspaper reports about some CBI team going somewhere or the other, filing some paperwork in some place or another, but nothing seems to emerge from those exercises. Few in the Opposition parties are willing to take on the government because they are as much revelers in the "mad widow's wedding" as the greediest ones in the administration.

It is therefore left to so-called mavericks like Subramanian Swamy to take up the thankless and almost futile tasks of finding out who ate how much and regurgitated where. The letters on the 2G scam that Dr Swamy sent the Prime Minister seem to have led to the chain of events that have put Raja and Kanimozhi in Tihar jail, and brought tears to the eyes of the old bandicoot Karunanidhi, but the decades-long skeleton-probing that Dr Swamy has done of the Sonia Gandhi household has made little headway and produced no results.

That he is the only one with the gumption to publicly accuse Sonia Gandhi of a variety of corrupt deeds without being taken to court for his allegations says something both about Dr. Swamy's courage as well as a lot about the weakness of Indian society and system.[50]

Where do these and many other aspects of the soft and corrupt Indian system lead us? People quote only the latter half of the Sanskrit adage, "Religion destroyed, destroys; religion protects those who protect it" to plead that if they abide by religion (dharma), they will truly prosper. What we need to invoke more often have been warning us is the threat that if dharma is destroyed, it destroys — individuals and societies.

---

[50] Ramesh Rao (2011), "Dharma Destroyed, Destroys", The Pioneer, June 4, 2011

The Rise of Populist measures

TRAVELING in Europe last week, it seemed as if every other conversation ended with some form of this question: Why does it feel like so few leaders are capable of inspiring their people to meet the challenges of our day? There are many explanations for this global leadership deficit, but I'd focus on two: one generational, one technological.

Let's start with the technological. In 1965, Gordon Moore, the Intel co-founder, posited Moore's Law, which stipulated that the processing power that could be placed on a single microchip would double every 18 to 24 months. It's held up quite well since then. Watching European, Arab and U.S. leaders grappling with their respective crises, I'm wondering if there isn't a political corollary to Moore's Law: The quality of political leadership declines with every 100 million new users of Face book and Twitter.

The wiring of the world through social media and Web-enabled cell phones is changing the nature of conversations between leaders and the led everywhere. We're going from largely one-way conversations — top-down — to overwhelmingly two-way conversations — bottom-up and top-down. This has many upsides: more participation, more innovation and more transparency. But can there be such a thing as too much participation — leaders listening to so many voices all the time and tracking the trends that they become prisoners of them?

This sentence jumped out from a Politico piece on Wednesday: "The Obama and Romney campaigns spend all day strafing each other on Twitter, all while decrying the campaign's lack of serious ideas for a serious time. Yet at most junctures when they've had the opportunity to go big, they've chosen to go small."

Indeed, I heard a new word in London last week: "Popularism." It's the über-ideology of our day. Read the polls, track the blogs, tally the Twitter feeds and Face book postings and go precisely where the people are, not where you think they need to go. If everyone is "following," who is leading?

And then there is the exposure factor. Anyone with a cell phone today is paparazzi; anyone with a Twitter account is a reporter; anyone with YouTube access is a filmmaker. When everyone is a paparazzi, reporter and filmmaker, everyone else is a public figure. And, if you're truly a public figure — a politician — the scrutiny can become so unpleasant that public life becomes something to be avoided at all costs. Alexander Downer, Australia's former foreign minister, remarked to me recently: "A lot of leaders are coming under massively more scrutiny than ever before. It doesn't discourage the best of them, but the ridicule and the constant interaction from the public is making it more difficult for them to make sensible, brave decisions."

As for the generational shift, we've gone from a Greatest Generation that believed in save and invest for the future to a Baby Boomer generation that believed in borrow and spend for today. Just contrast George W. Bush and his father George H.W. Bush. The father volunteered for World War II immediately after Pearl Harbor, was steeled as a leader during the cold war — a serious time, when politicians couldn't just follow polls — and as president he raised taxes when fiscal prudence called for it. His Baby Boomer son avoided the draft and became the first president in U.S. history to cut taxes in the middle of not just one war, but two.

When you have technologies that promote quick short-term responses and judgments, and when you have a generation that has grown used to short-term gratification — but you have problems whose solutions require long, hard journeys, like today's global credit crisis or jobs shortage or the need to rebuild Arab countries from the ground up — you have a real mismatch and leadership challenge. Virtually all leaders today have to ask their people to share burdens, not just benefits, and to both study harder and work smarter just to keep up. That requires extraordinary leadership that has to start with telling people the truth.

Dov Seidman, the author of the book "How" whose company LRN advises C.E.O.'s on leadership, has long argued that "nothing inspires people more than the truth." Most leaders think that telling people the truth makes that leader vulnerable — either to the public or their opponents. They are wrong.

Seidman explains: The most important part of telling the truth is that it actually binds you to people, because when you trust people with the truth, they trust you back. Obfuscation from leaders just gives citizens another problem — more haze — to sort through. Trusting people with the truth is like giving them a solid floor," adds Seidman. "It compels action. When you are anchored in shared truth, you start to solve problems together. It's the beginning of coming up with a better path."

That is not what we're seeing from leaders in America, the Arab world or Europe today. You'd think one of them, just one, would seize the opportunity to enlist their people in the truth: about where they are, what they are capable of, what plan they need to get there and what they each need to contribute to get on that better path. Whichever leader does that will have real "followers" and "friends" — not virtual ones.[51]

---

[51] THOMAS L. FRIEDMAN (2012), "The Rise of Popularism", The New York Times, June 23, 2012

INDIA:
Central Bureau of Investigation (CBI)

In its 70th anniversary year the CBI is not exactly covering itself with glory. Rather, seminal questions are being asked of its role in Indian policing, and whether the cancer, which is eating away its entrails, has rendered the once-proud investigative organisation moribund.

2011 will always be remembered as one of the worst years in the 70- year history of the Central Bureau of Investigation, which began its career in 1941 as the Special Police Department with the task of probing cases of bribery and corruption in transactions with the War & Supply Department during World War II.

Today, though that aspect of CBI's work remains largely controversy free, it is in its post-1965 additional role as a super-cop body promising surefire results in complicated murders, terrorism, etc, that this "premier" police body has been found wanting.

Last week, the nation was saturated with insights handed out by the media into the CBI's internal weaknesses after India faced international embarrassment on several fronts simultaneously. First, on May 16, the lawyer defending Niels Holck, alias Kim Davy, the Danish gun runner wanted in the Purulia Arms Drop case, objected to a warrant produced by the CBI which clearly stated it had expired on January 3 this year. India is struggling to get Holck extradited to face a trial in a Kolkata court for his role as principal organizer of the mysterious 1995 incident in which six others have already been convicted, sentenced and then let off with Presidential pardon.

Since the proceedings of this court were in the Danish language, the small exchange between the judges and the lawyers were not quite grasped by the Indian journalists present. So, it was a Danish paper, which reported it first. From there, the news travelled to an India paper. After that, Times Now TV picked it up and all hell broke loose. Since CBI had by then admitted to "oversight" and clarified that a fresh and valid warrant was on its way from Copenhagen, any amount of backtracking later with words to the effect that expiry date was a non-issue fell on deaf ears.

But by Wednesday May 18, the lords and masters at CBI, the Home Ministry, the PMO, the Congress party (in that order) were ducking for cover on not just Kim Davy, but two highly damaging issues. On that day, Home Minister P Chidambaram admitted to a "genuine mistake" in including the name of terror accused Wazhul Qamar Khan in the "50 most wanted" list which India had submitted to Pakistan recently. Alas, the man was found to be living in Thane, a suburb of Mumbai. The Home Minister had attributed the oversight to the Mumbai Police and also a "lapse" on the part of the Intelligence Bureau.

Even before the dust could settle on this, news arrived of a second blunder, this one of unforgivable proportions because it exposed the deepest vulnerability in India's security establishment -- lack of coordination. It concerned Feroz Abdul Khan, an accused in the 1993 Bombay blast, who the CBI presumed was enjoying life under the ISI's benign eye in Pakistan, but was actually in a cell in Mumbai's Arthur Road Jail. This only goes to prove that where multiple agencies are concerned, the Indian system simply collapses and gets reduced to a public joke.

As usual, excuses of the most pathetic nature were offered. And, of course, the top officers whose duty it was to ensure flawless delivery were left untouched. A humble inspector of police was suspended while a SP and Deputy SP of Delhi's Interpol wing were transferred. As for the Kim Davy blunder, the CBI actually had the gall to claim that the Judges of Denmark's Eastern High Court did not lend weight to the expired warrant -- without waiting for the judgment which is expected only in July.

In the same week, in fact hours after the "third goof-up", there surfaced another howler. By now enthusiastic journalists were up to a "spot the howler" contest and it wasn't long before one of them struck gold -- this time on the website of the CBI which had a page featuring a list of Indians out on the Interpol's watch. Now, because the journalist concerned happened to be somebody familiar with north- east insurgency, the glaring fact could not be suppressed. The website mentioned the name "Rajkumar Meghen" as a "most wanted" (not to be confused with the list handed to Pakistan). Lo behold, Meghen was found to be in the custody of the National Investigation Agency (NIA) since October 2010. He was arrested from the Nepal-Bihar border. Of course, this was a case of failure to update a website. But it is also very likely that the NIA people did not bother to inform the CBI. And, even if they did, the development was not passed on to the website handling department -- which goes to prove how casually the all-important matter of coordination with Interpol is taken.

Therefore, it is no exaggeration that few things are going right for the CBI in the new decade. The series of scams that came into public limelight last year inevitably dragged in the CBI. As The Pioneer's J Gopikrishnan (Main) points out, the Supreme Court blew a hole through the premier police organization's claims to be pursuing the spectrum scam sincerely by responding to lawyer Prashant Bhushan and political activist Subramanian Swamy's petition that the apex court itself take up the monitoring of the CBI's investigation.

In February, B Ramalinga Raju, author of the infamous Sathyam scam, almost walked free thanks to another botch up in coordination between the CBI and Enforcement Directorate, which were simultaneously probing the case. As usual, the politicians jumped into the ring and began to blast each other. While the BJP self-righteously attached the Congress, the latter took the usual stand -- "why did you do this?" or "why didn't you do that?" -- In allusion to the 1998-2004 period when too there were the usual comedies of errors. But that is not going to help matters.[52]

How to end Political Corruption

Why do liberals always point to the corporate influence into our government as a problem with corporations, which they say should be more heavily regulated and robbed of first amendment rights? Instead, why don't they see this as a problem with government, which in all reality should be more heavily regulated? The way our democratic republic was set up, the government was to have very little power and their job was to protect the rights of the individual. With the government having little power, there is no reason for a company to invest money in them because they have little power to help them. The place they would need to invest, to benefit them, is with the American people. Then we all benefit!

One prime example of this is the Oil Spill Liability Trust Fund, which was set up in 1986 but not funded until the government passed the Oil Pollution Act of 1990, which taxed oil companies at $.08 per barrel of oil produced in the U.S. or imported from outside the country. This allowed oil companies to face no more than $75 million in liability for damages that result

---

[52] Swarn Kumar Anand (2011), " CBI's annus horribilis ", The pioneer, May 28, 2011

from oil spills. The rest was to be paid for out of the "trust fund." The problem is that this trust fund now holds approx. $1.6 billion, which will be a drop in the bucket towards cleaning up the oil spill we are fighting in the Gulf of Mexico.

The liberals in this country are pointing to this as an example of deregulation when in fact; this is another prime example of a bad government regulation. The government had the power to set up this insurance policy for a company and help prop it up in case of a problem, but then the American people end up being the ones to pick up the tab. This is why limiting the governments power to do special favors and impose ridiculous regulations, would go a long way towards stomping out political corruption.

This has never made sense to me. Why regulate business and restrain them from creating wealth, which creates jobs, and improves the lives of people everywhere. Why not limit and regulate the government, which cannot create wealth, which seldom inspires innovation, which cannot grant rights, but can only protect rights, or infringe upon rights, and which has a record of absolute inefficiency? The second choice seems to be the obvious one to grow our nation in every aspect, and provide a stronger economy, free from political corruption. But do we honestly think our government will ever willingly give up their power, no matter how much it would benefit us all?[53]

A Complete Solution:

It is possible to end poverty and corruption

Let me be candid; I wish to propose an economic revolution. A carefully carved out revolution will fundamentally alter the face of India. A simple two steps technical solution, in line with the spirit of the

[53] You are Liberal. Com, June 14, 2010

constitutional directives, promises a complete answer to poverty, corruption, inequality and its consequences. We call it Economic Revolution.

While rubbing our hands gleefully at the solidity of the Indian state vis-à-vis the state of the economy of the crisis- struck developed countries, our attitude reinforces the adage "If it isn't broke, why fix it?" Yet, we cannot forget some unpleasant facts: The Indian per capita GDP at PPP of about $ 3275 places it at the 112th rank out of 162 countries (equivalent numbers for USA and China is $46,400 and $6,800). About 77 percent of India's population lives on consumption of less than 20 INR per head per day and the inequality is growing - with inflation hitting the have-nots hard, while the rich are getting the advantage of the high growth story of India.

The parallel economy is now almost equivalent to the regular economy. The flight of capital to tax havens and foreign banks is also a result of the same. Thus the total revenue collected in the coffers of the Union, State as well as Local governments is just about 11.5 Trillion Indian rupees (INR), which is far short of the current needs.

There has never been a more opportune time for a paradigm shift in economic thinking, to lead India out of the morass and to show the beacon of light to the rest of the world. India with its unique democracy, economy and challenges is an extremely complex country. A deeply researched unique solutions which does not resolve just the manifestations, but the core causes has to be crafted which is practical, optimistic, holistic and institutionalized.

The Arthakranti Mission, in a decade of its implementation can lead to growth of Per Capita Income nine to ten times over the present. These are:

(a) The end of poverty, hunger and poverty driven suicides with reduction in prices, social security and increased employment
(b) Reduction of income disparity.
(c) End of black money and parallel economy, stop flight of money to tax havens and foreign banks.
(d) Drastic reduction in Corruption.
(e) Cleansing of the political system with incentive for the best and brightest and creating conditions for politics becoming a tool for service instead of exploitation and self growth
(f) No manipulation in accounting, release of creative energy for new businesses.
(g) Global funds coming in big way to India due to increasing growth.
(h) No funding to terrorists, reduction in threat of fake currency.
(i) India becoming globally competitive with surging trade.
(j) Improvement of credit worthiness of Indian society as a whole.
(k) India becoming a role model for developed as well as developing economies.

The Economic Revolution (Arthakranti) Mission with its hundreds of serious volunteers has been working on the study, research, documentation and presentation of its practical suggestions for the past ten years. It has been well received by some of the most eminent economists, academics, political leaders and bureaucrats in India. While vested interests and inertia would resist this new paradigm shift, I hope that the people of this great nation will come together to influence the government to consider the Arthakranti proposal as a tool to seek a better quality of life. [54]

---

[54] Mayank Gandhi (2011), "A Complete Solution: It is possible to end poverty and corruption", Economic Times, 24 January 2011

The authors have neither given concrete proposals in detail nor have they cited any success events so far. The country would be happy with a growth rate of 9 percent or 10 percent. But they have expressed 9 times or ten times. How many families have achieved this growth rate?

INDIA: **End of Political Corruption:** With Finance Reform

Our state faces more challenges today than ever before. And yet at the very moment when we most need our elected officials to come together, Lansing has become a shouting match and nothing is getting done. Why? Because far too many politicians today serve special interests, the party line, and personal ambition, rather than the people they are suppose to represent.

The consequences are devastating. In the last three years we've witnessed state government shut down twice because both sides refused to talk. Every year we struggle to find adequate funding for education as personal egos and partisan purity take center stage. We need to be investing in our children - a moral and economic priority - and we need to make Michigan more attractive for job-creators. But we'll never make any progress on these or other priorities without decisive change at two levels: our institutions and the individuals we send to Lansing. At the institutional level I'm more convinced than ever that we need to control the flow of money in politics if we're going to have a legislature accountable to the people. The U.S. Supreme Court's decision last term to let corporations spend freely on elections was a step in the wrong direction.

But we can start with reforms at home. While Michigan has campaign finance laws, the system is a charade: meant to give the appearance of limits while concentrating power in the hands of political parties and special interests. Our laws place stringent limits on what individuals can give to candidates, but no limits whatsoever on contributions to party coffers and special interest PACs. This money often translates into unlimited spending to favor or defeat a candidate. If the candidate wins, the message is clear: a debt is owed. Reform must begin with meaningful limits.

In addition to campaign finance reform, we must also end the lawmaker-to-lobbyist revolving door. Too many legislators spend their time jockeying for a high-paying lobbyist post once they leave office. We should immediately enact a moratorium on formers legislators registering as lobbyists for at least two years after leaving office.

And we must eliminate the free lifetime health benefits after just six years in office that the politicians have given themselves. These extravagant benefits make our leaders less able to relate to the struggles of everyday working families. The rest of us have to work 30 years to enjoy this type of benefit, and then hope we can hold onto what we earned. This reform would have immense symbolic value, sending the message that legislators should serve the people, not themselves.

But let me be clear: institutional failures do not excuse Lansing gridlock. At the end of the day every legislator has a choice to serve the common good and the people they represent, or to serve the special interests, the party line, and themselves. Money corrupts when politicians choose to let it determine who has their ear. Returning to a politics that puts people first will require compromise. Finding workable solutions by talking with the other side doesn't make for easy sound bites. And the more partisan political donors may not reward such an approach.

Compromise forces elected officials to confront difficult decisions. In this day of 24/7 news and extreme political pundits, focusing on results instead of rhetoric may not be good politics. But it's the only way to get things done in a democratic system. The votes our legislators cast affect the lives of real people. Hopes and dreams are at stake - ours, our children's, our neighbors'. When Lansing grinds to a stop or a politician votes with a big donor instead of listening to the people, families suffer and kids don't get the education they need. Old-school politics has to go. Now is the time for a new generation of leadership. It's what our state needs and our community deserves.[55]

CAG indicts Prime Minister's Office

The Comptroller and Auditor General's (CAG) report on Commonwealth Games, tabled in Parliament on Friday, has directly indicted Prime Minister's Office, Delhi Chief Minister Sheila Dixit and former chairman of CWG Organizing Committee Suresh Kalmadi for various irregularities, wasteful expenditures and bending norms to benefit contractors.

The PMO has been indicted for "recommending" Suresh Kalmadi for heading the Organisation Committee, Delhi Chief Minister Sheila Dikshit for her "active involvement" in import of lighting equipment causing "avoidable expenditure of more than `300 million INR, and Delhi Government headed by her for "wasteful expenditure" of ONE billion INR (Indian Rupees) in streetscape and beautification.

The report indicted Kalmadi for series of violations in the administration of the Games, and favouritism in awarding contracts. The CAG also exposed manipulation to favour the controversial firm Emaar

---

[55] Mark Totten, Michigan Liberal. Com, Wednesday, July 7, 2010

MGF in awarding the contract for residential complex in the Games Village.

The report punctures the recent claims of the PMO and Government spokespersons that previous NDA Government was responsible for Kalmadi becoming the OC chairman. During the NDA regime in May 2003, the Organizing Committee (OC) was envisaged as a Government-owned registered society with Chairman of the OC Executive Board being a Government appointee. The Indian Olympic Association (IOA) president was to be the vice-chairman.

Exposing the claims of the UPA Government, CAG report says: "The OC was ultimately set up in 2005 as a non-Governmental registered society with IOA president Suresh Kalmadi as the Chairman of the OC Executive Board. This change was orchestrated through a sequence of events, commencing with a document titled as an 'updated bid' of December 2003 (which had no legal sanctity or relevance), indicating a changed structure, which surface only in September 2004."

Blaming the PMO for Kalmadi's appointment even after the objections by the Sports Ministers, the report said: "Despite strenuous objections from then Sports Minister Sunil Dutt, Kalmadi was appointed the OC Chairman, based on a PMO recommendation of December 2004. Attempts in 2007 by the Sports Minister by Mani Shankar Aiyar and Government Secretary SK Arora to the PMO, the Group of Ministers and the Cabinet Secretariat, highlighting the ineffective position of the Ministry in exercising control over the OC, met with strong resistance from the Chairman of the OC (Kalmadi) and were unfruitful."

With the available receipts of accounts, the CAG had found a "wasteful expenditure" of One billion INR by the Delhi Government in streetscape and beautification and directly indicted Chief Minister for awarding contract for a once disqualified vendor in street lighting, leading to the "avoidable expenditure of more than 300 million INR".

Finding Dikshit's role in favouring the disqualified vendor Space age and its highly inflated rate on importing lighting equipments, the CAG said: "However, the decision to use imported luminaries on selected A category of roads was not based on technical parameters, but was taken with the `active involvement' of the Chief Minister; this resulted in avoidable expenditure of more than 300 million INR. Further, the procurement of price of imported luminaries was far higher than the fair prices."

The CAG report said the lighting equipment from Saudi Arabia cost only Rs.5040 per unit. But the vendors supplied to PWD for an unjustifiable exorbitant rate of 25,704 INR.

Finding "arbitrary and non-transparent" procedures in streetscape and beautification projects, the CAG said: "We found the average awarded works for streetscape and beautification works of Rs.48 million INR /km to exorbitant, with total estimated wasteful expenditure of more than ONE billion INR." The auditors have found the discrepancies in comparing the rates of NHAI and Indian Railways for the same projects.

The report also blames the Delhi government for irregularities in Road Signage's project and manipulating the tendering procedures to favour two companies - 3M and Avery-Dennison. The CAG also found "discrepancies" in seven key road and flyover projects.

The Report also blamed the Delhi Government and NDMC for the exorbitant escalation of cost in the renovation of Co -naught Place. "The original estimated cost of 760 Million INR went up nearly nine-fold," said the auditors.

Addressing media, Deputy CAG Rekha Gupta said that the bills and accounts on several projects were still not available. "So we can't find the actual loss. How can you expect us to find the actual loss, when accounts were not available," she said, adding that the CAG will pursue with the accounting works.

As expected, Kalamdi faced scathing attack from the auditors for highly irregular and deficient management of the Organizing Committee.

"The contract management by the OC was highly irregular and deficient. The processing of certain sensitive contracts/ cases was allocated in an arbitrary and adhoc manner to certain officials who had no linkages with the concerned functional area. There was enormous bunching of high value contracts in 2010, particularly in the second and third quarters."

The Kalmadi-headed Organizing Committee was caught in the wrong for engaging SMAM as the consultant for sponsorship and merchandising / licensing rights, violations in signing broadcasting rights with Prasar Bharati, "suspicious payments" in Queen's Baton Relay, catering contract irregularities, awarding contracts to Swiss Timing Omega, Games Management System.

"The argument of urgency was used to obviate the regular process of tendering for award of contracts. We found numerous instances of single tendering, award on 'nomination basis', award of contracts to ineligible vendors, inconsistent use and restrictive practices to favour certain vendors, limiting competition, inexplicable delays in contract finalization, all of which seriously compromised transparency and economy.

"Further, there were numerous deficiencies in the appointment and management of the multiplicity of contracts for external consultant and advisors," said CAG pinpointing the irregularities and lack of transparency in recruitment by Kalmadi headed Organizing Committee.

CAG also found serious violation in awarding contracts to controversial Emaar MGF Consortium Pvt. Ltd for development and building flats in games village. "We found serious irregularities in the award of the contract to Emaar MGF Consortium, which was not qualified. There were series misrepresentations in their bid documents," said the report exposing the fraudulent ways to make bid to favour the controversial firm. (The Pioneer August 6, 2011 - News)

INDIA:

On way to being banana republic

As an ordinary citizen with no political affiliation, I felt disillusioned while listening to the high voltage recent debate in Parliament on foreign direct investment in multi-brand retail. In an open society one can legitimately have contrary views on any issue. There was merit on both sides during the debate in Parliament. It is a matter of individual preference to concur with the views of either. The standard of debate per se was high, particularly the debating skill of leaders of Opposition like Sushma Swaraj and Arun Jaitley. The ruling party through dubious floor management won the day but the Opposition managed to expose the former's feet of clay. The pyrrhic victory of the ruling party was hardly anything to gloat over. The Opposition parties may have lost the battle in 2012 but it may help them to win the war in 2014 or earlier. Be that as it may, my reaction — and that surely of many others — was that we witnessed the destruction of the fundamental fabric of democracy and moral values getting buried five fathoms deep.

We won our independence under the leadership of the Father of the Nation. He encouraged the Indian people wallowing in the dust of poverty, ignorance and slavery to demand — and succeed in gaining — independence, forcing the mightiest and largest empire known to history, to quit this country. And this was achieved through the unique weapon of non-violence in politics, breaking an altogether new ground. He demonstrated how politics can be played by a saint, keeping both the means and the end noble. When success appeared to be within grasp, to the dismay of his followers he called off the non-co-operation movement due to the unfortunate Chauri Chaura incident.

Today the 'grand old party' once led by the Mahatma himself and which he wanted to be disbanded after Independence, has now been virtually been done so by the present lot of Congressmen. Thus, we now have a new brand of Gandhi and a new brand of Congress. The complete metamorphosis of both took place from the time of Indira Gandhi. That was the era in which then president of Congress, Dev Kant Baruah, had maintained, 'India is Indira and Indira is India'.

He was formulating the North-East policy of the Congress in regard to illegal migrants from Bangladesh. He was being assisted in this by Fakruddin Ali Ahmed, then Cabinet Minister and later President of India, and Moinul Haq Chowdhry, then Cabinet Minister who till 1947 had been Private Secretary to Mohammad Ali Jinnah. B K Nehru, closely related to the Congress first family, was then Governor of Assam and veteran Congress leader BP Chaliha was the Chief Minister of the State. Their recommendation on curbing illegal migrants was summarily dismissed by the Congress High Command. BK Nehru in his autobiography, Nice Guys Finish Second, laments that the old Congress gave priority to national interests but the priority of the new Congress was entirely different; now, party interest came before national interest.

In 1989, there was a clash between the old brand Gandhi and the new brand Gandhi in the electoral battle at Amethi. Rajmohan Gandhi, grandson of the Mahatma Gandhi, lost to Rajiv Gandhi by a large margin. I wonder what would be the reaction of Jawaharlal Nehru and his mentor, the Mahatma, watching from heaven the contest between their grandsons. A recent remark by a Cabinet Minister that he would sacrifice his life for the sake of Sonia Gandhi shows the new culture of loyalty in the party. Though the Mahatma was deeply revered by the nation, no one in the party staked a claim to sacrifice his life for his sake. Sacrificing one's life for the motherland is left to the lowly soldier and not the high and mighty in the Congress.

In the wake of the recent Parliamentary debate, one saw yet another metamorphosis of the Congress. A Cabinet Minister of the Coalgate fame had the audacity to declare that democracy is run by numbers and not on moral principles. In Britain, Lloyd George had asserted that what is morally wrong cannot be politically right. The values practiced by past Congress leaders like Jawaharlal Nehru, Sardar Vallabhbhai Patel and Lal Bahadur Shastri have now become totally irrelevant for the Congress.

Uttar Pradesh is the largest State of India. It has always dominated politics at the Centre. Today, the duo of Mulayam Singh Yadav and Mayawati is providing life-support to the tottering Government at Delhi. By saying one thing during the Parliamentary debate on FDI and acting in another way when the time came to vote, they have reduced Parliamentary proceedings to a theatre of the absurd. Of course this does not bother them as they are confident that their caste-based vote bank will remain unaffected. These regional leaders have prime ministerial ambitions and so have some other regional party leaders. Sometimes I wonder if one is now witnessing the re-enactment of the later Mughal period with powerful regional subedars being beyond the control of Delhi. That had led to the eventual disintegration of India.

The main Opposition party, the BJP, is in disarray. It has a galaxy of able leaders with integrity but they are perceived to be squabbling amongst themselves. The party with a difference has now become a party with differences. Its crusade against mind-boggling numerous corruption cases of the ruling party stands compromised by alleged corruption within its own ranks. For the last few years it had chosen to co-exist with its blatantly corrupt Chief Minister of Karnataka and failed to take prompt action against him. The latter kept blackmailing the party high command for a long time, and has now broken away from the BJP to form his own outfit. Thus, for the sake of retaining power in Karnataka, the party has tarnished its chances of gaining power in Delhi. On top of this, its past president is now serving a jail sentence for corruption, and a can of worms has opened involving its present president. Thus, the perception among many people is that there is little to choose between the Congress and the BJP. It is a case of six of one and half a dozen of the other.

The Assembly election in Gujarat is of great significance. It is not only a tussle for power in the State but is being seen as preparing for the contest between the challenger and the heir apparent in the Parliamentary election. From all accounts, Chief Minister Narendra Modi won a third successive win in the State's Assembly election. As for the coming Parliamentary election, it is difficult to predict its results at this stage. The result of the Gujarat

Assembly election will have a definite impact on the former.

No matter which party comes to power at the Centre in 2014 or earlier — the Congress-led UPA, the BJP-led NDA or a Third Front of regional parties with or without the support of a national party — the great challenge will be to rejuvenate our democracy, revive the majesty of Parliament and restore moral values. All of these suffered a beating in the recent Parliamentary debate on FDI. If we fail to do so, India will be seen to have become a banana republic.[56]

INDIA: **The denial of justice:**
Some fundamental reforms we need to carry out

A festering sense of injustice invites anarchy. Most importantly, it diminishes fear to vanishing point, and while a 'fearless' society is the acme of true democracy, a society without fear (of authority) is a sure recipe for anarchy. The Indian state - in each of its judicial, executive and legislative organs - has to implement drastic structural changes and realise that the time for cosmetic surgery is long over.

In the Indian criminal justice system, major crimes are likely to remain unreported; if reported, frequently not registered; if registered, the true perpetrator not found; if found, not prosecuted; if prosecuted, not charged; if charged, usually not convicted; if convicted, frequently not adequately punished. At each crucial stage, the system has enough loopholes and inefficiencies to allow the guilty to walk away with impunity.

Where will these judicial additions - fast-track courts for rape cases, special courts for intellectual property right and patent cases, special judges for arbitrations

---

[56] S K Sinha (2012), " On way to being banana republic", the Pioneer, December 17, 2012

and commercial disputes - come from when at all times since Independence, a minimum of 25 percent - often 33 percent - of the country's aggregated judicial strength at high court level has been vacant! That too when that total sanctioned number for a 1.25 billion population is a mere 850?

The lower judiciary - those who decide rape cases and all other serious crimes - fares no better. At least 25 percent of such posts are always vacant - and the total sanctioned strength for the whole country is only 15,000!

Our psyche is used to delay; it is endemic and entrenched and we all take it for granted. A parliamentary report of 2002 accounted five hundred thousands cases in all high courts as being over 10 years old. Also cited were a Madhya Pradesh high court case of 1950, a 1951 case in Patna, a 1955 case in Kolkata and a 1956 case in Rajasthan. One hopes someone has simply screened and disposed of these cases for the sake of optics and statistics, if nothing else. Unfortunately, it is likely these hopes are misplaced. Would it otherwise be possible for actor Salman Khan's payment of 1.9 million Indian rupees in a drunken driving case - mandated by a court order in 2002 - yet to be disbursed to the dead victims' families?

The solutions (and this is not rape specific) are simple and need no high-powered committees or seminars.

Firstly, it needs a prioritization and a listing of 10 or 15 things which the system, without change, without mid-course correction or interruption, will implement for a minimum of five years. That consistency is vital for results. Secondly, the judiciary must lay down a procedural protocol which initiates the appointment procedure and navigates it through different collegian well in time to result in the official notification of a successor's name at least 30 days before the retirement date of the incumbent.

This protocol must specify specific time limits for each stage of the file movement and must designate a dedicated official to monitor it for the hundreds of such file movements involved. I am inclined to suggest that unless the successor is ready to take over from the incumbent, the latter must be deemed to continue. Thirdly, a similar protocol must be put in place for appointments to the lower judiciary with the involvement of the state government and the relevant high court.

Fourthly, the current judge per million population ratio of approximately 15 must immediately jump to at least 25 (the US has 50 and a 2002 Indian Supreme Court judgment exhorts us to progressively reach that figure; from 1987 to now we have crawled from 10.5 to 14-15!).

This needs, fifthly, a quantum leap in planned expenditure for the judiciary. It is amazing that prior to 1993; the judiciary was not even put under planned expenditure. The judiciary has crawled to 0.01 percent of GNP in the 11th Plan (2007-12), marginally above where it was in the 9th Plan. This is one area crying out for attention, even if increased Plan allocation creates a "planned deficit".

Sixthly, the highly underused 'brahmastra' of costs must be used proactively to combat the scourge of adjournments. Not only that, for civil cases, costs must follow the event, i.e. the loser must pay the full actual costs of the winner. This has proved a huge deterrent globally to frivolous and irresponsible litigation.

Finally, all the laws of the country must be standardized to have a maximum of one primary trial and one full appeal on facts and law. Second appeals and revisions, called by whatever name, and must be eliminated. Special leave petitions to the apex court will remain anyway, unless eliminated by a constitutional amendment.

I can guarantee that these seven measures alone - along with a host of reforms already under implementation - will make the three or 35 million arrears in cases in India collapse like a house of cards within less than five years of their implementation. Do we have the will, the political consensus and the dynamism to implement them?[57]

Right to recall is not practical in India

(a) Will render elections redundant:

Rashid Alvi opines that 'Right to Recall' to the elected Members of Parliament or the State Assemblies would render elections redundant in a democratic country.

I have argued on earlier occasions too that the "right to recall" is not practical to implement, and definitely not at this point of time. This is due to the fact that out of the roughly 1.3 million voters in a typical parliamentary constituency, we get to see, at best, about 60 to 70 per cent of the electorate voting. A candidate who gets, let's say, a mere 25 per cent of the total votes, which amounts to just about three hundred thousand votes, could still win the election. This means that there are about 1 million voters against the winning candidate. This reality makes the proposition of "right to recall" null and void the very day the verdict is out.

"Right to recall" should also be examined in the existing reality of caste-based politics. There are political parties which are dependent on particular

---

[57] Abhishek Singhvi (2012), " The Denial of Justice", The Times of India, December 28, 2012

castes to win elections. Though it's not good to have caste-based politics, yet, we have to consider the possibility and ramifications of other caste groups joining hands against an elected representative who may have won by using the "right to recall" option.

How would we react if the very next day after the election, someone starts a signature campaign against the winning candidate? It will make the whole process of fighting elections superfluous and redundant.

Had there been 100 per cent polling in elections and the winning candidates were to bag 50 per cent plus one votes and if the voters were educated enough to understand the nuances of the electoral system, one could understand and even opt for "right to recall". That, unfortunately, is not the case right now. Also consider the expenses involved.

There are a couple of states in the US where "right to recall" is in practice. I have visited those places and met people's representatives there. I have not seen any cases of "right to recall". Rather, I will say, that we need to promote the right kind of environment in the country before we can try such a mechanism. I do not mean to say that this is never possible in India. It is a serious issue and we need to find a way out. [58]

Electoral reform is necessary in the country and we should take steps to address issues raised by the civil society. Those who are elected do not feel that they are accountable to the people for the five years that they are in power. This is wrong. The very fact that only about one-third of the existing members of Parliament manage to win and two-third of them lose elections each time clearly indicates that we do have

---

[58] Rashid Alvi (2011), "Will render elections redundant" The Deccan Chronicle. November 24, 2011.

a very strong system of accountability which the electorate fully utilizes.

(b) **Find a way to make it work**:

Manish Sisodia emphasizes that let us find ways how "Right to Recall" to the elected Members would be possible.

First and foremost, let me clearly state the fact that there are good people in politics too but there are a number of people who should not have been part of the political system. We have many examples before us. On a number of occasions even Anna Hazare has maintained that after people's representatives are elected, they behave as if they are the masters, while in reality and in a real democracy they should work like the servants of the people.

The existing political realities are grim reminders of the fact that our elected representatives are in the habit of usurping the will of the people for a duration of five years, during which they are hardly accountable to the electorate. People at large get a perception as if they have mortgaged their will to these elected representatives.

They hardly take people in confidence over the legislation they pass in Parliament. And if an elected representative turns out to be a bad choice, people have no option but to bear him or her for five years. Why should people suffer due to a bad elected representative?

There are two issues concerning whether people should get the power of "right to recall". First is the issue of whether such a measure is practical or not and the second is of the possibilities such a measure will offer.

As far as the question of possibilities of having "right to recall" is concerned, the answer is a clear "yes" in the backdrop of the prevailing political conditions. When you see politicians like the jailed DMK MP and former communications minister A. Raja and others, one would definitely feel the pressing need for giving people the power of "right to recall". Coming to the issue of how to make the option of "right to recall" work, critics continuously say that such a measure is not practical because there are large parliamentary constituencies with a large number of voters. Let me say at the very outset that there is no sure-shot solution to the practical issue of how to implement the option of "right to recall".

The government has at its disposal various facilities to commission studies, which can look at some of the models in other countries and examine their effectiveness. Of course, the government has to find ways to address concerns about the possibilities of any misuse of the option as well. There is a need to seriously begin working on it so that we can arrive at a model which can be implemented in specific Indian conditions. But one cannot say that it's impossible to implement it. This can be done and the government should have the will to do it. [59]

Civil Society can't blackmail Government

T N Madan opines that social evolution is a continuous process. A society is diverse and vibrant in India; so India's is bound to undergo changes in the course of time. In the process, it ends up expanding the horizon of sociology. With liberalisation, new elements emerged into the existing social structures and processes, thus giving the society newer tone and appearance. We can also find some old beliefs and structures losing their relevance to the new patterns. At the same time, some key structures of Indian society and its ethos still remain

---

[59] Manish Sisodia (2011), "Find a way to make it work", The Deccan Chronicle, November24, 2011

intact, although they have definitely got modified over the years. So, in the case of Indian society, it's a matter of both continuity and change.

The Indian system follows a model where the state plays an important role in the religious affairs and formulates laws governing the inter-communal and state-religion relations. The state also gives financial supports to religious communities and often gets both criticized and admired for these 'subsidies'.

Our model is different from, say, the French model, which is regarded as the closest to the standard secular model. In the French system, religion has no space in the public sphere and the state never participates in the religious affairs. Our system is said to be a bit closer to the American model where religion has a definite presence in the public realm but where the state mechanism does not provide any support to any community or group on the basis of religion.

Our model goes a step further. It not only ensures and recognizes religious presence in the public sphere, but also assures legitimate support to these groups when the situation arises. Civil society is independent of the state, but it should not become a substitute for the state.

Of course, it is an important part of our democracy and the issue that it is raising today is also important that must be addressed. But that does not mean that it should take up the role of any branch of the government in any form or blackmail the government in a democratic country. It can or should, at best, act only as a reasonable pressure group.[60]

---

[60] T N Madan (2011), "Civil Society can't blackmail Government", The Pioneer, July 24, 2011

India's Dirtiest Elections Ever 2014

The bandwagons thunder along the road to 2014 through a slush of invective-spewing dirt and mud, staining khadi and saffron. The political discourse of this dirtiest election ever fought has taken an irreversible path, hurtling through shrapnel of abuse and personal attacks—'maut ka saudagar,' 'khooni panja,' 'poison of power' and more. Across states, sting operations by politically partisan news outfits, vicious personal attacks thick with allegories of blood and character assassinations form the thesaurus of current electoral rhetoric. Last year, when Gujarat went to the polls upon which rode the prestige of the Congress party's arch enemy Narendra Modi, Sonia Gandhi's departure from courtesy to revilement showed that the dynasty and its outfit were veering away from the path of its forebears; in an uncharacteristic broadside against the one she perceives as a Mephistopheles striking a Faustian bargain with Indian secularism, she invoked the spectre of the 2001 riots by calling Modi a "maut ka saudagar." The speechwriters have abandoned Emily Post for Marquis de Sade, in a sadistic attempt to demolish the enemy with invective.

Modi returned the favour a few months later, naming the Congress election symbol "in Dongargarh Rajnandgaon on November 7, promising protection from "the bloody hand" should they vote for the lotus—after the Maoist attacks on the Congress state leadership that had led to an internecine vilification campaign within the state Congress party. He had referred to Ajit Jogi's chief ministership as one led by a "zalim". In the South, Marxist paterfamilias V S Achyuthanandan wasn't being cute naming Rahul Gandhi an Amul baby; Karnataka's BJP president Eswarappa questioned Rahul's "manhood"; sex cases were splattered all over Kerala's politics; Naresh Agarwal, senior Samajwadi Party leader in Uttar Pradesh called Modi a "chaiwala" and questioned how "koi chaiwala Hindustan jaise bade desh ko chala sakta" (how can a person of stature of a tea vendor, run a huge and complex country like India). In a retort to Sonia Gandhi calling the BJP "a party of poisonous people," Modi reminded listeners at an election rally in Banswara, Rajasthan that Rahul Gandhi had once referred to Sonia comparing power to poison. "Madam's Shehzada once said in Jaipur that his mother told him that power is poison. They ruled the country for almost 50 years since Independence... then who has tasted poison for longer period... it is Congress...then who else can be more poisonous?"

No Holds Barred

The poison, in this election, has infected all political parties. In Andhra Pradesh, where a bitter battle looms after the Telengana bifurcation, Telugu Desam chief Chandrababu Naidu called YSR Congress scion Jagan Mohan Reddy a "monkey" and a "dog." A fellow traveller of many ideologies in his chequered career, Raj Babbar's exhibited his Bollywood prowess through excoriating dialogue, calling Madhya Pradesh Chief Minister Shivraj Singh Chouhan "a juggler" who wears colourful underpants. Madhya Pradesh became a bitter battlefield of contumelious cannonade—Digvijay Singh accused Shivraj of being Feku No 2, in a reference to Narendra Modi's mocking twitter name.

'Shehzada' Rahul Gandhi is a favourite target with the saffron Sardar Patel and he hits below the belt. Referring to Sonia's reported illness, he lashed out "Agar Madam beemar hain to bachche ko kaam do (If madam is unwell, hand over the work to her child)." He didn't spare former chief minister Ajit Jogi either calling him an "apahij" (cripple)—"He is in wheelchair...," implying a disabled leader cannot take his party to victory. He compared the Congress leadership with a Bollywood movie where a family introduced their beautiful daughter while finalising a marriage proposal but later switched sisters by bringing in the one with disability (Jogi) for the marriage ceremony. Modi, though widely hailed as an effective orator, has proved time and again that he is not in the mould of A B Vajpayee—who was genteel of tone and disarming in wit. The BJP's Chhattisgarh campaign is in bad taste, based on Jogi's infirmity, with posters warning people against the "handicapped" governance of the Congress. Rahul responded by calling the BJP a party of "chor-lootere". "Kya aap apne mama ke ghar se laakar de rahe ho (Are you getting the funds from your maternal uncle's home?)" was Modi's riposte.

BJP vs. Congress

The hatred between Modi and the Congress dominates the election. In April, Rashid Alvi called Modi "Yamraj", and was removed from his post as Congress spokesman (these were early days in the poll campaign and Modi was unsure of his national standing in his own party, and the Congress at that point did not wish to give him importance by taking him head-on). In Delhi, as both mainstream political parties treat the rise of Aam Aadmi Party's as a cause for worry, a sting operation surfaced indicating that the political outsider was using illegal funds. Party boss Arvind Kejriwal called the tape "doctored" and alleged that 1.40 billion Indian rupees was given to some media houses to tarnish his image. Undoubtedly, this election is not even a battle between parties, but between personalities who have a polarizing effect. No border, however absurd, is inviolable. Even Pakistan became part of political diatribe when Rahul spoke about ISI agents wooing the youth of riot-hit Muzaffarnagar, quoting an intelligence briefing. Facing widespread criticism from both, opponents and Muslim clerics, the Congress leader could not respond convincingly.

A vicious battle is being fought on the ground zero of mutual hate between Modi and JD (U) boss Nitish Kumar in Bihar. Though the bomb blasts at Modi's Hunkar Rally in Patna on October 27 did not harm the BJP's general, insinuations were made that Nitish wanted his opponent assassinated. A senior BJP leader questioned the Centre's soft approach to terrorism, "Are we going to be soft on security because some state governments want to be seen as soft on terror for collateral reasons?" alluding that Nitish Kumar's vote bank was encouraging terror to flourish in Bihar. Ironically Nitish indirectly blamed Modi for the fiasco, accusing him of "criminal negligence of security" and said terrorists in a way helped BJP in its "otherwise flop" rally. Modi was quick to point out that the chief minister—whom he calls "a backstabber and traitor"—did not visit the families of those killed and chose to "feast" at a party meeting. Oblivious to the irony, Kumar retorted he was attending a yoga convention.

Courtesy to Cudgels

The contorted asanas of political yoga as practiced by the current crop of demagogues contrast sharply with the behaviour of many stalwarts. A few days ago, Sharad Pawar gave reporters the sort of polished quip that is in danger of becoming extinct: where subtlety and irony join together in a perfect union with context. After a visit to a doctor, said the Maratha strongman with a wide grin to waiting journalists, "The test conducted on me proves that I have both, head and heart." I accept: A random piece of self-deprecating humour? No, uttered by Pawar, it perhaps carried extra freight: an oblique allusion to the criticism he was copping, as agriculture minister, for the spiralling food prices. At 73, Pawar is fast becoming the representative of an older political culture where even bitter animosities were marked by serviceably polite and civil exchanges, if not actually elevated by wit and mature sarcasm. Everyone abided by basic minimum courtesies; there was an inviolable protocol, a tacit line of control.

BJP spokesperson Nirmala Sitharaman says: Ideally political discourse should maintain standards so that people don't lose faith in leaders that they are not up to the mark. But after a point, if attacks continue unabated; expressions are couched in metaphors, and then your followers ask you why we are not reacting. We explain to them that this could be dirty tricks department of the other party. So sometimes we have to reply. However restraint should be there from all sides."

Future Shock

Beset by scandals, the first sign of the purple times to come were visible during Anna Hazare's fast in April 2011 for the Lok Pal Bill. The then Congress spokesman and current I&B minister Manish Tewari accused Anna of being corrupt "from head to toe." He had also referred to Anna's associates as a combination of "armchair fascists, over-ground Maoists, closet anarchists funded by invisible donors." Kapil Sibal, one of the interlocutors appointed to deal with the Anna brigade called the aged freedom fighter a "Pied Piper." In the current atmosphere of, even Prime Minister Manmohan Singh isn't being spared—his opponents have dragged his name into the Coalgate affair.

It takes only the briefest of glances to see the epidemic nature of bad language in politics—either in the form of personalised slurs, or verbal violence that Varun Gandhi's notorious speech in Pilibhit or the TMC-Left exchanges in West Bengal are illustrative of, and devoid of grace. In last week's civic body elections in Odisha, state Finance Minister Prasanna Acharya of the BJD threatened voters: "I am Odisha's finance minister. Funds are in my hands. If you vote for the Congress, I shall lock the funds." About a fortnight ago, Karnataka's former deputy CM K S Eshwarappa called the Prime Minister a "hijra" over bilateral relations with Pakistan. "The Congress lacked manhood in the past, they don't have it now either. Only those who have drunk their mother's milk will have manhood."

Sex CDs have forced ministers out of office; shady operators are linked to the chief minister's office in Kerala. The irascible Mamata Banerjee who took pleasure in humiliating the prime minister showed her political nature, asking "Should I beat up the prime minister?" over rising fertiliser prices.

Historian Ramachandra Guha sees it in terms of the new competitiveness: The political animosity is too much. That is why the level of discourse too has come down so. It's not a normal electoral battle...but we can take heart from the fact that it's no better in the US. In fact, we have come to match their levels.

P C Chacko, AICC spokesperson say: When there is nothing positive to campaign, they (leaders) resort to personal vilification.

Changing Times

The composition of the political class reflects in the deteriorating nature of political attacks—criminal cases are pending against 30 per cent of Lok Sabha MPs and 17 per cent of Rajya Sabha members. Naturally, venom has given way to wit, and hatred to humour. In Parliament, Bharatiya Jan Sangh founder Shyama Prasad Mukherjee, a practiced Nehru baiter of the 1950s said, "I saw with my own eyes how powerfully the resources of the government can be made to operate for the purpose of winning the elections. I can tell the Prime Minister some time later. He does not know that money and wine played their part in many a sphere."

The era of Nehru and Indira had no shortage of personalities but their endorsement and rejection were grounded in issue-based political debates. The BJP grew out of the strong anti-Congress ideological pool. Modi is its inheritor, trying to mould the party in his own image as the now ubiquitous masks show; idolatry minus ideology is the mood de jour at his rock star-like receptions. It's not just the traditional BJP vote base that's rooting for him, but sections of the apolitical middle class, too, which is the new claimant on a newborn political space. Social scientist Ashsis Nandy says:

Sarcasm is misunderstood now. Only crude and direct language works. There's no scope of subtlety. The middle class has expanded in terms of money, but their value system has persistently eroded. Many people in public life are first-generation leaders...they don't have the political vocabulary.

A senior BJP think-tanker was inclined to read it in terms of free speech. "There can be no 'standard' for electioneering," he says. "We can't have a situation where the EC decides the political discourse and intimidates leaders and parties. Even the most outrageous ideas get play. We can't move towards a controlled democracy."

Sophistication is out

Outrageous ideas notwithstanding, outrageous comments were examples of political wit. Nehru, when confronted with the red flag of the undivided Communist Party on a trip to Kerala, quipped: "What is this foreign flag doing here?" When Nehru's finance minister T T Krishnamachari called Feroze Gandhi a "lapdog" of the PM, he responded with elan: "Sir, you are a pillar of society. And today I will do to you what a dog does to a pillar." After India was trounced by China in 1962, and lost a large chunk of territory Nehru remarked in Parliament, "There is really no loss, though our territory has been annexed. Not a blade of grass grows there." Congress MP Mahavir Tyagi asked the speaker if Nehru could to remove his cap. Nehru did so. Tyagi said, "Mr. Speaker Sir, not a single blade of hair grows on Mr. Nehru's head. So let us cut it off, it is of no consequence and no loss to us." Now, not a single Congressman would dare challenge a Gandhi in public.

Indira Gandhi was vitriolic towards her enemies, even throwing them in jail but she rarely launched personal attacks on her opponents. When the Bofors scandal was gathering momentum against her son Rajiv Gandhi—whose majority in Parliament remains unbeaten— VP Singh was called a Jaichand. Rajiv made the phrase "Naani yaad dila denge" part of Indian political lampoon.

In the bonfire of inanities that is Indian politics today; respect is being lost in the ruins of the past.[61]

Conclusion

Corruption, black money and money laundering could be checked or minimized with the existing law provided the legal procedure is completed within a year. If the case is not completed the court should declare the culprit free of charges. The aggrieved petitioner could be awarded decree order, as the bureaucracy is corrupt, insincere and anti-people.

The peoples' representatives must submit Income-tax statement and property statement to the election commissioner and income-tax department each financial year. The CBI or FBI (highest bureau of Investigation) must verify their reports.

---

[61] Santwana Bhattacharya (2013), "Filth Fest", the New Sunday Express, December 01, 2013

India needs revision of Indian Penal Code, revision of service code, and correction of the constitution without any change to the fundamentals. The right to land of the farmers, extent of forest coverage, retirement benefits of all the senior citizens including peasants must be looked into.

Corruption gallops in all democratic countries and low-income countries. Politicians and bureaucrats nourish corruption openly. If judiciary system is quicker and efficient, corruption could be limited or abolished. The corruption penal code must be re-written and punishment should be spectacular and quicker.

All court cases against elected political leaders must be finalized within three months. If elections would be free from corruption, a stable and efficient government would be possible.

The Governments must undertake special enquiry to check corruption in Mining, Industry, Politics, Export-Import business, land deal, environment loss, small finances, government schemes and subsidies.

It is a fact that 162 Members of Parliament (out of 547 MPs) in India are facing criminal cases on grounds of murder, rape, cheating, dacoit and theft cases in different criminal courts. Hence, the Election Commission of India, must see that only 'clean leaders' should be elected in the Elections. The tainted leaders would create problems in the parliament. If two or three political parties (United Political Alliance) could not give stability to the government, the law should permit all parties should form the government to run the government with clean MPs as ministers.

Political leaders should not be decorated with honorary degrees; it speaks ill of politics and education. The political party in Government should bring all Universities under the administrative control of central government.

All colleges and schools must function under the administrative control of state governments. All deemed universities and research institutes can award training certificates; not degrees and honorary degrees of university.

The honorary degrees such as Doctor of Science and Doctor of Literature should not be traded for business purposes.

The Election Commission should grant permission to political parties for ensuring democracy. But some of these political parties paralyze the government and governance through road-shows, strikes and obstructing railways for self publicity. These political parties close even the school and colleges. The EC must record their activities.

The Election Commission of India must take political parties to task for violating the Model Code of Conduct during election process. There should be a maximum of seven political parties. An independent candidate must be denied to contest elections as people do not know his capacity and capability. Moreover, his political ideology is also unknown.

The political parties should say; what they have done or what they want to do. They cannot call their rivals monkeys, back stabbing anti-nationals or names with ugly words. They cannot call their names, profession, religion or caste during elections meets in different places.

They cannot meet the voters after 10 PM to transact illegal funds with them. The Central Bureau of Investigation must start inspecting and completing their property statements six months before the due date of Election.

Chapter V

POLITICS AND WAR

An eye for an eye leaves the whole world blind.
------ Mahatma M. K. Gandhi

War and the large military establishments are the greatest sources of violence in the world. Whether their purpose is defensive or offensive, these vast powerful organizations exist solely to kill human beings. We should think carefully about the reality of war. Most of us have been conditioned to regard military combat as exciting and glamorous - an opportunity for men to prove their competence and courage. Since armies are legal, we feel that war is acceptable; in general, nobody feels that war is criminal or that accepting it is criminal attitude. In fact, we have been brainwashed. War is neither glamorous nor attractive. It is monstrous. Its very nature is one of tragedy and suffering.

His Holiness Dalai Lama says that war is like a fire in the human community, one whose fuel is living beings. I find this analogy especially appropriate and useful. Modern warfare waged primarily with different forms of fire, but we are so conditioned to see it as thrilling that we talk about this or that marvelous weapon as a remarkable piece of technology without remembering that, if it is actually used, it will burn living people. War also strongly resembles a fire in the way it spreads. If one area gets weak, the commanding officer sends in reinforcements. This is throwing live people onto a fire. But because we have been brainwashed to think this way, we do not consider the suffering of individual soldiers. No soldiers want to be wounded or die. None of his loved ones wants any harm to come to him. If one soldier is killed, or maimed for life, at least another five or ten people - his relatives and friends - suffer as well. We should all be horrified by the extent of this tragedy, but we are too confused.

Frankly as a child, I too was attracted to the military. Their uniform looked so smart and beautiful. But that is exactly how the seduction begins. Children starts playing games that will one day lead them in trouble. There are plenty of exciting games to play and costumes to wear other than those based on the killing of human beings. Again, if we as adults were not so fascinated by war, we would clearly see that to allow our children to become habituated to war games is extremely unfortunate. Some former soldiers have told me that when they shot their first person they felt uncomfortable but as they continued to kill it began to feel quite normal. In time, we can get used to anything.

It is not only during times of war that military establishments are destructive. By their very design, they were the single greatest violators of human rights, and it is the soldiers themselves who suffer most consistently from their abuse. After the officer in charge have given beautiful explanations about the importance of the army, its discipline and the need to conquer the enemy, the rights of the great mass of soldiers are most entirely taken away. They are then compelled to forfeit their individual will, and, in the end, to sacrifice their lives. Moreover, once an army has become a powerful force, there is every risk that it will destroy the happiness of its own country.

There are people with destructive intentions in every society, and the temptation to gain command over an organisation capable of fulfilling their desires can become overwhelming. But no matter how malevolent or evil are the many murderous dictators who can currently oppress their nations and cause international problems, it is obvious that they cannot harm others or destroy countless human lives if they don't have a military organisation accepted and condoned by society. As long as there are powerful armies there will always be danger of dictatorship. If we really believe dictatorship to be a despicable and destructive form of government, then we must recognize that the existence of a powerful military establishment is one of its main causes.

Militarism is also very expensive. Pursuing peace through military strength places a tremendously wasteful burden on society. Governments spend vast sums on increasingly intricate weapons when, in fact, nobody really wants to use them. Not only money but also valuable energy and human intelligence are squandered, while all that increases is fear.

I want to make it clear, however, that although I am deeply opposed to war I am not advocating appeasement. It is often necessary to take a strong stand to counter unjust aggression. For instance, it is plain to all of us that the Second World War was entirely justified. It "saved civilization" from the tyranny of Nazi Germany, as Winston Churchill so aptly put it. In my view, the Korean War was also just, since it gave South Korea the chance of gradually developing democracy. But we can only judge whether or not a conflict was vindicated on moral grounds with hindsight. For example, we can now see that during the Cold War, the principle of nuclear deterrence had a certain value. Nevertheless, it is very difficult to assess al such matters with any degree of accuracy. War is violence and violence is unpredictable. Therefore, it is better to avoid it if possible and never to presume that we know beforehand whether the outcome of a particular war will be beneficial or not.

For instance, in the case of the Cold War, through deterrence may have helped promote stability, it did not create genuine peace. The last forty years in Europe have seen merely the absence of war, which has not been real peace but a facsimile founded dear. At best, building arms to maintain peace serves only as a temporary measure. As long as adversaries do not trust each other, any number of factors can upset the balance of power. Lasting peace can assure secured only on the basis of genuine trust.[62]

The United States of America

Senator Byrd (2003) opines that the United Nations is in diplomatic disarray today as the foreign ministers from the world's most powerful nations scramble to find some scrap of common ground on the question of war with Iraq.[63]

What a difference a few months makes. Last November, under the leadership of the United States, the 15-member U.N. Security Council unanimously approved **Resolution 1441,** strengthening the weapons inspection regime and giving Iraq a final

---

[62] His Holiness the 14th Dalai Lama Of Tibet, Dalai Lama Com

[63] Senator Byrd (2003), "America the Peacemaker Becomes America the Warmonger", Senate Remarks, Information Clearing House, March 11, 2003

opportunity to comply with its disarmament obligations.

The rapidity with which that unity has unraveled is astounding. What began as a constructive process to gain international support for war against Iraq has disintegrated into insults, accusations, and finger pointing among the key members of the Security Council? Instead of forging an international coalition to deal with Iraq, as it set out to do, the Administration has managed to turn much world opinion against United States. With his insistence that the United Nations declare the inspection regime a failure and immediately authorize war against Iraq, the President has opened a chasm between the U.S. and Great Britain on one side and the remaining permanent members of the Security Council on the other.

The White House is declaring the United Nations irrelevant if it does not authorize immediate war against Iraq, and U.N. Secretary General Kofi Annan is countering that a U.S.-led invasion of Iraq without the sanction of the United Nations will violate the U.N. charter.

The knock-down, drag-out in the Security Council has tarnished the images of both the United Nations and the United States, and it has imperiled the political career of at least one world leader, President Bush's staunchest ally, British Prime Minister Tony Blair.

What a high price to pay for the President's insistence on blindly following a war-first, war-now policy on Iraq.

Despite feverish activity this week on the part of the U.S. and Great Britain to persuade a majority of members of the Security Council to support a second resolution authorizing war with Iraq, the President and his chief advisers have made it clear that the activity is merely window dressing and that the United States is prepared to act with or without U.N. support. For the Bush Administration, war with Iraq seems to be no longer a question of if, but when -- and the window on "when" is rapidly closing.

Dr. Condoleezza Rice, the President's National Security Advisor, declared over the weekend, "There is plenty of authority to act. We are trying very hard to have the Security Council one more time affirm that authority. But it's important to know that we believe the authority is there."

In other words, the die has been cast. The rhetoric has hardened. U.S. forces are in place and poised to attack. The U.N. Security Council has been relegated to a classic Greek chorus of tragic protest while the United States takes center stage. The President has stopped listening.

The Administration's strategy for war with Iraq is so far advanced that not only does the President have war plans on his desk; he also has a blueprint for the post-war reconstruction of Iraq.

On Monday, *The Wall Street Journal* reported that the U.S. Agency for International Development is soliciting bids from a handful of U.S. firms for a contract worth as much as $900 million dollars to begin the reconstruction of Iraq. According to the *Journal*, the contract would be the largest reconstruction effort undertaken by the United States since the reconstruction of Germany and Japan after World War II. With post-war contracts already in hand, can the onset of war be far behind?

My views, by now, are well known. I believe this coming war is a grave mistake, not because Saddam Hussein does not deserve to be disarmed or driven from power, not because some of our allies object to war, but because Iraq does not pose an imminent threat to the security of the United States.

There is no question that the United States has the military might to defeat Saddam Hussein, but we are on much shakier ground when it comes to the question of why this nation, under the current circumstances, is rushing to unleash the horrors of war on the people of Iraq.

In many corners of the world, the United States is seen as manufacturing a crisis in Iraq, not responding to one. Key members of the U.N. Security Council, including France and Russia, have vowed to veto any move to secure the imprimatur of the UN on war with Iraq. The UN weapons inspectors have pleaded for more time to do their work. Citizens by the thousands have taken to the streets in countries around the globe, including the United States, Europe, and the Middle East, to protest the war.

The day after the September 11 terrorist attacks on America, the French newspaper *Le Monde* proclaimed, "We are all Americans!" Eighteen months later, the United States and France are hurling insults at each other, and the French are leading the opposition to the war against Iraq. In country after country, the United States has seen the outpouring of compassion and support that followed September 11 dissolve into anger and resentment at this Administration's heavy-handed attempts to railroad the world into supporting a questionable war with Iraq.

The latest report of the U.N. weapons inspectors only heightened the tensions in the Security Council and helped to precipitate the current scramble for a new resolution. On Friday, (March 7) Chief U.N. weapons inspector Hans Blix reported progress in the disarmament of Iraq and predicted that the inspection process could be completed in months -- "not years, nor weeks, but months."

At the same meeting, Mohamed El Baradei, the director general of the International Atomic Energy Agency, threw cold water on a key assertion of the Bush Administration, that Iraq is actively pursuing a nuclear capability on two fronts -- by importing high-strength aluminum tubes which could be used as part of a centrifuge to produce enriched uranium and by attempting to buy uranium from Niger. Dr. El Baradei said the inspectors have found no evidence that Iraq is attempting to revive its nuclear weapons program, concluding that the aluminum tubes were for a rocket engine program, as Iraq claimed, and that the documents used to establish the Niger connection were faked.

Not even reports of a chilling discovery by U.N. weapons inspectors of a new type of rocket in Iraq that appears to be designed to carry chemical or biological agents has swayed the hardening opposition in the United Nations to authorizing an immediate war against Iraq.

The world is awash in anti-Americanism. The doctrine of preemption enshrined in the Bush Administration's national security strategy -- the policy on which the war with Iraq is predicated -- has turned the global image of the United States from that of a world class peacemaker into what many believe is dangerous warmonger.

The President is on the wrong track in insisting on rushing into war without the support of the international community, and specifically the United Nations. Not only is America's reputation on the line, but so is our war on terror. The recent arrest of Khalid Sheikh Mohammed and two of his cohorts in Pakistan is evidence that the United States is making slow but steady progress in dismantling the al Qaeda organization and that we are reaping huge dividends from the anti-terrorism efforts we have undertaken in cooperation with other nations in the Middle East.

Pakistan's cooperation is particularly important in the war on terror, yet the majority of the Pakistani people are opposed to war with Iraq. How or whether Pakistani opposition to the war against Iraq will affect the war against terror is one of many unknowns.

The United States cannot bring down al Qaeda alone. We need support and cooperation from friendly nations in the region. We risk losing their friendship, and possibly causing major upheavals in the Middle East, if the President defies world opinion and launches a U.S. led invasion of Iraq. The cost of war and the potential casualties -- not only to American military personnel but also to innocent civilians in and around Iraq -- are unknowns. The impact of war on the fragile fabric of the Middle East is also unknown. The Administration seems to think that war with Iraq will pave the way to peace and democracy in the Middle East, but I believe that is merely wishful thinking. Saddam Hussein is not the cause of the strife between the Israelis and the Palestinians, and his downfall will not erase the deeply rooted conflict between the two sides.

War against Iraq may prove to be a fatal distraction from the war on terror. The danger to Americans today is from al Qaeda. Intelligence officials predict that war with Iraq will precipitate new wave terrorism against the United States and its allies, and will serve as a powerful recruiting tool for anti-American extremists.

We need to keep the pressure on al Qaeda. We need to strengthen our defenses against a terrorist attack here at home. We need to focus the resources of our nation on the war on terror and dismantle the al Qaeda network before it can mount another catastrophic attack on the United States.

The hour is late, the clock is ticking, but if the President would only listen to voices outside his war cabinet, he might discover that it is not too late to stop the rush to war. There is still a chance that Saddam Hussein can be disarmed and neutralized short of war. As long as that possibility exists, the United States should drop its resistance to any slowdown in the march to war and should begin to talk with, and listen to, the other members of the Security Council. The prospect of regaining unanimity within the United Nations on the question of Iraq is dim at best, but as long as there remains even a glimmer of hope, it is in the best interests of both the United States and the other members of the Security Council to regroup and strive to achieve that goal. The world community deserves nothing less.

How Lincoln Could Have Prevented Civil War

Abraham Lincoln was an extraordinary man with many wonderful qualities. He is greatly admired by many and is generally considered one of America's greatest Presidents. Since the era of the founding fathers, he is certainly one of the most influential Americans. Yet he was President during a brutal Civil War in which an estimated **625,000 Americans died**. This is nearly as many as all the Americans who have died in all the other wars of the United States. Although Lincoln was obviously not the only cause of the Civil War, he was probably more responsible for the nature of the war than any other individual.[64]

The purpose of this essay is to examine briefly how President Lincoln handled this crisis and then to learn the lessons of history by imagining how he might have prevented the military conflict that had such terrible consequences. By looking at the probable consequences of other policies we may be able to find ways to resolve conflicts more successfully, especially

---

[64] Sanderson Beck, "How Lincoln Could Have Prevented Civil War", San Beck Org / Lincoln Civil War

now in an age when total war could mean mass suicide.

The horrible institution of slavery was obviously the issue that provoked the conflict between the southern slave states and the northern states, where slavery had been almost completely abolished by 1860. Lincoln was a politician, and he did not consider himself a radical abolitionist. Lincoln definitely hated slavery, and he believed it is wrong. He took the political position that the United States Constitution had authorized slavery in the states where it already existed; but he strongly opposed extending it into the territories of the United States or to other states. He made this policy clear in his speeches and reiterated it in his first inaugural address on March 4, 1861. By then seven states had already seceded from the United States and had formed the Confederate States of America. It is ironic that the slave states would have had a better chance of preserving their nefarious institution if they had remained in the Union during Lincoln's presidency. But Lincoln represented the new Republican Party that was formed by northerners, and he was the first President to be strongly opposed to the extension of slavery. In the election of 1860 he was one of four candidates and won a majority in the Electoral College even though he got less than forty percent of the popular vote.

Many politicians in both the South and the North believed in the sovereignty of the states that had come together after the War of Independence to form a "more perfect Union" under the Constitution of the United States of America. In 1776 the thirteen colonies had essentially seceded from the British Empire in order to establish that sovereignty and to make sure that they were not taxed without representation. The US Constitution does not mention secession, does not state that the Union is to be perpetual, and defines no procedure for states to withdraw or become independent. Many abolitionists had advocated that northern states could secede in order to form a nation that would be free of slave states. During the transition between Lincoln's election and his inauguration the Buchanan administration allowed seven of the southern states to withdraw.

John Pendleton Kennedy, an ex-congressman from Maryland, advocated a "separate confederacy of the border states" in his pamphlet *The Border States*, which was published on December 15, 1860. On January 2, 1861 Governor Thomas Hicks of Maryland took the position that a central confederacy of Border States could solve Maryland's problems. On that day he met with three members of a Union meeting and wrote to Governor William Burton of Delaware. Hicks also wrote to the governors of New York, Pennsylvania, New Jersey, Virginia, Missouri, and Ohio about the idea of forming a central confederacy if the Federal Union were disrupted. Like many, Governor Hicks opposed the use of force to keep Maryland or any other state in the Union. While the seven states in the Deep South were seceding, the border slave states of Maryland and Delaware were considering seceding and forming a Central Confederacy with New Jersey, Pennsylvania, and New York. Many Democrats and newspapers in these five states advocated this proposal until the forces of South Carolina attacked Fort Sumter on April 12, 1861. Then sentiment in the northern states quickly turned to patriotic support for the Union and its war against the southern rebels. Believing that the war made peaceful secession impossible, they abandoned the plan for a central confederacy.

Then why did seven southern states secede when Lincoln had promised to protect slavery in their states and even enforce the controversial Fugitive Slave Law in the other states? The South also felt exploited by the North because of the high tariffs that were the largest source of Federal taxation that resulted in southern taxes being used in other parts of the country. As a former Whig, Lincoln was a strong advocate of high protective tariffs. The Morrill Tariff Act was passed on March 2, 1861, and tariffs were increased early in Lincoln's presidency to raise revenues to pay for the war. Politicians are naturally ambitious, and the southern politicians also wanted to control their own destiny. Some had imperial ambitions to enlarge their new nation by expanding into territories and by conquering Cuba and portions of Mexico. They did not want their slave states to be restricted by Lincoln's policies.

South Carolina seceded on December 24, 1860, and by February 1, 1861 Mississippi, Florida, Alabama, Georgia, Louisiana, and Texas had also voted and declared secession. Six days later these seven states adopted a constitution for the Confederate States of America in Montgomery, Alabama, and they elected Jefferson Davis president. If these were revolutions, they were quite peaceful so far. They went through some democratic process by conventions and in the state legislatures, and apparently their state governments accepted the new nation with little resistance.

The most difficult bones of contention became the federal forts and installations in the southern states and the collection of tariff revenues in southern ports. The Federal forces in Charleston harbor withdrew from other forts and moved into the most defensible Fort Sumter, which was a customs house used to collect duties. South Carolina had sent three commissioners, who had arrived in Washington on December 26 to negotiate a treaty between the new republic and the United States in order to resolve disputes over the forts, the arsenal, and lighthouses, to divide the public property and apportion the public debt, and to settle any other issues necessary to establishing South Carolina as an independent state. President Buchanan took the weak position that he had no authority to decide any of these questions, and he declined to make any preparations to fight over them. In fact by his negligence some weapons of the United States were moved to the South by their sympathizers in his Democratic administration.

Lincoln took the strong position, which some would call tyrannical, that states have no right to secede from the Union. He believed it was his obligation as President to enforce the laws that would keep the states in the Union even against their will as expressed by democratic conventions and state legislatures. His policy is ironic and even hypocritical because this position conflicts with Lincoln's own doctrine of the right of revolution that he expressed in Congress on January 12, 1848 during the Mexican War when he said:

"Any people anywhere, being inclined and having the power, have the right to rise up and shake off the existing Government and form a new one that suits them better. This is a most valuable—a most sacred right—a right, which we hope and believe, is to liberate the world. Nor is this right confined to cases in which the whole people of an existing government may choose to exercise it. Any portion of such people that can may revolutionize and make their own so much of the territory as they inhabit. More than this, a majority of any portion of such people may revolutionize, putting down a minority, intermingled with or near about them, who may oppose their movement. Such minority was precisely the case of the Tories of our own revolution.

It is a quality of revolutions not to go by old lines or old laws, but to break up both and make new ones."

In his inaugural address President Lincoln warned against a civil war while promising that he would not invade the South. Yet he indicated that the Federal Government would continue to occupy its property in the South and would attempt to collect "duties and imposts." He promised he would not impose "obnoxious strangers" in Federal offices in hostile regions. The mails would continue unless repelled. He called for "a peaceful solution of the national troubles and the restoration of fraternal sympathies and affections." However, in his view this came to mean only by the retention of the states in the Union.

Early in his presidency Lincoln rejected the option of letting the southern states withdraw peacefully. He took the position that secession is illegal and that the use of force against the Federal Government was rebellion and treason against the United States. He refused to recognize the Confederate States as legal entities and would not let anyone in his administration negotiate with their representatives. He also rejected an offer of mediation by Napoleon III of France. In March 1861 Jefferson Davis sent peace commissioners to Washington with an offer to pay for all Federal property in the South and to take on the southern portion of the national debt. However, Lincoln refused even to acknowledge them, thus blocking any attempt to resolve the conflicts by peaceful means. He took the hard line that the southern states must return to the Union. Unless they did so, or unless he relinquished the forts and tariffs, it became inevitable that the two sides would fight. His position has been compared to that of the British Empire, which demanded that their American colonists pay their taxes.

Lincoln was careful to avoid beginning the war with an attack. However, he managed to instigate an attack on Fort Sumter by refusing to negotiate with South Carolina or to withdraw Federal forces from there. He informed the government of South Carolina that he was sending in supplies to his besieged men with the warning that he would retaliate against an attack. President Jefferson Davis and his cabinet authorized the attack by the forces of South Carolina that began the fighting. Lincoln had provoked it by insisting on keeping control over Federal forts in their territory. He took the position that a minority who lost an election should not be allowed to withdraw from the nation, and he jumped to the erroneous conclusion that to do so would destroy democracy. Yet from the other point of view, he was denying democracy to the seceding states. If he had recognized their right to be independent states, surely both nations could have co-existed as republics. I do not believe that we should be blind to these democratic rights, as he was, simply because we believe that slavery is wrong or because we have a desire that the Union should be perpetual. Clearly the main motive for the South's withdrawal from the Union was a bad one, but that does not mean that they did not have sovereign rights as states.

Lincoln called for 75,000 volunteers for three months to add to the small Union army of 17,000, and he proclaimed a naval blockade of southern ports in May, excluding even drugs and medicine. By June 8 the states of Arkansas, North Carolina, Virginia, and Tennessee had also seceded and joined the Confederate States. On June 26 the *New York Tribune* published "The Nation's War Cry," urging capture of the new Confederate capital of Richmond, Virginia. The next day the Republican *Chicago Tribune* repeated the same cry. Nearly four years later on February 23, 1865 when *Chicago Tribune* editor Joseph Medill and others pleaded with Lincoln not to draft more men, the President reminded them that Chicago was one of the cities that had called for war, and he told them to go home and raise the men. The Union Army began robbing and plundering in the disastrous battle at Manassas (or Bull Run) on July 21, 1861, and the next day Lincoln called for the enlistment of 500,000 men for three years. This military victory gave the South hope that they could win the war despite their disadvantages because they believed the northerners would eventually give up the task as not worth the costs. However, Lincoln had extraordinary determination, and he eventually found generals ruthless enough to win battles while suffering enormous losses. During the Civil War about 2,100,000 men served in the Union Army, and about 850,000 were in the Confederate Army.

On April 22 Rev. Richard Fuller had led a delegation of 35 delegates of the Young Men's Christian Association from Baltimore, and he asked President Lincoln to avoid war by recognizing the independence of the southern states; but Lincoln obstinately referred to Washington, Jackson, and manhood in refusing to consider a peaceful approach. He complained that people in Baltimore had harassed Federal troops on their way to Washington, and five days later he suspended the writ of habeas corpus so that such people could be arrested without being charged with a crime. Conflicts in Missouri led to the imposition of martial law there. In May a list of more than a hundred newspapers that opposed the war was published, and Lincoln ordered Postmaster General Blair to deny those papers mail delivery, the usual means of circulating newspapers at that time. President Lincoln widened the suspension of habeas corpus, and during the summer of 1861 Maryland legislators who favored secession were imprisoned so that they could not even meet to decide the issue.

Lincoln was a pragmatic commander-in-chief, and he was afraid that if Maryland seceded, Virginia and Maryland would surround his capital at Washington. General Nathaniel Banks reported to Lincoln that Maryland legislators who advocated peace had been arrested, and in their November elections judges were instructed to disallow votes for candidates who opposed the war. Peace Party ballots were a different color so that they could be thrown out, and those carrying them were arrested. In the first ten months of the war the Federal Government arrested 854 civilians.

After suffering several defeats by the Confederates led by General Stonewall Jackson, General John Pope began waging war on civilians in Virginia. His General Order No. 11 was issued on July 23, 1862 and required men behind Union lines to take a loyalty oath to the United States; those suspected of breaking their oath could be shot and have their property confiscated. Hundreds of southern churches were burned, and ministers who refused to pray publicly for Lincoln were imprisoned. On July 25 Pope issued General Order No. 13, which ordered soldiers not to guard private homes or property of those who were hostile to the Federal Government. This and the previous General Order No. 5 allowed Union soldiers to rob and mistreat civilians.

Two days after he announced the Emancipation Proclamation on September 22, 1862, Lincoln suspended the writ of habeas corpus throughout the nation. Careful research by scholars, such as Mark E. Neely, Jr., indicates that during the Civil War the Federal Government imprisoned more than 14,000 civilians for opposing the Government or its war in some way. Lincoln authorized military officers to shut down newspapers if they were disrupting recruiting or the war effort. The Provost Marshal General's Bureau was organized in 1863 and by the end of the war two years later they had arrested and returned to the Union Army 76,526 deserters. During the draft 161,286 citizens failed to report to the Union Army, but how many of them were arrested is unknown.

Lincoln also had imperial ambitions for the United States, and he used Government subsidies to finance the transcontinental railroad to the west coast. In 1862 a crop failure caused starvation to the Santee Sioux because the Federal Government refused to pay them the $1,410,000 owed them from the sale of 24 million acres in 1851. When the Sioux revolted, General John Pope tried to exterminate them. Hundreds of Indians were held as prisoners of war and were given military trials that sentenced 303 to death. President Lincoln commuted most of these sentences, but thirty-nine were put to death in the largest mass execution in the history of the United States. After Lincoln's death under mostly Republican administrations the experienced military would be used to attack any Indians who were in the way of the railroads and the western expansion of the United States. Lincoln was ambitious on behalf of the United States and did not want to see the empire divided. He developed the power of the imperial presidency as commander-in-chief by arrogating to himself extra-constitutional "war powers."

In 1863 at Geneva efforts were made to codify an international convention on the conduct of war, and on April 24 President Lincoln issued General Order No. 100 on proper conduct during war. Written by his advisor Franz Lieber, this was issued as "Instructions for the Government of Armies of the United States in the Field." However, this code allowed military commanders to make exceptions when they believed it was necessary. Specifically the code allowed them to destroy property and withhold the means of subsistence from the enemy and to appropriate whatever the country afforded for the subsistence of the army. This code also endorsed military retaliation, and Union commanders were allowed to take hostages to deter guerrilla action.

While General George McClellan and other generals in the east tended to be more conciliatory, in the west Generals Ulysses S. Grant, William T. Sherman, and others soon began foraging and burning towns and crops. Sherman declared all people in the South enemies and traitors so that he could justify waging war against civilians. As they closed in on Vicksburg in 1863, the Union Army stripped the surrounding land in Mississippi of crops and burned the houses. Sherman ordered Jackson bombarded every five minutes day and night, and then his soldiers sacked and destroyed the city. Sherman told Grant that they had devastated the land for thirty miles around. Sherman's forces also destroyed the city of Meridian.

In the late summer of 1864 Sherman's army bombarded Atlanta and then destroyed ninety percent of the city. As they marched to Savannah robbing and plundering, Sherman ordered randomly chosen civilians killed in retaliation for attacks by Confederate soldiers. Because South Carolina began the secession movement, Sherman ordered his men to pillage, plunder, and sack cities there even more ruthlessly. His chaplain James Stillwell reported that a majority of the cities, villages, and county houses were burned to the ground. In late 1864 the Union cavalry led by Philip Sheridan ravaged the Shenandoah Valley by pillaging, plundering, and burning. Lincoln was overjoyed by the "victories" of Sherman and Sheridan because they assured his re-election that November.

The question I am raising is whether war was the best way to resolve these conflicts. To answer this question as best we can, let us explore various scenarios of what might have happened if Lincoln had allowed the South to secede. In the 19th century most nations in the world abolished slavery by peaceful means. The British freed all the slaves in their empire in six years, completing the process in 1840. Most Latin American nations emancipated all their slaves between 1813 and 1854, and the gradual liberation of slaves in Brazil was completed in 1888. The only other violent emancipation of slaves was the slave uprising in Haiti in 1794.

Clearly the historical trend in this era was toward emancipation and the abolition of slavery. The proportion of slaves in the population had been declining for three decades in Delaware, Maryland, Kentucky, Missouri, and most of Virginia. The American Civil War, which Lincoln called the War of the Rebellion and others called the War Between the States, cost $6.6 billion and was borne about equally by both sides. The greatest cost of the Civil War was the death of 625,000 people—one-third in combat and two-thirds by disease. In the South one out of four males between the ages of twenty and forty perished in the war. Hundreds of thousands were also wounded, and tens of thousands were crippled. Nearly forty percent of the American economy was destroyed directly by the war. From the monetary costs alone all the slaves could have been freed by compensating their former owners while providing each of the former slaves with forty acres.

If Lincoln had agreed to negotiate the settlement of the Federal installations in the seceded states and their portion of the national debt, and if he gave up the exploitative taxes, then most of the costs of the war probably could have been saved. The remaining northern states may have lost some of the wealth they were exploiting from the South by the tariffs, but that would have been a small loss compared to the war costs. The greatest advantage of a peaceful settlement would have been saving the **625,000** lives that were lost and the other injuries. One can hardly overestimate the psychological trauma caused by young men being forced to kill their fellow countrymen in miserable conditions that caused so many to die of disease. Many civilians were also killed, wounded, or imprisoned.

If some of the slave states had remained in the Union, then they would have continued as before. Gradual emancipation with compensation to the former owners might have been negotiated so that the Union would eventually have become free of slavery. The question is how long the Confederate States would have maintained their "peculiar institution" of slavery against the trend of modern history. Instead of being forced to emancipate the slaves without compensation, they could have worked out some sort of gradual emancipation eventually. Without a war surely almost all those staying in the Union would have been much better off. Also the whites in the seceded states would have been more prosperous and safe compared to the utter defeat they suffered in the war and during the military occupation referred to as "Reconstruction."

One can argue that the slaves in the seceded states would have been worse off. Yet they also suffered in the devastating war. The southern slaves liberated by the North were given a period of twelve years to reconstruct their lives during which they were favored with exceptional political opportunities because of the Union occupation that disenfranchised the rebels. Yet the resentment of the white southerners to having this forced on them led to a strong reaction after Reconstruction was ended in 1877. The whites then developed the segregation system of Jim Crow laws that perpetuated hatred between the races for the next century. So for several generations this discrimination lowered the quality of life for the slaves' descendants.

If there had been no war, the northern abolitionists could have found ways to help the slaves in the South, and most likely the Fugitive Slave Law would not have been enforced. If all the slave states seceded, then slaves could have run away to the northern states. One could argue that this might also have led to a war. Yet the North could simply defend its borders. It seems to me that in this situation it would have been much less likely that either side would have significantly invaded the other's territory. The northerners might have used economic pressures to urge the southerners to emancipate their slaves. Eventually the southern states would have learned what all other countries had found out—that free labor is more productive and more socially desirable than slavery.

After the Confederate States emancipated their slaves, they would likely have wanted to be readmitted into the United States. Thus the nation could have been reunited with less resentment than after a war because the northerners would have respected the right of the southerners to exercise their own sovereignty and learn their own lessons their own way without having them forced upon them. Americans claim to value freedom greatly, but the military tradition of fighting and winning wars is the opposite of the respect for the freedom of others. The history of the United States since then would probably have been more peaceful. The United States might not have gone to war against the Spanish empire in 1898. If the United States had not gone abroad to join the useless carnage of the First World War in Europe, some historians have argued that the peace may not have caused the resentments in Germany that led to the Second World War.

Understanding this tragic flaw in Lincoln's character that led to the terrible Civil War is especially significant because his virtues of honesty, intellect, integrity, compassion, mercy, humor, determination, diligence, and sense of justice make him one of America's greatest heroes. His talents would have been much better put to use in using diplomatic and political skills rather than in prosecuting a brutal war. Because of Lincoln's imperialistic approach to this crisis, the Federal Government of the United States was greatly strengthened and centralized. Without the war the people in the states would have retained more local control. He also developed the role of the President as commander-in-chief in perhaps the largest war in western civilization up to that time. This war was a transition to modern warfare in which the industries of nations are pitted against each other, and millions of people are put in harm's way.
These lessons are important now when the United States has become bogged down in two unnecessary wars in Iraq and Afghanistan. When are we going to

learn that it does not spread freedom to force others to do what we want? Force is the opposite of freedom. If we used a fraction of what we waste on military spending to help people in other nations, they would be our friends as well as being much more prosperous. Humanity needs to learn how to solve its conflicts in peaceful ways because otherwise we are likely to destroy ourselves and ravage the environment of this planet with the possible consequence of leaving a desolate place to those who may survive.

As Americans maybe we need to ask ourselves why we allowed the terrible injustice of slavery to lead to such a destructive war when every other nation except Haiti managed to resolve this issue without horrendous violence. Why is the United States continuing to arrogate to itself the role of policing the world with our military might? Huge military spending since World War II and especially since 1981 has led to a national debt that has passed ten trillion dollars.

The United States is now spending more on the military than the rest of the world combined. The United States Government is currently teetering on the brink of bankruptcy because we have been wasting our resources and living beyond our means.

Let us pray and work hard in peaceful ways so that the day of reckoning for our country can be faced and resolved without massive violence and suffering. Let us work together for a world that is peaceful, just, free, prosperous, and ecologically sustainable.

Myths of the Kennedy cult

The cult of John F. Kennedy has the resilience of a horror-movie villain. No matter how many times the myths of Camelot are seemingly interred by history, they always come shambling back to life — in another television special, another Vanity Fair cover story, another hardcover hagiography.

It's fitting, then, that the latest exhumation comes courtesy of Stephen King himself. King serves a dual role in our popular culture: He's at once the master of horror and the bard of the baby boom, writing his way through the twilit borderlands where the experiences of the post-World War II generation are stalked by nightmares and shadowed by metaphysical dread.

In this landscape, the death of JFK looms up like the Overlook Hotel. The gauzy fantasy of the Kennedy White House endures precisely because the reality of the assassination still feels like a primal catastrophe — an irruption of inexplicable evil as horrifying as any supernatural bogeyman.

At its best, King's new Kennedy assassination novel, 11/22/63 — which sends its protagonist back in time to change that November day's events — offers an implicit critique of this generational obsession. But its narrative power still depends on accepting the false premises of the Kennedy cult — premises that will no doubt endure so long as the 1960s generation does, but still deserve to be challenged at every opportunity.

The first premise is that Kennedy was a very good President, and might have been a great one if he'd lived. Few serious historians take this view: It belongs to Camelot's surviving court stenographers, and to popularize like Chris Matthews, whose new bestseller Jack Kennedy: Elusive Hero" works hard to gloss over the thinness of the 35th President's actual accomplishments. Yet there is no escaping the myth's hold on the popular imagination. In Gallup's "greatest President" polling, JFK still regularly jostles with Lincoln and Reagan for the top spot.

In reality, the kindest interpretation of Kennedy's presidency is that he was a mediocrity whose death left his final grade as "incomplete". The harsher view would deem him a near disaster — ineffective in domestic policy, evasive on civil rights and a serial blunderer in foreign policy, who barely avoided a nuclear war that his own brinksmanship had pushed us towards. (And the latter judgment doesn't even take account of the medical problems that arguably made him unfit for the presidency, or the adulteries that eclipsed former US President Bill Clinton's for sheer recklessness.)

The second false premise is that Kennedy would have kept us out of Vietnam. Or as a character puts it in 11/22/63, making the case for killing Lee Harvey Oswald: "Get rid of one wretched waif, buddy, and you could save millions of lives."

Actually, it would be more accurate to describe the Vietnam War as Kennedy's darkest legacy. His Churchillian rhetoric ("pay any price, bear any burden...") provided the war's rhetorical frame as surely as George W. Bush's post-9/11 speeches did for our intervention in Iraq. His slow-motion military escalation established the strategic template that Lyndon Johnson followed so disastrously. And the war's architects were all Kennedy people: It was the Whiz Kids' mix of messianic and technocratic confidence, not Oswald's fatal bullet that sent so many Americans to die in Indochina.

The third myth is that Kennedy was a martyr to Right-wing unreason. Writing on JFK in the latest issue of New York magazine, Frank Rich half-acknowledges the mediocrity of Kennedy's presidency. But he cannot resist joining a generation of liberals in drawing a connection between the Right-wing "atmosphere of hate" in early-1960s Dallas and the assassination itself — and then linking both to today's anti-Obama zeal. Neither can King, whose

11/22/63 explicitly compares Right-wing Dallas to his own fictional territory of Derry, Maine — home of the murderous Pennywise the Clown from It, among other demons.

This connection is the purest fantasy, made particularly ridiculous by the fact that both Rich and King acknowledge that Oswald was a leftist — a pro-Castro agitator whose other assassination target was the far-Right segregationist, Edwin Walker. The idea that an atmosphere of Right-wing hate somehow inspired a Marxist radical to murder a famously hawkish Cold War President is even more implausible than the widespread suggestion that the schizophrenic Jared Lee Loughner shot his congresswoman because Sarah Palin put some targets on an online political map.

This last example suggests why the JFK cult matters — because its myths still shape how we interpret politics today. We confuse charisma with competence, rhetoric with results, and celebrity with genuine achievement. We find convenient scapegoats for national tragedies, and let our personal icons escape the blame. And we imagine that the worst evils can be blamed exclusively on subterranean demons, rather than on the follies that often flow from fine words and high ideals.[65]

Wars could be avoided

It's military stalemate in Libya. It will be a long war of attrition by both sides. The troops of the Libyan president, Muammar Gadhaffi, have the upper hand. Unlike the NATO countries they have boots on the ground, always a prerequisite for success in warfare; his troops are well armed and reasonably trained with a clear command structure. His opponents are a rag

---

[65] Ross Douthat (2011), " Myths of the Kennedy cult", The Deccan Chronicle, November22, 2011

tag bunch, if less rag tag than they were at the beginning. But they are organised enough to keep Gadhaffi away from the important town of Benghazi and can effectively force a division of the country between west and east. But what happens next is anybody's guess.

Wouldn't it have been better to accept from the onset that toppling the regime in Libya would be a long haul business? Sanctions were never given time to bite, although earlier sanctions against Libya over its downing of two civilian airliners, one American and one French, did eventually have an effect.

Too many national leaders resort to war too quickly. War ravaged the twentieth century from 1914 on. It was the bloodiest century in the world's history. But it had been preceded by a long peace from 1815 to 1914, disturbed only by the three years of the Crimean War. (However, many historians say it was also broken by the war between Russia and Turkey. But since Russia and Turkey have always had a doubtful status as "European", it can be safely put on one side.)

It is widely believed that the First World War that ended the 100 years of unprecedented peace in Western Europe, Korea and Vietnam were unnecessary wars. But the Second World War is still judged as a "just war".

The great Oxford historian, the late A. J. P. Taylor, wrote in his seminal book "The Origins of the Second World War" that we should be careful in assuming that at the beginning it was unavoidable- although he also says that once it started it had to be finished with the defeat of Germany and Japan. In his introduction he makes the biting comment, "In 1938 Czechoslovakia was betrayed (by the British). In 1939 Poland was saved. Less than one hundred thousand Czechs died during the war. Six and a half million Poles were killed. Which was better – to be a betrayed Czech or a saved Pole?"

The British finally declared war on Germany because it invaded the Polish-ruled "Danzig corridor" a sliver of land, separated from Poland by German territory. The Versailles Treaty had created the corridor on the grounds that the port of Danzig was essential to the Polish economy. But later, with the construction of the port of Gdynia, Danzig needed Poland more than Poland needed Danzig.

Before the German march into Czechoslokia most British opinion thought the German claim to take back Danzig was reasonable and that the corridor was an anomaly of the Versailles Treaty, widely considered to be unjust. The British hand was forced by Poland once Prime Minister Neville Chamberlain had declared that if Poland felt driven to war Britain would come to its aid. Poland, believing that it was a great power, instead of compromising, insisting on principal, had refused to even begin negotiations with Germany, yet it could probably have negotiated a compromise such as a corridor across the corridor. For his part Hitler mistakenly thought that Britain would never declare war over such a small issue. Moreover, his ambition was a peaceful alliance with Poland, not its destruction. But Britain, ashamed by its role over Czechoslakia, when it failed to honour its guarantee to protect it, believed it could not go back on its word again. London declared war on Germany.

Jonathan Power, A. J. P. Taylor and Basil Liddell Hart were of the view that the World War II could have been avoided.

Hitler did not want a major war in Europe. He wanted to solve what he believed mistakenly was Germany's living space problem and the anomalies of the Versailles Treaty by a series of small wars which would not involve Britain or France.

Of course, even if the British had not gone to war over Danzig, Hitler would have remained a tyrant. He would have persecuted the Jews, homosexuals and Gypsies. But the German people with their growing economic contentment, whilst turning a blind eye to this policy, would have continued as they did before hostilities broke out to resist war. The memories of the destructiveness of the First World War were still deep in their consciousness.

Can we avoid war in the future? Have our fingers been burnt over Iraq, Afghanistan and Libya. Probably for this generation the answer is "yes". But can we work for the next? Memories are short and history is too often twisted.[66]

Dealing with Dictators

Today, even the most wicked and ruthless rulers must take international opinion into account and conversely the global community expects them to behave much better than dictators did in the bad old days. They may not always live up to expectations, but that is the standard by which they will be judged.

The 'Prague Spring' of 1968 was a gallant attempt at a non-violent democratic revolution, but Soviet tanks crushed it. Eighteen years later, in the Philippines, the first 'people-power' revolution succeeded, and since 1986 non-violent revolutions have driven a great many dictators from power. The most recent was in Egypt, in February — but there never was a guarantee that these revolutions would turn out well.

It depends partly on how bad the ethnic and religious cleavages are in a country: Bulgaria and Romania were okay, but Yugoslavia was a blood bath. It depends to some extent on how poor and illiterate

---

[66] Jonathan Power, The Tenerife News, Tues day, May 10, 2011

the population is, although even very poor countries have made a successful transition to democracy. And it depends on good leadership and good luck, too. But it is the dominant political phenomenon of our time.

The revolution in the Philippines succeeded because by the late 1980s, everything was happening in real time on global television. Oppressive regimes that had never had much compunction about killing people who challenged them didn't feel confident about doing it before a global audience. They no longer felt free to use massive force unless the protesters gave them an excuse by resorting to violence themselves.

The Marcos regime that was overthrown in the Philippines in 1986 was a mere kleptocracy with little ideology beyond a vague 'anti-communism'. When the infection spread to China in 1989, the outcome was different, because a disciplined Communist dictatorship was willing to kill large numbers of its own people in front of the television cameras. It understood that if it failed that test, it would not survive.

Less ruthless Communist dictatorships in Europe, longer in power and ideologically exhausted, did fail the test. The non-violent revolutions that began in East Germany in November 1989, and ended Communist rule in the old Soviet Union itself by late 1991, could have been stopped if the local Communist regimes had been willing to follow the Chinese example, but none of them had the stomach for killing on that scale.

So about 350 million Europeans got their freedom and almost nobody died. At almost exactly the same time, the apartheid regime in South Africa released Mr. Nelson Mandela and began the talks that led to majority rule in 1994. A very well connected African friend of mine told me later what had actually happened.

In late 1989, after the East German, Czech and Romanian regimes had fallen with scarcely a shot being fired, the head of the National Intelligence Service, the South African secret police, went to State President FW de Klerk and warned him that if the African National Congress put half-a-million people on the street in Johannesburg, he would only have two options: To kill ten thousand of them, or to surrender power unconditionally.

If he didn't like either of those options, he should start negotiating the transfer of power now. So Mr. Mandela was released, and eventually there was a peaceful transition from apartheid to majority rule.

Then there's a long gap, perhaps partly explained by the fact that the number of dictatorships in the world had already shrunk considerably. An attempted non-violent revolution in Iran in 2009 was mercilessly crushed. People worried that repressive regimes might have finally figured out how to counter non-violent revolution. And then along came the 'Arab spring'.

So the technique is still alive, and it worked in Tunisia and in Egypt. On the other hand, it has been stamped out in Bahrain, whose fate resembles that of Prague in 1968. And while the revolt in Yemen has probably displaced the old regime, it has been very violent, and the new regime may be no more democratic than the old.

The same goes for Syria, and of course for Libya. There are no one-size-fits-all techniques for revolution or for anything else. But the desire for democracy, equality and fairness survives everywhere, and the least bad technique for trying to achieve those things is still non-violence. Even if sometimes the revolution succeeds but the aftermath doesn't.

The original 'people power' revolution in the Philippines was followed by two decades of political turbulence. Yugoslavia splintered into half-a-dozen warring fragments. Russia, though it escaped mass violence, is not exactly a model democracy.

On the other hand, South Korea, Indonesia and South Africa are now all democracies. So are Poland, Romania and Taiwan. The aftermath may not be what most people hoped for in Egypt, and it probably won't be in the case of Syria. But non-violent revolution works often enough, and its results are positive often enough, that it is still the most hopeful political development of the past quarter-century.

The glass is half-full, and getting fuller. Even the most wicked and ruthless rulers must now take world public opinion into account, and we expect them to behave much better than dictators did in the bad old days. They may disappoint our expectations, but that is the standard by which they will be judged, and they know it.[67]

INDIA: **Political Will Is Missing**

The time for lighting candles is over. People must demand security. And, national security must be insulated from vote-bank politics.

India is the top contender for the Nobel Peace Prize for Strategic Restraint. Its tolerance level to accept punishment is rated the highest in the world. This inglorious distinction it has held for 20 years. Terrorists strike with predictable regularity and impunity. The latest assault in Mumbai (13/7) comes after five unsolved attacks since 26/11.

India has managed to terrorize itself, doing the job of

---

[67] Gwynne Dyre (2011), "Dictators no longer immune to criticism", The Pioneer, Bhubaneswar, June 14, 2011

the Lashkar-e-Tayyeba, the Indian Mujahideen and other terrorist groups. In his book *Psychology of Strategic Terrorism*, Ben Sheppard says the way Governments and societies respond to terrorism exacerbates or mitigates its effects. The less said about the Government the better. Political leaders made bizarre statements after 13/7. Here are some: "We had no prior information as terrorists work clandestinely. But this was no intelligence failure"; "all cities are vulnerable"; "we stop 99 per cent of attacks — but it is impossible to stop all".

The Prime Minister put some balm: "Government will do everything in its power to prevent such attacks in the future". Yet, after the next attack, Delhi Police will be on high alert, plant barriers on the roads and do nothing. People have come to accept the inevitability of their fate. Speaking to IPS probationers in December 2010, Mr. Singh admitted that home grown terrorism is a bigger threat than externally driven terrorism though little has been done to home in on local groups. Instead, intelligence and investigating agencies took their eyes off the IM which is believed to be involved in all five terrorist strikes since 26/11.

Two facts are clear. Even in a Congress-led State, internal security reforms as promised after 26/11 have not been implemented. Regrettably the focus is on being better prepared after the event than on its prevention or pre-emption. The British Government's latest counter-terrorism strategy, 'PREVENT', mandates the primary task is to stop terrorist attacks, stop growth of homegrown terrorism, protect cities and citizens and mitigate the impact of attacks. The US, the UK and Germany have prevented terrorist attacks. The blur between external and internal security has disappeared.

The last war was in 1971 and Kargil in 1999 was a border skirmish. Pakistan, where it is difficult to distinguish between state and non-state actors, has finessed its strategy of cross-border terrorism after 26/11. No mass casualty attacks which can be traced to it; instead, it has been outsourcing mid-intensity strikes to its terror affiliates like the IM. Clearly India needs an internal security doctrine with a counter-terrorism strategy to prevent terrorism, including overt and covert means to punish Pakistan.

Unfortunately the Constitution of India mandates law and public order is a State subject. The police are designated to handle internal disturbances and words like 'internal security' or 'national security' are not used in the Constitution. Full-blown insurgencies, including the Maoist uprising, and terrorism are not law and order issues. They require a political and professional military response, which has myriad problems, not the least of Centre-State cooperation and coordination. In a federal set-up this conflict has to be resolved, preferably through an amendment to the Constitution.

The recommendations of the Task Force on Internal Security, headed by Mr. N N Vohra and set up during the NDA regime, have not been implemented. China, which spends $89 billion on defense, has invested $100 billion on law enforcement and internal security. By comparison, despite Mr. Singh recognizing the grave challenges of Maoism and homegrown terrorism, India's resource investment is a pittance. The combined State and central funding is less than a quarter of the amount spent on defense. The Government has provided to States 20 billion INR (Indian rupees) over five years for training and strengthening of police infrastructure. But the States will do their own, having failed to implement police reforms ordered by the Supreme Court. Progress in establishing homeland security architecture has lagged behind. This is typical — akin to constituting a sub-optimal Integrated Defense Staff without a CDS.

In 2009, Home Minister P Chidambaram announced one year after 26/11: "India must decide now to go forward in setting up the National Counter-Terrorism Centre by the end of 2010." He said this while addressing Intelligence Bureau officers at Vigyan Bhavan. While the NIA and a truncated NatGrid are in place, the NCTC received qualified approval last month, though the media has reported otherwise. Intra-party schisms on combating Maoism and terrorism have confirmed that coalition Governments can never be decisive on internal security.

By being hailed as the best Minister in this Government, Mr. P Chidambaram has turned Ministerial colleagues into adversaries. The Government has been overly focussed on externally driven terrorism. The 32-month lull engendered complacency, instead of shifting focus inwards. Intelligence, surveillance, policing, investigation and prosecution skills are below par, especially human intelligence. On these pillars must rest the goals of prevention of terrorist strikes without turning into a police state; reduction of the impact of attacks; and a visible and viable deterrent by raising the cost for the perpetrators and their sponsors.

The country needs special anti-terror laws and fast-track anti-terror courts, but most of all, it needs the political will to hang culprits. The Constitution provides for the security of every citizen. The police-public partnership has to be a key element of securing cities and States. The time for lighting candles is over. People must demand security. Internal security, indeed national security, must be insulated from vote-bank politics.

Mr. N N Vohra's 1994 report on the nexus between politicians, the underworld mafia and criminals is revealing. Insurgency and terrorism do not fall under the purview of law and order and are beyond the current capacities of the States. The shortfall in police is to be made good by recruiting 400,000 annually for the next three years. The intervention of the Supreme Court in ordering the rollback of *Salwa Judum* will make even military operations justifiable. Remember the Hazratbal siege!

Given these obstacles it is a miracle that India has not become a disturbed state. The dormant unrest in Nagaland has earned the title of the oldest insurgency of the world. But India has shown political steel in subduing terrorism in Punjab and insurgencies in Tripura and Mizoram though in the non-coalition era. If India is to find its place under the Sun, it must have a separate Ministry of Internal Security and set its house in order. India must implement pending reforms to prevent the next terrorist attack.[68]

IRAQ: **War could have been avoided**

The Dalai Lama has said that the US-led war in Iraq could perhaps have been avoided through negotiations with Saddam Hussein.

Responding to a question about the wars in Iraq and Afghanistan, the exiled leader of Tibetan Buddhists said that Hussein was "not such a foolish person to wage War against America. He knew he couldn't win."

The Dalai Lama has criticized the Iraq war effort in the past. He did not offer any solutions to continued violence there. He said, "Now, I don't know".

The Nobel Prize winner appeared at the Cathedral of St John the Divine after wrapping up four days of teaching at Radio City Music Hall. Nearly 2,000 people, including actors Richard Gere and Naomi Watts, filled the cavernous Gothic cathedral to hear the man whom followers believe to be the

---

[68] Ashok K Mehta (2011), " Political will is missing", The Pioneer, July 20, 2011

reincarnation of his predecessors. Billed as a panel discussion on 'Kinship and its Meaning in Our World Today', the event was more of a free-floating ecumenical meditation.

As is his usual practice, the 74-year-old Dalai Lama smiled broadly and chuckled at his own remarks. He said, laughing, "Whether you like it or not, there are different traditions. And no one can change that."

Recalling a 2001 visit to the Roman Catholic shrine of Our Lady of Fatima in Portugal, the Dalai Lama said the statue of the Virgin Mary appeared to smile at him. "Maybe, my eyes, something wrong" But he said that although he is a Buddhist, "Mary I always revere as a symbol of compassion."

The Dalai Lama dropped names of Christian leaders including Mother Teresa, South African Archbishop Desmond Tutu and the Trappist monk Thomas Merton. "His boot was very big, like Army boot," he said of Merton, who died in 1968. "His hat was very shiny."

Joining the Dalai Lama on the panel were two Muslims, American Eboo Patel, a member of the Obama administration's Faith Advisory Council, and Sakena Yacoobi, executive director of the Afghan Institute of Learning, which provides education and health care in Afghanistan.

Patel, the founder of the Chicago-based Interfaith Youth Core, said, "I think one of the great questions of our era is this:

Is religion going to be a barrier of division? Is it going to be a bomb of destruction? Or is it going to be a bridge of cooperation?"

He called the Dalai Lama "perhaps the greatest world leader, the most beloved global citizen, shining a light on the issue of **religion as a bridge of cooperation."** [69]

Was Hiroshima Bombings Necessary?

On August 6, 1945, the world dramatically entered the atomic age: without either warning or precedent, an American plane dropped a single nuclear bomb on the Japanese city of Hiroshima. The explosion utterly destroyed more than four square miles of the city center. About 90,000 people were killed immediately; another 40,000 were injured, many of whom died in protracted agony from radiation sickness. Three days later, a second atomic strike on the city of Nagasaki killed some 37,000 people and injured another 43,000. Together the two bombs eventually killed an estimated 200,000 Japanese civilians.

Between the two bombings, Soviet Russia joined the United States in war against Japan. Under strong US prodding, Stalin broke his regime's 1941 non-aggression treaty with Tokyo. On the same day that Nagasaki was destroyed, Soviet troops began pouring into Manchuria, overwhelming Japanese forces there. Although Soviet participation did little or nothing to change the military outcome of the war, Moscow benefited enormously from joining the conflict.

In a broadcast from Tokyo the next day, August 10, the Japanese government announced its readiness to accept the joint American-British "unconditional surrender" declaration of Potsdam, "with the understanding that the said declaration does not compromise any demand which prejudices the prerogatives of His Majesty as a Sovereign Ruler."

A day later came the American reply, which included these words: "From the moment of surrender the authority of the Emperor and the Japanese

[69] Zee News, New York, Last updated May 24, 2010

Government to rule the State shall be subject to the Supreme Commander of the Allied Powers." Finally, on August 14, the Japanese formally accepted the provisions of the Potsdam declaration, and a "cease fire" was announced. On September 2, Japanese envoys signed the instrument of surrender aboard the US battleship Missouri in Tokyo Bay.

A Beaten Country

Apart from the moral questions involved, were the atomic bombings militarily necessary? By any rational yardstick, they were not. Japan already had been defeated militarily by June 1945. Almost nothing was left of the once mighty Imperial Navy, and Japan's air force had been all but totally destroyed. Against only token opposition, American warplanes ranged at will over the country, and US bombers rained down devastation on her cities, steadily reducing them to rubble.

What was left of Japan's factories and workshops struggled fitfully to turn out weapons and other goods from inadequate raw materials. (Oil supplies had not been available since April.) By July about a quarter of all the houses in Japan had been destroyed, and her transportation system was near collapse. Food had become so scarce that most Japanese were subsisting on a sub-starvation diet.

On the night of March 9-10, 1945, a wave of 300 American bombers struck Tokyo, killing 100,000 people. Dropping nearly 1,700 tons of bombs, the warplanes ravaged much of the capital city, completely burning out 16 square miles and destroying a quarter of a million structures. A million residents were left homeless.

On May 23, eleven weeks later, came the greatest air raid of the Pacific War, when 520 giant B-29 "Super fortress" bombers unleashed 4,500 tons of incendiary bombs on the heart of the already battered Japanese capital. Generating gale-force winds, the exploding incendiaries obliterated Tokyo's commercial center and railway yards, and consumed the Ginza entertainment district. Two days later, on May 25, a second strike of 502 "Super fortress" planes roared low over Tokyo, raining down some 4,000 tons of explosives. Together these two B-29 raids destroyed 56 square miles of the Japanese capital.

Even before the Hiroshima attack, American air force General Curtis Le-May boasted that American bombers were "driving them [Japanese] back to the stone age." Henry H. ("Hap") Arnold, commanding General of the Army air forces, declared in his 1949 memoirs: "It always appeared to us, atomic bomb or no atomic bomb; the Japanese were already on the verge of collapse." The former Japanese Prime Minister Fumimaro Konoye said: Fundamentally, the thing that brought about the determination to make peace was the prolonged bombing by the B-29s.

Japan Seeks Peace

Months before the end of the war, Japan's leaders recognized that defeat was inevitable. In April 1945 a new government headed by Kantaro Suzuki took office with the mission of ending the war. When Germany capitulated in early May, the Japanese understood that the British and Americans would now direct the full fury of their awesome military power exclusively against them.

American officials, having long since broken Japan's secret codes, knew from intercepted messages that the country's leaders were seeking to end the war on terms as favorable as possible. Details of these efforts were known from decoded secret communications between the Foreign Ministry in Tokyo and Japanese diplomats abroad.

In his 1965 study, Atomic Diplomacy: Hiroshima and Potsdam (pp. 107, 108), historian Gar Alperovitz writes:

Although Japanese peace feelers had been sent out as early as September 1944 (and [China's] Chiang Kai-shek had been approached regarding surrender possibilities in December 1944), the real effort to end the war began in the spring of 1945. This effort stressed the role of the Soviet Union.

In mid-April 1945, the [US] Joint Intelligence Committee reported that Japanese leaders were looking for a way to modify the surrender terms to end the war. The State Department was convinced the Emperor was actively seeking a way to stop the fighting.

A Secret Memorandum

It was only after the war that the American public learned about Japan's efforts to bring the conflict to an end. Chicago Tribune reporter Walter Trohan, for example, was obliged by wartime censorship to withhold for seven months one of the most important stories of the war.

In an article that finally appeared August 19, 1945, on the front pages of the Chicago Tribune and the Washington Times-Herald, Trohan revealed that on January 20, 1945, two days prior to his departure for the Yalta meeting with Stalin and Churchill, President Roosevelt received a 40-page memorandum from General Douglas MacArthur outlining five separate surrender overtures from high-level Japanese officials. (Source: Trohan's article vide the Winter 1985-86 Journal, pp. 508-512)

This memo showed that the Japanese were offering surrender terms virtually identical to the ones ultimately accepted by the Americans at the formal surrender ceremony on September 2 -- that is, complete surrender of everything but the person of the Emperor. Specifically, the terms of these peace overtures included:

(a) Complete surrender of all Japanese forces and arms, at home, on island possessions, and in occupied countries.
(b) Occupation of Japan and its possessions by Allied troops under American direction
(c) Japanese relinquishment of all territory seized during the war, as well as Manchuria, Korea and Taiwan.
(d) Regulation of Japanese industry to halt production of any weapons and other tools of war
(e) Release of all prisoners of war and internees
(f) Surrender of designated war criminals

Peace Overtures

In April and May 1945, Japan made three attempts through neutral Sweden and Portugal to bring the war to a peaceful end. On April 7, acting Foreign Minister Mamoru Shigemitsu met with Swedish ambassador Widon Bagge in Tokyo, asking him "to ascertain what peace terms the United States and Britain had in mind." But he emphasized that unconditional surrender was unacceptable, and that "the Emperor must not be touched." Bagge relayed the message to the United States, but Secretary of State Stettinius told the US Ambassador in Sweden to "show no interest or take any initiative in pursuit of the matter." Similar Japanese peace signals through Portugal, on May 7, and again through Sweden, on the 10th, proved similarly fruitless.

By mid-June, six members of Japan's Supreme War Council had secretly charged Foreign Minister Shigenori Togo with the task of approaching Soviet Russia's leaders "with a view to terminating the war if possible by September." On June 22 the Emperor called a meeting of the Supreme War Council, which included the Prime Minister, the Foreign Minister, and the leading military figures. "We have heard enough of this determination of yours to fight to the last soldiers," said Emperor Hirohito. "We wish that you, leaders of Japan, will strive now to study the ways and the means to conclude the war. In doing so, try not to be bound by the decisions you have made in the past."

By early July the US had intercepted messages from Togo to the Japanese ambassador in Moscow, Naotake Sato, showing that the Emperor himself was taking a personal hand in the peace effort, and had directed that the Soviet Union be asked to help end the war. US officials also knew that the key obstacle to ending the war was American insistence on "unconditional surrender," a demand that precluded any negotiations. The Japanese were willing to accept nearly everything, except turning over their semi-divine Emperor. Hirohito, the king of Japan, was the heir of a 2600 year-old dynasty. People of Japan regarded him as a "living God" and who personified the nation. (Until the August 15 radiobroadcast of his surrender announcement, the Japanese people had never heard his voice.) Japanese particularly feared that the Americans would humiliate the Emperor, and even execute him as a war criminal.

On July 12, Hirohito summoned Fumimaro Konoye, who had served as prime minister in 1940-41. Explaining, "It will be necessary to terminate the war without delay," the Emperor said that he wished Konoye to secure peace with the Americans and British through the Soviets. As Prince Konoye later recalled, the Emperor instructed him "to secure peace at any price, notwithstanding its severity."

The next day, July 13, Foreign Minister Shigenori Togo wired ambassador Naotake Sato in Moscow:

"See (Soviet foreign minister) Molotov before his departure for Potsdam ... Convey His Majesty's strong desire to secure a termination of the war ... Unconditional surrender is the only obstacle to peace..."

On July 17, another intercepted Japanese message revealed that although Japan's leaders felt that the unconditional surrender formula involved an unacceptable dishonor, they were convinced that "the demands of the times" made Soviet mediation to terminate the war absolutely essential. Further diplomatic messages indicated that the only condition asked by the Japanese was preservation of "our form of government." The only "difficult point," a July 25 message disclosed, "is the ... formality of unconditional surrender."

Summarizing the messages between Togo and Sato, US naval intelligence said that Japan's leaders, "though still balking at the term unconditional surrender," recognized that the war was lost, and had reached the point where they have "no objection to the restoration of peace on the basis of the (1941) Atlantic Charter." These messages, said Assistant Secretary of the Navy Lewis Strauss, "indeed stipulated only that the integrity of the Japanese Royal Family be preserved."

Navy Secretary James Forrestal termed the intercepted messages "real evidence of a Japanese desire to get out of the war." "With the interception of these messages," notes historian Alperovitz (p. 177), "there could no longer be any real doubt as to the Japanese intentions; the maneuvers were overt and explicit and, most of all, official acts. Koichi Kido, Japan's Lord Privy Seal and a close advisor to the Emperor later affirmed: "Our decision to seek a way out of this war was made in early June before any atomic bomb had been dropped and Russia had not entered the war. It was already our decision."

In spite of this, on July 26 the leaders of the United States and Britain issued the Potsdam declaration, which included this grim ultimatum: "We call upon the government of Japan to proclaim now the unconditional surrender of all Japanese armed forces and to provide proper and adequate assurance of good faith in such action. The alternative for Japan is prompt and utter destruction."

Commenting on this draconian either-or proclamation, British historian J.F.C. Fuller wrote: "Not a word was said about the Emperor, because it would be unacceptable to the propaganda-fed American masses." (A Military History of the Western World [1987], p. 675)

America's leaders understood Japan's desperate position: the Japanese were willing to end the war on any terms, as long as the Emperor was not molested. If the US leadership had not insisted on unconditional surrender -- that is, if they had made clear a willingness to permit the Emperor to remain in place -- the Japanese very likely would have surrendered immediately, thus saving many thousands of lives.

The sad irony is that, as it actually turned out, the American leaders decided anyway to retain the Emperor as a symbol of authority and continuity. They realized, correctly, that Hirohito was useful as a figurehead prop for their own occupation authority in postwar Japan.

Justifications

President Truman steadfastly defended his use of the atomic bomb, claiming that it "saved millions of lives" by bringing the war to a quick end. Justifying his decision, he went so far as to declare: "The world will note that the first atomic bomb was dropped on Hiroshima, a military base. That was because we wished in this first attack to avoid, insofar as possible, the killing of civilians."

This was a preposterous statement. In fact, almost all of the victims were civilians, and the United States Strategic Bombing Survey (issued in 1946) stated in its official report: "Hiroshima and Nagasaki were chosen as targets because of their concentration of activities and population."

If the atomic bomb was dropped to impress the Japanese leaders with the immense destructive power of a new weapon, this could have been accomplished by deploying it on an isolated military base. It was not necessary to destroy a large city. And whatever the justification for the Hiroshima blast, it is much more difficult to defend the second bombing of Nagasaki.

All the same, most Americans accepted, and continue to accept, the official justifications for the bombings. Accustomed to crude propagandistic portrayals of the "Japs" as virtually subhuman beasts, most Americans in 1945 heartily welcomed any new weapon that would wipe out more of the detested Asians, and help avenge the Japanese attack on Pearl Harbor. For the young Americans who were fighting the Japanese in bitter combat, the attitude was "Thank God for the atom bomb." Almost to a man, they were grateful for a weapon whose deployment seemed to end the war and thus allow them to return home.

After the July 1943 firestorm destruction of Hamburg, the mid-February 1945 holocaust of Dresden, and the fire-bombings of Tokyo and other Japanese cities, America's leaders -- as US Army General Leslie Groves later commented -- "were generally inured to the mass killing of civilians." For President Harry Truman, the killing of tens of thousands of Japanese civilians was simply not a consideration in his decision to use the atom bomb.

Critical Voices

Amid the general clamor of enthusiasm, there were some who had grave misgivings. "We are the inheritors to the mantle of Genghis Khan," wrote New York Times editorial writer Hanson Baldwin, "and of all those in history who have justified the use of utter ruthlessness in war." Norman Thomas called Nagasaki "the greatest single atrocity of a very cruel war." Joseph P. Kennedy, father of the President, was similarly appalled.

A leading voice of American Protestantism, Christian Century, strongly condemned the bombings. An editorial entitled "America's Atomic Atrocity" in the issue of August 29, 1945, told readers:

The atomic bomb was used at a time when Japan's navy was sunk, her air force virtually destroyed, her homeland surrounded, her supplies cut off, and our forces poised for the final stroke ... Our leaders seem not to have weighed the moral considerations involved. No sooner was the bomb ready than it was rushed to the front and dropped on two helpless cities ... The atomic bomb can fairly be said to have struck Christianity itself ... The churches of America must dissociate themselves and their faith from this inhuman and reckless act of the American Government.

A leading American Catholic voice, Commonweal, took a similar view. Hiroshima and Nagasaki, the magazine editorialized, "are names for American guilt and shame."

Pope Pius XII likewise condemned the bombings, expressing a view in keeping with the traditional Roman Catholic position that "every act of war directed to the indiscriminate destruction of whole cities or vast areas with their inhabitants is a crime against God and man." The Vatican newspaper

Osservatore Romano commented in its August 7, 1945, issue: "This war provides a catastrophic conclusion. Incredibly this destructive weapon remains as a temptation for posterity, which, we know by bitter experience, learns so little from history."

Authoritative Voices of Dissent

American leaders who were in a position to know the facts did not believe, either at the time or later, that the atomic bombings were needed to end the war.

General Dwight Eisenhower was deeply troubled when Secretary of War Henry L. Stimson informed the decision to use the atomic bomb in mid-July 1945. He disclosed his strong reservations about using the new weapon in his 1963 memoir. (The White House Years: Mandate for Change, 1953-1956, pp. 312-313)

During his (Stimson's) recitation of the relevant facts, I had been conscious of a feeling of depression and so I voiced to him my grave misgivings, first on the basis of my belief that Japan was already defeated and that dropping the bomb was completely unnecessary, and secondly because I thought that our country should avoid shocking world opinion by the use of a weapon whose employment was, I thought, no longer mandatory as a measure to save American lives. It was my belief that Japan was, at that very moment, seeking some way to surrender with a minimum loss of "face."

"The Japanese were ready to surrender and it wasn't necessary to hit them with that awful thing ... I hated to see our country be the first to use such a weapon," Eisenhower said in 1963.

Shortly after "V-J Day," the end of the Pacific war, Brig. General Bonnie Fellers summed up in a memo for General MacArthur: "Neither the atomic bombing nor the entry of the Soviet Union into the war forced Japan's unconditional surrender. She was defeated before either these events took place."

Similarly, Admiral Leahy, Chief of Staff to presidents Roosevelt and Truman, later commented:

It is my opinion that the use of the barbarous weapon at Hiroshima and Nagasaki was of no material assistance in our war against Japan ... The Japanese were already defeated and ready to surrender because of the effective sea blockade and the successful bombing with conventional weapons ... My own feeling was that in being the first to use it, we had adopted an ethical standard common to the barbarians of the Dark Ages. I was not taught to make war in that fashion, and wars cannot be won by destroying women and children.

If the United States had been willing to wait, said Admiral Ernest King, US Chief of Naval Operations, "the effective naval blockade would, in the course of time, have starved the Japanese into submission through lack of oil, rice, medicines, and other essential materials."

Leo Szilard, a Hungarian-born scientist who played a major role in the development of the atomic bomb, argued against its use. "Japan was essentially defeated," he said, and "it would be wrong to attack its cities with atomic bombs as if atomic bombs were simply another military weapon." In a 1960 magazine article, Szilard wrote: "If the Germans had dropped atomic bombs on cities instead of us, we would have defined the dropping of atomic bombs on cities as a war crime, and we would have sentenced the Germans who were guilty of this crime to death at Nuremberg and hanged them."

US Strategic Bombing Survey Verdict

After studying this matter in great detail, the United States Strategic Bombing Survey rejected the notion that Japan gave up because of the atomic bombings. In its authoritative 1946 report, the Survey concluded:

The Hiroshima and Nagasaki bombs did not defeat Japan, nor by the testimony of the enemy leaders who ended the war did they persuade Japan to accept unconditional surrender. The Emperor, the Lord Privy Seal, the Prime Minister, the Foreign Minister, and the Navy Minister had decided as early as May of 1945 that the war should be ended even if it meant acceptance of defeat on allied terms...

The mission of the Suzuki government, appointed 7 April 1945, was to make peace. An appearance of negotiating for terms less onerous than unconditional surrender was maintained in order to contain the military and bureaucratic elements still determined on a final Bushido defense, and perhaps even more importantly to obtain freedom to create peace with a minimum of personal danger and internal obstruction. It seems clear, however, that in extremis the peacemakers would have peace and peace on any terms. This was the gist of advice given to Hirohito by the Jushin in February, the declared conclusion of Kido in April, and the underlying reason for Koiso's fall in April, the specific injunction of the Emperor to Suzuki on becoming premier which was known to all members of his cabinet...

Negotiations for Russia to intercede began the forepart of May 1945 in both Tokyo and Moscow. Konoye, the intended emissary to the Soviets, stated to the Survey that while ostensibly he was to negotiate, he received direct and secret instructions from the Emperor to secure peace at any price, notwithstanding its severity...

It seems clear ... that air supremacy and its later exploitation over Japan proper was the major factor, which determined the timing of Japan's surrender and obviated any need for invasion.

Based on a detailed investigation of all the facts and supported by the testimony of the surviving Japanese leaders involved, it is the Survey's opinion that certainly prior to 31 December 1945 and in all probability prior to 1 November 1945 [the date of the planned American invasion], Japan would have surrendered even if the atomic bombs had not been dropped, even if Russia had not entered the war, and even if no invasion had been planned or contemplated.

Historians' Views

In a 1986 study, historian and journalist Edwin P. Hoyt nailed the "great myth, perpetuated by well-meaning people throughout the world," that "the atomic bomb caused the surrender of Japan." In Japan's War: The Great Pacific Conflict (p. 420), he explained:

The fact is that as far as the Japanese militarists were concerned, the atomic bomb was just another weapon. The two atomic bombs at Hiroshima and Nagasaki were icing on the cake, and did not do as much damage as the firebombing of Japanese cities. The B-29 firebombing campaign had brought the destruction of 3,100,000 homes, leaving 15 million people homeless, and killing about a million of them. It was the ruthless firebombing, and Hirohito's realization that if necessary the Allies would completely destroy Japan and kill every Japanese to achieve "unconditional surrender" that persuaded him to the decision to end the war. The atomic bomb is indeed a fearsome weapon, but it was not the cause of Japan's surrender, even though the myth persists even to this day.

In a trenchant new book, The Decision to Drop the Atomic Bomb (Praeger, 1996), historian Dennis D. Wainstock concludes that the bombings were not only unnecessary, but were based on a vengeful policy that actually harmed American interests. He writes (pp. 124, 132):

By April 1945, Japan's leaders realized that the war was lost. Their main stumbling block to surrender was the United States' insistence on unconditional surrender. They specifically needed to know whether the United States would allow Hirohito to remain on the throne. They feared that the United States would depose him, try him as a war criminal, or even execute him...

Unconditional surrender was a policy of revenge, and it hurt America's national self-interest. It prolonged the war in both Europe and East Asia, and it helped to expand Soviet power in those areas.

General Douglas MacArthur, Commander of US Army forces in the Pacific, stated on numerous occasions before his death that the atomic bomb was completely unnecessary from a military point of view: "My staff was unanimous in believing that Japan was on the point of collapse and surrender."

General Curtis Lemay, who had pioneered precision bombing of Germany and Japan (and who later headed the Strategic Air Command and served as Air Force chief of staff), put it most succinctly: "The atomic bomb had nothing to do with the end of the war."[70]

---

[70] Mark Weber (1997), "Why the Atomic Bombings Could Have Been Avoided? Was Hiroshima Necessary?" The Journal of Historical Review, May-June 1997 (Vol. 16, No. 3), pages 4-11, Institute for Historical Review

Iraq and Iran: Can Try for World Peace

The Iranian president has called for more cooperation between Iran and Iraq, saying that the two can promote peace, justice, and freedom throughout the world. Mahmoud Ahmadinejad made the remarks on Saturday in a meeting with his visiting Iraqi counterpart Jalal Talabani, IRNA reported.

The Iraqi president arrived in Tehran to attend a ceremony celebrating Nowruz, which marks the beginning of the New Year in Iran. Ahmadinejad praised the increasing ties between Tehran and Baghdad, saying the mutual collaboration is very constructive for both countries.

The Iranian president lauded Nowruz as one of the ways to increase cultural relations among the countries who celebrate the ancient festival. Talabani, in his turn, voiced his country's interest for long-term and strategic relations with the Islamic Republic.

The two also discussed the latest regional developments, and underlined the important role of the two neighboring nations in the new political structure of the region. Iran is hosting senior officials from 20 countries at the International Nowruz Celebrations. High-ranking officials from the Persian-speaking states of Tajikistan and Afghanistan will join representatives from the countries that celebrate Nowruz such as Turkmenistan, Azerbaijan, Kazakhstan, Kyrgyzstan, Iraq, Albania, and Turkey.

Kyrgyz First Deputy Prime Minister Omurbek Babanov, Qatari Crown Prince Sheikh Tamim bin Hamad Al Thani and Omani Foreign Minister Youssef bin Alawi bin Abdullah will also attend the event. According to head of the International Affairs Office for Iran's Cultural Heritage, Handicrafts and Tourism Organization Shahbaz Yazdani, participating officials will discuss opening a permanent Nowruz secretariat.[71]

A Changing Balance of Power in Asia

Aaron Friedberg says the U.S. is endangering of losing its predominant status in Asia because of Chinese defense advancements:

After nearly two decades of double digit increases in defense spending, China is beginning to acquire capabilities that could pose a serious challenge to our long-standing position as Asia's preponderant military power. Unless we respond in a prudent and timely fashion, we could find that our commitments to defend our friends and interests in the region are no longer regarded as credible. Over time this could eat away at the foundations of our alliances and diminish our ability to deter conflict.

Friedberg's has been the conventional wisdom in Washington when it comes to the disposition of America's defenses. Like all conventional wisdom, it's high time to reexamine it. It's unnatural for the U.S. to be the predominant military power in Asia and China's investment in her military capabilities is a natural reflection of this and her growing economy. Insofar as it's a "long-standing" U.S. position to be the dominant military power in Asia, it was one born of the Cold War imperative to deny the Soviet Union access to Asia's industrial capacity and out of a justified fear that a re-militarized Japan would go on another imperial rampage. It was, in other words, a means to an end - not an end of itself.

Both of the threats that propelled America's military dominance in Asia are gone. Yet it remains important that the balance of Asian power favors the kind of open, international system in which both America and

---

[71] Press TV, March 26, 2011

Asia have thrived. The real question is whether China poses a threat to that system akin to the Soviet Union. To date I think we can conclude that they are not a threat to world order, and let's credit the Bush administration and Robert Zoellick for working to make China a "stakeholder" in the system.

Still, there's uncertainty as to how China will behave as she accumulates even more power and so it's necessary to hedge. But rather than focus on the unsustainable, unnatural, and undesirable goal of being the lone Asian hegemon, the U.S. should, as Michael Lind suggests, ensure that the combined weight of America and her Asian allies stays well ahead of any state that wishes to overturn the balance to our detriment. As Elbridge Colby has observed, an essential component of this strategy is to incentivize our Asian allies to invest more in their own defenses. That's not done by continuing to divert more American tax dollars to the Pentagon, but by quietly stepping back and forcing our allies to shoulder more responsibility.[72]

Conclusion

Can't a country find clean (corruption free) leaders to lead the country as President or Prime Minister? He/ she should hold the office for only two terms.

Brazil and Turkey are casting off decades of weakness and stepping into strategic vacuums left by failed Western-led strategies in development, climate change and the Iranian nuclear challenge.

If the United Nations would be more powerful and promulgate international laws for cooperation, trade, development and war-free environment with consent of all countries, the world could avoid terrorism, boundary disputes and war.

---

[72] Chris Hardwick, Real Clear Politics, February 20, 2009

The United Nations should forcefully request each country to allocate 10 percent lower budget for defense expenditure in each annual budget.

The companies that manufacture guns, pistols, arms and ammunitions should be de-recognized in all countries to save the humanity.

The boundary disputes must be finalized as on January 1, 2016 or any date to be fixed by the Security Council and General Assembly.

The World would never face WORLD WAR III, but has to meet the challenges of Terrorists, Maoists, and Naxalites. So each country should cooperate with each other to bring these organizations into the peace world. The members of these fighting organizations need justice of human rights.

When food security, right to education, right to healthcare to all people would be possible in all countries, the causes of fighting against governments would be minimized or zeroed and they would come back to the society for happy living with parents and family members. The respective governments should withdraw all pending cases against these youths with sureties of family members.

Each country should give each Maoist, Terrorist or Naxalites a piece of land, where he can have a hut to reside and some monetary help to start retail trade to earn an income.

+++++

Chapter VI

POLITICS AND FOREIGN POLICY

Man needs peace for self and for family members. If a young man feels hungry and cannot fill his belly, his anger increases and he feels that he has been cheated by his near and dear friends. If his friends feel the same problem in his village, they make up mind to steal food or valuables from the rich people in his village.

A hungry youth cancels his hopes and ambitions in life and turns violent. This causes him to join the camps of Terrorist, Maoist or Naxalites. And they become anti-socials and anti-government and exercise revenge against rich people and ultimately rich countries.

So the governments must see that each youth must be associated with services or employment opportunity to earn his bread and butter. This would lead to a safe area of life. They can earn their livelihood. Their problems would be solved and they would the assets of the country and the world.

This episode explains that the policy adopted by the respective government is at fault in many countries. It is because politics, political parties and political leaders are corrupt, inefficient and the government machinery is more corrupt and self-centered. They are worried to amass wealth for their future generations, but they forget the hungry people of the world. The world has enough food for each man, but the state is unable to distribute food among all.

The politicians must be honest, knowledgeable and people friendly. Politics should not be treated as a trade, business or profession.

It is late but there is still time to have friendship with all countries. But, it is not so easy a task. All the countries are making friendship only for defense collaborations. The developing countries are more worried for availing high amount finance for rural development. And these leaders are pocketing more funds in their personal accounts than investing in a productive way.

If the foreign policy of each country should be for cooperation in food production, rural health and education, each one would get food, education and enjoy health security. Let us discuss how politics could award peace to all.

Wars are not caused by people and the soldiers.

Wars are initiated by the governments and retaliated by governments. So an intelligent, highly educated, woman politician should be External Affairs Minister of each country to do justice to the people and country. And, it is possible.

The USA:
Foreign Policy and the Crisis Mentality

In his *Crisis* papers of the American Revolution, Thomas Paine observed: "it is surprising to see how rapidly a panic will sometimes run through a country." Yet Paine was so fearful of the tendency of men to become indifferent or weary in times of crisis and conflict that he believed even panics produce "as much good as hurt."

If he were permitted to review our own time, he would doubtless conclude that the problem of maintaining a proper course between panic and complacency has taken on new dimensions, for the thirteen colonies which leveled their muskets against the established order have evolved into the world's mightiest power in a highly dangerous nuclear age. This is a responsibility, which demands a rare capacity to distinguish between fundamental forces at work around the globe and localized crises of uncertain significance.

But there is a disturbing American tendency to overreact to certain ideological and military factors while overlooking issues of vastly greater relevance to our safety and welfare. A civil insurrection in Santo Domingo or Vietnam is dramatic, but what is its significance compared with such quiet challenges as the proliferation of nuclear weapons, the surging of nationalism and social upheavals in the developing world, or the mounting crisis of hunger and population? What, too, is the relationship of the quality and strength of our own society to our position in the world? How will the world see us if we succeed in pacifying Vietnam but fail to pacify Chicago?

Many Americans, having grown impatient with the frustrations of the cold war, see each international tension as an urgent crisis calling for a direct and decisive attack on the enemy. Moreover, there must be no halfway measures: "Either get in or get out!" Those who suggest that there may be a proper limit to American power are branded as "neo-isolationists." A preference for the peacekeeping actions of the United Nations over a freewheeling unilateral interventionism is, for example, a sure sign of "neo-isolationism."

I believe that, in fact, we are in danger of seeing the isolationists of the 1920s and 1930s replaced by the neo-imperialists, who somehow imagine that the United States has a mandate to impose an American solution, the world around. Those who see the United States in this role not only want U.S. police action in each trouble spot, but with decisive speed. The old isolationists and the new imperialists may be cut from the same cloth in that both look with disdain on the claims of the international community in contrast with the American way.

For example, the neo-imperialists' solution to the long, inconclusive struggle in Vietnam is a crushing military onslaught. They reject the outlook expressed not so long ago by General Maxwell Taylor when, as ambassador to Saigon, he said that the issue here is "very largely a political, economic, and psychological problem." They would prefer the approach of former Senator Goldwater, who said of Vietnam: "I would turn to my Joint Chiefs of Staff and say: 'Fellows, we made the decision to win. Now it's your problem.'"

In this scheme of things, the Soviet Union and Mainland China are viewed not as major world powers with which we must live, but as diabolical conspiracies that sooner or later we must face in battle. The answer to other lesser threats, such as Fidel Castro, is the U.S. Marine Corps. If a political rebellion occurs in the Dominican Republic, send in American troops and worry about such international niceties as the UN and the OAS later. The answer to the Berlin problem is simple: "Tear down the wall."

There are doubtless many explanations for the crisis outlook.

For one thing, America is a comparatively new country that has been largely separated from the turmoil of world politics for most of our history. During the nineteenth century, we relied on the British to put out the fires that flared from time to time in out-of-the-way places. We were free to concentrate on the development of our own economy and institutions. Pulled into World War I by the course of events, we swung back to an even more ardent isolationist course in the 1920s and 1930s. It is thus not surprising that faced with a vastly greater international involvement after World War II, we have frequently overreacted to incidents that an older, more mature society would have regarded as "business as usual."

Second, many Americans have not assimilated a sense of the world's diversity, nor do we look at events from an international vantage point. The older nations of Europe, steeped in the maelstrom of continental politics and with a century or more of colonial experience in every corner of the globe, have acquired a cosmopolitan view of the world. But when a political coup is attempted against an unpopular government in the Dominican Republic, or student rioting changes government policies in Japan, or De Gaulle seeks the leadership of Europe after liquidating hopeless French ventures in Asia and Africa, or a guerrilla movement threatens to bring down a much more generously armed American-backed regime in Saigon, we are unable to equate these events with our own experience. The revolution in mass communications instantly brings such developments into our living rooms, but there has been no corresponding increase in our capacity to evaluate the swift changes of our convulsive age.

Communist Devils

A third explanation of our tendency to react strongly to events is the unique power of Communism (as a general menace) and of the Soviet Union or China or Cuba or North Vietnam (as the precise devil) to challenge a variety of deeply felt American dreams and values at their core. For the democratically oriented American public, these are evil forces, which deny open political discussion, religious freedom, bona fide elections, and a framework of law and legal process. For those businessmen to whom a large portion of the world represents an essential area for expansion, Communism presents a dangerous challenge to capitalist ground rules. For Americans who dream of the United States exercising a dominant role in potentially unlimited areas of world development, to whom Theodore Roosevelt, and later, Henry Luce and others, have spoken, Moscow, Peking, Havana, and Hanoi are challenges to the American Century. And finally, for that sizable and vociferous minority whose views are premised on the assumption that conspiracies and dark alien powers sway world affairs--to which the late Senator Joseph McCarthy was the Angel Gabriel--Communist propaganda is tailor-made.

Thus, the American consensus against Communism--no matter the variety--is rooted in a very real set of challenges and denials. It is not easily dismissed as "hysteria." Its deep traditional sources lead to an almost irresistible identification of any event related to Communism as a crisis, a dire and fundamental threat to basic values. Our crisis tendency has been given additional force by the nature of our political leadership and our two-party political dialogue, especially since 1950.

In the years immediately following World War II, thanks to the leadership of men such as the late Senator Vandenberg, our foreign policy was conducted in a bipartisan manner largely free from political rancor and partisan duels. This was the period, which launched the United Nations, the Marshall Plan, Point IV, and the North Atlantic Treaty Organization.

But with the triumph of Communism in China in 1949, the North Korean attack of 1950, and the breaking of our nuclear monopoly by the Soviet Union, the comparative confidence and calm of post-war American foreign policy were shattered. The first strains of the postwar world were beginning to wear on the American public even before the Korean conflict.

It was these cold-war tensions, which set the stage for the poisoning of American political life by the late Senator McCarthy in the early 1950s. Many government officials and politicians still find it expedient to demonstrate their "Americanism" by frequent outbursts of rhetoric directed at the Communist enemy. The two political parties, having generally agreed on basic foreign policy objectives, wage a recurring battle over which party is taking the harder line against the Communists.

Fuel on the Fire

Foreign policy, more mysterious and remote than domestic issues, is ideal grist for the political mill. The average citizen knows enough about social security to be somewhat invulnerable to loose charges against the program. But a prediction of disaster in the Caribbean based on alleged evil in high places is beyond the capacity of our citizens to evaluate.

This kind of exercise has been a major cause of the crisis mentality. Having agreed for years on basic foreign policy assumptions and especially the containment of Communism, our political-party leaders has found it necessary to devise other areas of combat. Each side knows that it must capitalize quickly on even inconsequential events lest the opposition do so first with telling political results. Politicians out of power have found it expedient interpret each international incident as a mortal danger to the republic. Politicians in power must demonstrate that they are taking swift and forceful steps to save the nation from disaster.

No doubt the late President Kennedy benefited in the 1960 presidential campaign from the fact that Castro had come to power during a Republican Administration while at the same time the Russians were moving ahead of us in the missile race. Once in power, the new President was under pressure to take a hard, activist line on Cuba. Even after the nuclear showdown of October 1962, when the Russian missiles were withdrawn from Cuba--a sensational cold-war victory the United States--some politicians worked overtime to keep the crisis boiling. Any step to ease tension was quickly branded as a softening resolve.

American domestic political considerations have probably motivated our deepening involvement in Vietnam since the 1950s as much as any other factor. The Republicans accused the Democrats of "losing" China to the Communists in the 1940s; Secretary of State Dulles did not want to "lose" Southeast Asia in the 1950s and see the tables reversed. Whatever else was prudent, it was safest in terms of domestic politics to take a tough, militaristic stand toward revolutionary Asian leaders while embracing the comfortable despotisms.

Looking back on the Bay of Tonkin incidents of August, 1964, one wonders if a crisis was manufactured by the Administration to justify politically popular aerial reprisal against Hanoi backed by a strongly worded congressional resolution--all of this at the beginning of a national election when Administration firmness was being questioned by the political challenger.

Again in February 1965, American planes began bombing in both North and South Vietnam in response to nighttime Viet Cong attack that killed several Americans in one of our barracks near Pleiku. Senator Goldwater had earned a "trigger-happy" label in 1964 for recommending the use of American bombers in Vietnam, but Administration spokesmen rationalized the bombing in 1965 by dramatic references to the Viet Congo's dastardly "sneak attack"--implying that enemy troops should attack only in broad daylight after a fair warning. Apparently our spokesmen had forgotten our schoolboy pride in George Washington's "sneak attack" on the British after he and his rebel forces stole across the Delaware River.

An American Illusion

The meagerness of genuine discussion about fundamental issues and our tendency to magnify minor incidents have caused us to miss many opportunities for constructive new initiatives both at home and abroad. We have, for example, concentrated too heavily and too long on an all-out military response to the international challenge while neglecting the economic, political, and moral sources of our strength. Frequently we have confused means with ends and then argued about those means with all the passion ordinarily reserved for sacred principles. The crisis mentality and the emphasis on means always call for more and bigger weapons. The crisis addict becomes impatient when it is suggested that a nation's strength is measured as much by the quality of its schools, the health of its citizens, the vigor of its economy, and the treatment of minorities as by the size of its weapons. He lacks the perspective to realize that the steady, peaceful development of Asia, Africa, and Latin America is of far greater significance to American security than the political color of future regimes in Vietnam or in the Dominican Republic.

Foreign aid for underdeveloped countries is a favorite target of crisis-oriented citizens and legislators, who are much more comfortable appropriating $50 billion annually for arms than $2 billion for economic development. The results of foreign aid are too slow to satisfy the mind dominated by a sense of crisis. Indeed, even an economic boycott (Cuba) or limited military action (Korea and Vietnam) is frustrating and unsatisfying to the crisis-prone individual, who would prefer to "clean up the mess" overnight.

Foreign aid bills have been presented to Congress year after year as a stopgap against the spread of Communism rather than as an investment in social and economic development. Poverty-stricken countries have been encouraged by shipment of American arms to build military machines as part of "the free world" defense against Communist aggression. But in the summer of 1965, Pakistan threw its American-supplied Patton tanks into war with India's American-supplied Sherman tanks. The final irony came when the Soviet Union, theoretically a potential target of the tanks, mediated an end to the war. This was scarcely a convincing demonstration of U.S. wisdom in determining other countries' needs.

While recognizing our responsibility to influence world affairs in the direction of peaceful development as best we can, we will do well to heed D.W. Brogan's warning of "the illusion of American omnipotence."

There is a tendency for some Americans to assume that every distressing situation, no matter how remote, is the result of a failure on our part. During the late 1940s and early 1950s, we talked about "losing China," as though we had somehow been in command of China's destiny. But as Professor Brogan has reminded us, "A great many things happen in the world regardless of whether the American people wish them or not." For example, we ought to take every reasonable step to ensure the success of the Alliance for Progress and the defeat of Castro's in Latin America, but we must also recognize that the success of these efforts depends more on decisions that are made in Latin-American capitals than in Washington.

Furthermore, we must be willing to look at our own view of the world with at least as critical an eye as we apply to the views of others. Those who have suggested that college students protesting our Vietnam policy should be automatically drafted are, in effect, calling for a moratorium on conscience and freedom. It would be ironic indeed to surrender liberty in America in the name of its advancement in Vietnam. Instead of intimidating the public dissenter, we ought to welcome his independence and give his views a careful hearing. Instead of promoting the government official who plays it safe by avoiding thoughts that might irritate his superiors; we ought to encourage intellectual integrity and moral courage as the most precious qualities of the public servant.

Stop, Look, and Listen

If we are to strengthen our position in the world, we must be willing to look carefully and critically at all foreign policy assumptions, including our present course in Southeast Asia and our insistence that the world's largest nation be excluded from the United Nations.

We can well afford to listen thoughtfully to the views of experienced leaders abroad, including General de Gaulle, despite his peculiar faculty for irritating Washington. The French successfully and gracefully terminated self-defeating campaigns in Southeast Asia and North Africa; in the process they might have gained certain insights that are worth our evaluation.

America has achieved a position of power and influence in the world that is unprecedented. We have often used that power generously and courageously, perhaps more than any other nation of our age. I have no doubt had our capacity to respond effectively to a genuine crisis that calls for vigorous and decisive action. I should like to believe that we would also develop a talent for discovering and responding rationally to the underlying forces at work in our time. But to those innumerable tensions, struggles, and incidents of the future that we neither can nor should control, I hope we will manifest a measure of Ralph Waldo Emerson's wisdom: "Let him not quit his belief that a popgun is a popgun, though the ancient and honorable of the earth affirm it to be the crack of doom." [73]

The USA:

Foreign Policy of Democratic Party

Iraq: Seldom if ever has the hostility between academics and the U.S. president been so pronounced. Of course, political scientists always seem to complain about the occupant of the White House, and Republicans fare worse than Democrats: Herbert Hoover was called callous, Dwight Eisenhower a dunce, Richard Nixon evil, Ronald Reagan dangerous, and George H.W. Bush out of touch. But professors have consigned George W.

---

[73] George McGovern (1967), " Foreign Policy and the Crisis Mentality", The Atlantic Monthly; January 1967; Volume 219, No. 1; pages 55-57

Bush to a special circle of their presidential hell. And the White House seems to return the sentiment.

According to the academics, Bush's chief transgressions have had to do with foreign policy, especially the Iraq war -- a mess that could have been avoided if only the president and his advisers had paid more attention to those who devote their lives to studying international relations.

The irony of this argument is that few other presidents -- certainly none since Woodrow Wilson, a former president of the American Political Science Association, scribbled away in the Oval Office -- have tied their foreign policies more explicitly to the work of social science. The defining act of Bush's presidency was grounded in a theory that the political scientist Jack Levy once declared was "as close as anything we have to an empirical law in international relations," namely, that democracies do not fight one another.

The theory, which originated in the work of the eighteenth-century philosopher Immanuel Kant and was refined in the 1970s and 1980s by several researchers working independently, has, since the 1990s, been one of the hottest research areas in international relations. Although some skeptics remain and no one agrees about why exactly it works, most academics now share the belief that democracies have indeed made a separate peace. What is more, much research suggests that they are also unusually likely to sign and honor international agreements to become economically interdependent.

The administrations of Presidents George H.W. Bush and Bill Clinton made frequent appeals to the theory in public, and it seems to have informed their support for democratization in former communist lands and in Haiti. The current Bush administration, however, has gone much further in its faith in the idea, betting the farm that the theory holds and will help Washington achieve a peaceful, stable, and prosperous Muslim world as, over time, Iraq's neighbors, following Iraq's example, democratize. The United States' real motives for attacking Iraq may have been complex, but "regime change" -- the replacement of Saddam Hussein's gruesome tyranny with a democracy -- was central to Washington's rhetoric by the time it began bombing Baghdad in March 2003.

Why has a president who set his defining policy around one of political science's crown jewels come in for so much venom from the same academics who endorse the idea? After all, a host of peer-reviewed journal articles have implicitly supported the president's claim that a democratic Iraq would not threaten the United States or Israel, develop weapons of mass destruction, or sponsor terrorism. Are professors simply perpetual critics who refuse to take responsibility for the consequences of their ideas? Or does Bush hatred trump social science?

The Bush administration's desire to break with its predecessors and alter the authoritarian status quo in the Middle East was admirable. But the White House got its science wrong, or at least not completely right: the democratic peace theory does not dictate that the United States can or should remake Iraq into a democracy. In Electing to Fight: Why Emerging Democracies Go to War, the veteran political scientists Edward Mansfield and Jack Snyder make two critical points. Not only is turning authoritarian countries into democracies extremely difficult, much more so than the administration seems to have anticipated. The Middle East could also become a much more dangerous place if Washington and the rest of the world settle for a merely semi-democratic regime in Baghdad. Such an Iraq, Mansfield and Snyder imply, would be uncommonly likely to start wars -- a bull in the Middle Eastern china shop.

Unfortunately, such an Iraq may also be just what we are likely to end up with.

Illiberal Democracies: At first glance, the realists' critique of the Iraq war is easier to understand than that of the democratic peace theorists. Indeed, realism -- which holds that a country's type of government has no systematic effects on its foreign policy -- is enjoying a revival in Washington these days, precisely because of the war. According to the realists, the best way to have dealt with Saddam would have been not to overthrow him but to use coercive bargaining: to have threatened him with annihilation, for example, if he ever used nuclear weapons.

Even the democratic peace theory, however, does not necessarily prescribe the use of force to transform despotisms such as Iraq into democracies. Indeed, by itself, the argument that democracies do not fight one another does not have any practical implications for the foreign policymaker. It needs an additional or minor premise, such as "the United States can make Iraq into a democracy at an acceptable cost." And it is precisely this minor premise about which the academy has been skeptical. No scholarly consensus exists on how countries become democratic, and the literature is equally murky on the costs to the United States of trying to force them to be free.

This last part of the puzzle is even more complicated than it first appears. Enter Mansfield and Snyder, who have been contributing to the democratic peace debate for a decade. Their thesis, first published in 1995, is that although mature democracies do not fight one another, democratizing states -- those in transition from authoritarianism to democracy -- do, and are even more prone to war than authoritarian regimes. Now, in Electing to Fight, the authors have refined their argument. As they outline in the book, not only are "incomplete democratizing" states --

those that develop democratic institutions in the wrong order -- unlikely ever to complete the transition to democracy; they are also especially bellicose.

According to Mansfield and Snyder, in countries that have recently started to hold free elections but that lack the proper mechanisms for accountability (institutions such as an independent judiciary, civilian control of the military, and protections for opposition parties and the press), politicians have incentives to pursue policies that make it more likely that their countries will start wars. In such places, politicians know they can mobilize support by demanding territory or other spoils from foreign countries and by nurturing grievances against outsiders. As a result, they push for extraordinarily belligerent policies. Even states that develop democratic institutions in the right order -- adopting the rule of law before holding elections -- are very aggressive in the early years of their transitions, although they are less so than the first group and more likely to eventually turn into full democracies.

Of course, politicians in mature democracies are also often tempted to use nationalism and xenophobic rhetoric to buttress their domestic power. In such cases, however, they are usually restrained by institutionalized mechanisms of accountability. Knowing that if they lead the country into a military defeat or quagmire they may be punished at the next election, politicians in such states are less likely to advocate a risky war. In democratizing states, by contrast, politicians know that they are insulated from the impact of bad policies: if a war goes badly, for example, they can declare a state of emergency, suspend elections, and censor the press, and so on. Politicians in such states also tend to fear their militaries, which often crave foreign enemies and will overthrow civilian governments that do not share their goals. Combined, these factors can make the temptation to attack another state irresistible.

Mansfield and Snyder present both quantitative and case-study support for their theory. Using rigorous statistical methods, the authors show that since 1815, democratizing states have indeed been more prone to start wars than either democracies or authoritarian regimes. Categorizing transitions according to whether they ended in full democracies (as in the U.S. case) or in partial ones (as in Germany in 1871-1918 or Pakistan throughout its history), the authors find that in the early years of democratic transitions, partial democracies -- especially those that get their institutions in the wrong order -- are indeed significantly more likely to initiate wars. Mansfield and Snyder then provide several succinct stories of democratizing states that did in fact go to war, such as the France of Napoleon III (1852-70), Serbia between 1877 and 1914, Ethiopia and Eritrea between 1998 and 2000, and Pakistan from 1947 to the present. In most of these cases, the authors find what they expect: in these democratizing states, domestic political competition was intense. Politicians, vying for power, appeased domestic hard-liners by resorting to nationalistic appeals that vilified foreigners, and these policies often led to wars that were not in the countries' strategic interests.

Although their argument would have been strengthened by a few comparative studies of democratizing states avoiding war and of full democracies and authoritarian states starting wars, Mansfield and Snyder are persuasive. In part this is because they carefully circumscribe their claims. They acknowledge that some cases are "false positives," that is, wars started by states that have wrongly been classified as democratizing, such as the Iran-Iraq War, started by Iraq in 1980. They also answer the most likely objections to their argument. Some skeptics, for example, might counter that Mansfield and Snyder get the causality reversed: it is war or the threat of it that prevents states from becoming mature democracies. Others might argue that democratizing states become involved in more wars simply because their internal instability tempts foreign states to attack them -- in other words, that democratizers are more sinned against than sinning. Analyzing data from 1816 through 1992, Mansfield and Snyder put paid to these alternative explanations. Bad domestic institutions usually precede wars, rather than vice versa, and democratizing states usually do the attacking.

Where does Electing to Fight leave realism, the dominant theory of international conflict? The quantitative data support the realist claims that major powers are more likely to go to war than minor ones and that the more equal are the great powers, the more likely are wars among them. But democratization makes war more likely even after one takes these factors into account. Furthermore, the case studies suggest that democratizing states very often lose more than they gain from the wars they begin, which implies that they do not respond to international incentives as rationally as realism would expect. That said, notwithstanding its preference for viewing states from the inside, the Mansfield-Snyder theory is still "realist" in the general sense that it assumes that politicians and other actors are rationally self-interested. Their self-interest simply involves building and maintaining domestic power as well as external security -- and sometimes trading some of the latter in order to gain the former.

The authors' conclusions for foreign policy are straightforward. The United States and other international actors should continue to promote democracy, but they must strive to help democratizing states implement reforms in the correct order. In particular, popular elections ought not to precede the building of institutions that will check the baleful incentives for politicians to call for war. Mansfield and Snyder are unsparing toward well-intentioned organizations that have pressured authoritarian governments to rush to elections in the past -- often with disastrous consequences. As the authors show, for example, it was organizations such as the World Bank and the National Democratic Institute that pushed Burundi and Rwanda to increase popular sovereignty in the early 1990s -- pressure that, as Mansfield and Snyder argue, helped set off a chain of events that led to genocide. Acknowledging their intellectual debt to writers such as Samuel Huntington (particularly his 1968 book Political Order in Changing Societies) and Fareed Zakaria, Mansfield and Snyder have written a deeply conservative book. Sounding like Edmund Burke on the French Revolution but substituting statistics and measured prose for rhetorical power, the authors counsel against abruptly empowering people, since premature elections may well usher in domestic upheavals that thrust the state outward against its neighbors.

Back in Baghdad: This brings the conversation back to Iraq and in particular the notion that the United States can turn it into a democracy at an acceptable cost. In effect, Mansfield and Snyder have raised the estimate of these costs by pointing out one other reason this effort may fail -- a reason that few seem to have thought of. Forget for a moment the harrowing possibility of a Sunni-Shiite-Kurdish civil war in Iraq. Set aside the prospect of a Shiite-dominated state aligning itself with Iran, Syria, and Lebanon's Hezbollah. What if, following the departure of U.S. troops, Iraq holds together but as an incomplete democratizer, with broad suffrage but anemic state institutions? Such an Iraq might well treat its own citizens better than the Baathist regime did. Its treatment of its neighbors, however, might be just as bad.

Although Saddam was an unusually bellicose and reckless tyrant, attacking Iran in 1980 and Kuwait in 1990 and engaging in foolish brinkmanship with the United States, as Mansfield and Snyder imply, a democratic Iraq may be no less bellicose and reckless. In the near future, intensely competitive elites there -- secularists, leftists, moderates, and both Shiite and Sunni Islamists -- could compete for popularity by stirring up nationalism against one or more of Iraq's neighbors. And Iraq lives in a dangerous neighborhood. Already, Iraqi Shiite parties have been critical of Sunni-dominated Jordan; Iraqi Sunni parties, of Shiite-dominated Iran; and Iraqi Kurdish parties, of Turkey.

One hopes that the White House contemplated this scenario prior to March 2003. Whether it did or not, the possibility must be considered now, by U.S. civilian and military leaders, academics, and U.S. allies who agree with those academics. If Mansfield and Snyder are correct about the bellicose tendencies of young, incompletely democratized states, the stakes of Iraq's transition are higher than most have supposed. They are high enough, in fact, that those who called so loudly in the 1990s for an end to UN sanctions because Iraqis were dying but who are silent about the Iraqis who are dying now ought to reconsider their proud aloofness from the war. An aggressive Iraq, prone to attack Kuwait, Iran, Saudi Arabia, Syria, or Israel, is in no one's interest. The odds may be long that Iraq will ever turn into a mature democracy of the sort envisaged by the Bush administration. But those odds are lengthened by the refusal of those states in Europe and the Middle East that could make a difference actually to do so.[74]

---

[74] John M. Owen IV (2005), "Who says Democracies Don't Fight?" University of virginia, November/December 2005

The USA:
A Future Foreign Policy

In Tim Pawlenty's speech before the Council on Foreign Relations, the former Minnesota governor criticized America's decades old policy of cozying up to dictators in the Middle East, castigated America's behavior abroad during the Obama Administration -- it's allegedly wrong on Israel, Egypt, Libya, Tunisia, Syria, Saudi Arabia, Palestine, and Afghanistan and followed up with this non-sequester: "America is exceptional, and we have the moral clarity to lead the world."

It's an incoherent position: it cannot be that America wrongly propped up Middle Eastern and North African dictators over many decades, that its current policy is terribly wrongheaded, and that our elected leaders are uniquely possessed of the moral clarity to get things right in those regions. Pawlenty implicitly admits as much. "America already has one political party devoted to decline, retrenchment, and withdrawal," he notes. "It does not need a second one." In other words, he thinks that all Democrats and some Republicans have wrongheaded views about America's role in the world. It sure seems like what Pawlenty actually believes is that if elected; he would possess the moral clarity to lead the world.

Say that he's right. It's theoretically possible that Pres. Pawlenty would be the best leader the world has ever had. Even if that were true, however, his worldview would be obviously flawed for this reason: the U.S. is inevitably going to elect Democrats to the presidency, and other times it's going to elect Republicans with whom Pawlenty disagrees. Indeed, recent polls cast doubt on the likelihood that T-Paw is going to be elected in 2012. You'd think a guy who describes our current foreign policy as ineffective and incoherent -- someone who says our Middle East policy has been flawed for 60 years -- would argue for a more limited American role (you know, as a hedge in case voters don't wind up stocking the White House with right-thinking Republicans for the rest of time).

After what he describes as 60 years of failure in the region, Pawlenty continues to insist that more active engagement in North Africa and the Middle East is the right way forward. It's a foreign policy outlook he shares with Senators John McCain and Lindsey Graham, as my colleague Jeffrey Goldberg noted in a recent column. And with other conservatives who imagine that professing a belief in American exceptional is a coherent foreign policy posture. I've got a question for those hawks.

On the one hand, you assert that America is an exceptional nation, institutionally and morally superior to all others. It is for this reason that our global interventions and international supremacy are both necessary and justified. At the same time, many of you favor a muscular executive who is empowered to unilaterally wage war without first getting the approval of Congress.

Even if we accept that America is exceptional -- that its people and its institutions are uniquely suited to moral global leadership -- why would it follow that the particular person who occupies the White House possesses those same qualities? Wouldn't it be possible for a man unworthy of the presidency to take office, and lead exceptional America astray in ways that are unwise and immoral? Isn't it your contention that President Obama is doing just that thing?

If you believe that even unwise presidents who pursue immoral policies are empowered to wage war before receiving Congressional approval, and that they're appropriately scene as predominating on foreign policy matters generally, then how is the exceptional of America generally relevant to the question of whether America is fit to lead the world? After all, in your view, it's the occupant of that one office, rather than the people and their elected representatives that shapes foreign policy. Furthermore, you think the American people erred when it last selected that person. Doesn't it follow, Mr. Pawlenty and other hawks that agree with him, that your rhetoric fails on its own terms?[75]

In short, its core flaw: a belief that America has been wrong in the past, is wrong in the present, and alone knows what's best for the future.

An Upbeat View of America's 'Bad' Year

Among global big thinkers, never a bashful crowd, the notion of a United States in decline has become conventional wisdom. In late 2011, this narrative has crescendo, with experts arguing that China has surpassed the United States economically, Niall Ferguson declaring that we are at "the end of 500 years of Western predominance" and The National Interest proclaiming "the end of the American era." Even the National Intelligence Council's coming Global Trends 2030 study reportedly assumes an America in decline.

As 2011 draws to a close, the U.S. military's exit from Iraq and challenges in Afghanistan along with American vulnerability to the European crisis provide further confirmation of the decline narrative.

We agree with some of these views. The United States has neither the willingness nor the capability to provide the kind of global leadership that it has provided in the past several decades, and other countries are increasingly less willing to follow America's lead.

---

75 Conor Friedersdorf (2011), "Tim Pawlenty's Foreign-Policy Speech Refutes Itself", The Atlantic, June 29, 2011

But the conventional wisdom obscures as much as it reveals. Specifically, the declines overlook the inconvenient truth that global power is relative. And comparing America's year to that of our present and potential adversaries paints an interesting picture: 2011 was not the year when the United States fell off the wagon. Instead, a look back at the past 12 months suggests that U.S. power is more resilient than the narrative of inevitable decline portrays.

Take Al Qaeda, our most consistent adversary (by their definition and ours) since the 9/11 attacks. Despite some severe missteps, we have in 10 years degraded Al Qaeda's capabilities to the point that they are having difficulty mounting attacks against significant targets. In 2011, the United States killed Al Qaeda's most effective propagandist, Anwar al-Awlaki; its operating chief, Atiyah Abd al-Rahman; and of course its founder, chief executive and spiritual leader, Osama bin Laden. Moreover, the Arab Spring undercut the notion that political change in the Middle East requires the violent jihad that Bin Laden spent his career espousing.

The fight against extremist Islam is an impossible one in which to declare success. Yet the fact remains that while Al Qaeda began the War on Terror with a horrific assault on the foremost symbols of U.S. economic and military power, it leaves 2011 effectively leaderless, rudderless and reduced to boasting about kidnapping defenseless U.S. aid workers.

Iran's leaders also exit 2011 in worse shape than they entered it. Early in the year, they viewed the demise of Middle Eastern potentates as accelerating their rise to regional dominance. Turkish anger over the Mavi Marmara incident continued to draw Ankara closer to Tehran. Saudi anger at the perceived lack of U.S. support for Egypt's Hosni Mubarak seemed to threaten a permanent rupture in the U.S. relationship with a key ally, and Iran assumed that it would be the beneficiary of declining American influence in the Arab World.

But the Arab Spring has unfolded very differently. Iran's closest, most vital, and in some ways only Arab ally, Syria's Bashar al-Assad, ends the year leading an embattled, isolated regime facing a combination of civil war and economic sanctions that his government is unlikely to survive. Iran's relationship with Turkey has deteriorated sharply, and, along with Saudi Arabia, Ankara has in fact drawn closer to the United States. Indeed, the nascent U.S.-Turkey-Saudi troika is one of the most important but least noticed trends of the past few months.

Combined with another year without nuclear weapons — the program apparently thwarted significantly by covert operations — and a tightening vise of economic sanctions, these events have left Iran's leaders disoriented. After years of growing consensus, Iran's elites are now increasingly fragmented and at one another's throats.

Moreover, Tehran spent the past few months engaged in a stunning series of blunders: plotting with Mexican drug dealers to assassinate the Saudi ambassador to the United States and allowing regime supporters to storm the British Embassy in Tehran, the combination of which has re-energized global efforts to squeeze Iran financially. The assumption that Iran is the emerging regional power has shattered.

China, which most of the declines identify as America's greatest future rival, has likewise had a difficult 2011. With U.S. willingness to lead receding, the international spotlight has fallen on Beijing. And on every issue — the euro zone crisis, climate change and rebalancing the global economy — China has declined to take the lead, to criticism and dismay at home and abroad.

Beijing has failed to reconcile rising domestic nationalism with assuaging its neighbors' increasing alarm over Chinese economic sustainability and strategic hegemony. China's miscalculations in Northeast and Southeast Asia have allowed the United States to reassert traditional alliances in the region (with Japan and South Korea), establish new beachheads (placing a permanent U.S. Marine Corps presence in Australia), and create a process and institutions (the Trans-Pacific Partnership) for a balanced Asia–Pacific regional architecture, rather than one dominated by the Middle Kingdom.

Compared to this, 2011 has not been a bad year for America. It is a stretch to call the Iraq war a victory, but the endgame in the Afghan quagmire is slowly coming into focus. And for all our fiscal problems, global funding has to flow somewhere, and our capital markets are still unparalleled. China won't internationalize the renminbi, the euro is fragile and gold is not a country. As a result, the dollar remains the world's reserve currency, and U.S. Treasury bills the global financial safe haven.

This will inevitably change in the long term, but not for quite some time. The uni -polar moment is over. But for 2011 at least, the world order has remained the United States and the rest.[76]

The USA: **Shame on Them**

The Republicans are playing a cynical political game with hugely high economic stakes. IN THREE weeks,

---

[76] Ian Bremmer and David F Gordon (2011), "An Upbeat View of America's 'Bad' Year", The New York Times, Opinion Page, December 27, 2011

if there is no political deal, the American government will go into default. Not, one must pray, on its sovereign debt. But the country will have to stop paying someone: perhaps pensioners, or government suppliers, or soldiers. That would be damaging enough at a time of economic fragility. And the longer such a default went on, the greater the risk of provoking a genuine bond crisis would become.

There is no good economic reason why this should be happening. America's net indebtedness is a perfectly affordable 65 percent of GDP, and throughout the past three years of recession and tepid recovery investors have been more than happy to go on lending to the federal government. The current problems, rather, are political. Under America's elaborate separation of powers, Congress must authorise any extension of the debt ceiling, which now stands at $14.3 trillion. Back in May the government bumped up against that limit, but various accounting dodges have been used to keep funds flowing. It is now reckoned that these wheezes will be exhausted by August 2nd.

The House of Representatives, under Republican control as a result of last November's mid-term elections, has balked at passing the necessary bill. That is perfectly reasonable: until recently the Republicans had been exercising their clear electoral mandate to hold the government of Barack Obama to account, insisting that they will not permit a higher debt ceiling until agreement is reached on wrenching cuts to public spending. Until they started to play hardball in this way, Mr Obama had been deplorably insouciant about the medium-term picture, repeatedly failing in his budgets and his state-of-the-union speeches to offer any path to a sustainable deficit. Under heavy Republican pressure, he has been forced to rethink.

United States: Now, however, the Republicans are pushing things too far. The cut of budget for at least $2 trillion over the next ten years is supported by the Democrats. Assuming that the recovery continues, that would be enough to get the deficit back to a prudent level. As *The Economist* went to press, Mr. Obama seemed set to restart the talks.

The sticking-point is not on the spending side. It is because the vast majority of Republicans, driven on by the wilder-eyed members of their party and the cacophony of conservative media, are clinging to the position that not a single cent of deficit reduction must come from a higher tax take. This is economically illiterate and disgracefully cynical.

A gamble where you bet your country's good name

This newspaper has a strong dislike of big government; we have long argued that the main way to right America's finances is through spending cuts. But you cannot get there without any tax rises. In Britain, for instance, the coalition government aims to tame its deficit with a 3:1 ratio of cuts to hikes. America's tax take is at its lowest level for decades: even Ronald Reagan raised taxes when he needed to do so.

And the closer you look, the more unprincipled the Republicans look. Earlier this year House Republicans produced a report noting that an 85 percent - 15 percent split between spending cuts and tax rises was the average for successful fiscal consolidations, according to historical evidence. The White House is offering an 83 percent – 17 percent split (hardly a huge distance) and a promise that none of the revenue increase will come from higher marginal rates, only from eliminating loopholes. If the Republicans were real tax reformers, they would seize this offer. Both parties have in recent months been guilty of fiscal recklessness. Right now, though, the blame falls clearly on the Republicans. Independent voters should take note.[77]

China

Independent Foreign Policy of Peace

China unswervingly pursues an independent foreign policy of peace. The fundamental goals of this policy are to preserve China's independence, sovereignty and territorial integrity, create a favorable international environment for China's reform and opening up and modernization construction, maintain world peace and propel common development. The main content of this policy includes:

1. China has all along adhered to the principle of independence. With regard to all the international affairs, China will, proceeding from the fundamental interests of the Chinese people and the people of the world, determine its stand and policy in the light of the merits and demerits of the matter, without yielding to any outside pressure. China does not form an alliance with any big power or group of big powers. Nor does China establish military groups with other countries, or engage in arms race and military expansion.

2. China opposes hegemonies and preserves world peace. China believes that all countries, big or small, strong or weak, rich or poor, are equal members of the international community. Countries should resolve their disputes and conflicts peacefully through consultations and not resort to the use or threat of force. Nor should they interfere in others' internal affairs under any pretext. China never imposes its social system and ideology on others, nor allows other countries to impose theirs on it.

---

[77] American Debt: Shame on Them, The Economist, Jul 7th 2011

3. China actively facilitates the establishment of a new international political and economic order that is fair and rational. China holds that the new order should give expression to the demands of the development of history and progress of the times and reflect the universal aspirations and common interests of the peoples of all the countries in the world. The Five Principles of Peaceful Coexistence and the universally recognized norms governing international relations should serve as the basis for setting up the new international political and economic order.

4. China is ready to establish and develop friendly relations of cooperation with all the countries on the basis of mutual respect for sovereignty and territorial integrity, mutual non-aggression, mutual non-interference in each other's internal affairs, equality and mutual benefit, and peaceful coexistence.

It is an important component of China's foreign policy to actively develop good-neighborly relations of friendship with the surrounding countries. China has resolved problems left over by history with the overwhelming majority of neighboring countries. And China's mutually beneficial cooperation with its neighbors has witnessed a vigorous development.

It is the fundamental standing point of China's foreign policy to strengthen its solidarity and cooperation with numerous developing countries. China and these countries share common historic experiences and are faced with the common tasks of preserving national independence and achieving economic development. Therefore, their cooperation has a solid foundation and a broad prospect.

China sets store by improving and developing its relations with developed countries. It advocates that countries should surmount their differences in social system and ideology, respect one another, seek common ground and shelve differences and enhance their mutually beneficial cooperation. Their disputes should be appropriately solved through dialogue on the basis of equality and mutual respect.

5. China pursues a policy of all-dimensional opening up to the outside. It is ready to develop, on the basis of equality and mutual benefit, extensive trade relations, economic and technological cooperation and scientific and cultural exchanges with countries and regions of the world so as to promote common prosperity. At the end of 2001, China approved 390,000 overseas-funded enterprises with 745.9 billion dollars of contractual capital and 395.5 billion dollars of used capital. In 2001, China's import and export volume amounted to 509.8 billion dollars, ranking the sixth in the world.

After 15 years' talks, China finally acceded to the World Trade Organization on December 11, 2001. While enjoying the relevant rights, China has begun earnestly honoring its obligations within the framework of the WTO and its commitments. China remains ready to play a positive role, together with other countries, in improving world multilateral trade system and promoting prosperity and progress in the world.

The world economy is an inter-connected and inter-dependent whole. Economic globalization has brought both opportunities and big risks for the economies of various countries. It is a common challenge confronting the governments of all the countries to preserve financial stability, prevent financial crisis and ensure economic security.

6. China takes an active part in multilateral diplomatic activities and is a staunch force in preserving world peace and facilitating common development.

As a permanent member of the Security Council of the United Nations, China actively participates in the political solution of the problems of regional hot spots. China's peacekeepers have joined United Nations peacekeeping operations. China supports the reform of the United Nations and a continued important role of the United Nations and other multilateral organs in international affairs. China is firmly opposed to all forms of terrorism and has made important contributions to international anti-terrorism cooperation.

China devotes itself actively to pushing forward the cause of international arms control, disarmament and non-proliferation. To date, China has joined all the treaties related to international arms control and non-proliferation. With regard to non-proliferation, China has all along scrupulously abided by its international obligations and, thanks to its active efforts in enacting laws on non-proliferation, set up a relatively perfect export control system for non-proliferation.

The Chinese government has attached importance to human rights and made unremitting efforts in this regard. China has joined 18 human rights conventions, including the International Covenant on Economic, Social and Cultural Rights, and signed the International Covenant on Civil and Political Rights.

China remains ready, together with the international community, to enhance cooperation to address the global problems facing mankind including worsening environment, resources scarcity, unemployment, population explosion, narcotics spreading, AIDS and rampant transnational crimes.[78]

[78] Ministry of Foreign Affairs of the People's Republic of China, August 18, 2003

India

India's Foreign Policy - 50 Years of Achievement

The foundations of India's foreign policy were laid during the freedom movement when our leaders, even when fighting for independence, were engaged with the great causes of the time. The principles of India's foreign policy, that emerged then, have stood the test of time: a belief in friendly relations with all countries of the world, the resolution of conflicts by peaceful means, the sovereign equality of all states, independence of thought and action as manifested in the principles of Non-alignment, and equity in the conduct of international relations.

Under the leadership of Jawaharlal Nehru, India was the founder member of the Non-aligned Movement. India has played an active role in strengthening the Movement and making it an effective voice in representing the collective aspirations and interests o the developing countries on such vital issues as development, peace and stability. India hosted the 7th NAM Summit in New Delhi in 1983. In recent years, after the end of the Cold War, our foreign policy has been focused on strengthening the Movement by redefining its priorities in keeping with the changing times.

India has also been in the forefront of the world community in the struggle against colonialism. Indeed, the Independence of India itself played the role of a catalyst in removing the vestiges of colonialism in other parts of the developing world, particularly in Africa. India was also the first country to raise the question of racial discrimination in South Africa in 1946. It was at India's initiative that the AFRICA (Action for Resistance to Invasion, Colonialism and Apartheid) Fund was set up at the 8th NAM Summit in Harare in 1986. India was the Chairman of the AFRICA Fund Committee, which wound up in 1993.

A notable feature of Indian foreign policy has been its strong advocacy of general and complete disarmament, with nuclear disarmament being accorded the highest priority. Towards this end, India has taken several initiatives within the United Nations and outside. In 1988, India presented to the 3rd Session of the UN General Assembly devoted to Disarmament an Action Plan for Ushering in a Nuclear Weapons Free and Non-Violent World Order. In order to highlight international concern about the unprecedented nuclear arms race, India was also a member of the Six-Nation Five-Continent joint Initiative in the 1980s. But while India has, and will, remain committed to nuclear disarmament, to be achieved in a time-bound framework, it has consistently and in a principled manner opposed such discriminatory treaties as the Nuclear non-Proliferation Treaty (NPT) and Comprehensive Nuclear Test Ban Treaty (CTBT) and has refused to give up its nuclear options until all countries in the world including nuclear weapon states embrace the idea of nuclear disarmament in a phased manner.

As a founder member of the United Nations, India has been firmly committed to the purposes and principles of the United Nations and has made significant contributions to its various activities, including peacekeeping operations. India has been a participant in all its peacekeeping operations including those in Korea, Egypt and Congo in earlier years and in Somalia, Angola and Rwanda in recent years. India has also played an active role in the deliberations of the United Nations on the creation of a more equitable international economic order. It has been an active member of the Group of 77, and later the core group of the G-15 nations. Other issues, such as environmentally sustainable development and the promotion and protection of human rights, have also been an important focus of India's foreign policy in international forums.

Commensurate with national interests and security, the improvement of bilateral relations is an important component of any foreign policy, and India has succeeded in establishing a network of mutually beneficial relations with all countries of the world.

In particular, the improvement of relations with our neighbors has always been one of the pillars of India's foreign policy. India played an historic and unique role in the liberation of Bangladesh, which emerged as a sovereign nation in 1971. Through the implementation of the 1964 and 1974 Agreements, the issues of the stateless people of Indian origin in Sri Lanka were resolved. In 1988, India helped preserve the integrity of Maldives by coming to the assistance of that country and preventing an attempted takes over by armed mercenaries. The Indian government has taken recent initiatives to further strengthen ties with our neighbors, which have won international appreciation. These initiatives are based on five clear principles:

(a) First, with neighbors like Bangladesh, Bhutan, Maldives, Nepal and Sri Lanka, India does not ask for reciprocity but gives all that it can in good faith and trust.
(b) Secondly, no South Asian country should allow its territory to be used against the interests of another country of the region.
(c) Thirdly, none will interfere in the internal affairs of another.
(d) Fourthly, all South Asian countries must respect each other's territorial integrity and sovereignty.
(e) And finally, they should settle all their disputes through peaceful bilateral negotiations.

These tenets have paid rich dividends. A landmark Treaty has been signed with Bangladesh on the sharing of waters of the Ganges. With Bhutan and Nepal, major projects of economic collaboration have been advanced. Our relations with Sri Lanka have shown steady improvement. With Pakistan, India ha consistently pursued a policy seeking to improve relations under the framework of the Simla Agreement signed in 1972 which provided for the resolution of outstanding issues peacefully and bilaterally and for establishing durable peace in the Sub-continent. Bilateral discussions with Pakistan have resumed recently and India would continue efforts to have good neighborly relations with Pakistan.

An important achievement of India's foreign policy has been the strengthening of regional co-operation. India is an active member of the South Asian Association for Regional Cooperation (SAARC), which was launched in December 1985. With India's full support, SAARC has recently taken significant steps in accelerating the pace of economic co-operation. The South Asian Preferential Trade Arrangement (SAPTA) became operational in December 1995. At the 9th SAARC Summit in Male in May 1997, which was chaired by India, a historical decision has also been taken to strive for a South Asian Free Trade Area (SAFTA) latest by the year 2001 AD. The emergence of the Indian Ocean Rim Association for Regional Co-operation (IOR-ARC) in March 1997, as a major instrument of cooperation in the larger region, has also had the active support of India.

India's foreign policy has always regarded the concept of neighborhood as one of widening concentric circles, around a central axis of historical and cultural commonalties. From this point of view, it has always given due priority to the development of relations with South East Asia. In 1947, India organized the Asian Relations Conference. It chaired the International Control Commission in 1954 and was a major player in the organization of the Bandung Conference in 1955. Today, India is implementing a 'Look East' policy, which is underpinned by important economic considerations. Some significant steps in the pursuance of this policy have been taken with the admission of India as a full dialogue partner of ASEAN and a member of the ASEAN Regional Forum, in 1996.

An attribute of a dynamic foreign policy is the ability to respond to changing developments. The emergence of the Central Asian Republics in the aftermath of the break up of the Soviet Union was one such recent development, and India, given the strategic and economic importance of this region, has been quick to strengthen its bilateral relations with each of these Republics. The shift in recent years by the countries of Central and East Europe to political pluralism and market-oriented structures has also seen India trying to build upon existing business and institutional linkages so as to further strengthen the traditional ties of friendship with the countries of this region.

The countries of the Gulf have a political and strategic importance for India. The region is a major market for Indian exports. Three million Indians are employed in these countries. The strengthening of ties with this region, therefore, has been a priority of India's foreign policy.

With China the aim of Indian foreign policy has been of developing a relationship of friendship, cooperation and good neighborliness, exploiting the potential for favorable growth wherever it exists, even as we seek to find a fair, reasonable and mutually acceptable solution to the outstanding border issue. Towards this aim, a series of high level visits have been exchanged, bilateral trade and economic cooperation is growing, and an Agreement on Confidence Building Measures, as part of a wider dialogue on security, has been signed.[79]

---

[79] Ministry of Foreign Affairs, Government of India

India and the U S: **A dialogue between two democracies**

India values its bilateral relations with the US. As democracies, both countries have many shared ideals. Relations have also continued to grow with the 15 countries of the European Union, and with Japan. These countries are important economic partners of India, especially in the wake of our economic reforms. However, in pursuing bilateral relations, we have sought to preserve the independence of our viewpoint and protect our national interests from the pressures of conformity.

Our relations with Russia have grown over the years to constitute an important foreign policy priority for both countries. There is recognition in both counties to the strategic dimension of our multifaceted ties. The considerable goodwill for India in Russia has been further cemented in recent years.

Economic diplomacy has been a key component of India's foreign policy. Apart from long established Divisions in the Ministry to deal with economic issues, an Investment Publicity Unit (IPU) was specifically set up in 1990 with a view to disseminating economic information and coordinating the economic and commercial activities of Indian Missions abroad in the light of the recent economic reforms underway in the country. One aspect of economic diplomacy has been the promotion of South-South Cooperation. The Indian Economic and Technical Cooperation (ITEC) Program was established in 1964. Today it extends to 110 countries in Asia, East Europe, Africa and Latin America and facilitates the training of as many as 1000 foreign candidates in Indian institutions each year.

As many as 20 million people of Indian origin live and work abroad and constitute an important link with the mother country. An important role of India's foreign policy has been to ensure their welfare and well being within the framework of the laws of the country where they live.

The strength of any foreign policy depends also on the professional abilities of those who implement it, both at Headquarters and in the field. With a view to ensuring this, the Foreign Service Institute was established to undertake specialist training for entrants into the Indian Foreign Service, and conduct several other specialist courses for Indian and foreign diplomats.

It is difficult to enumerate the achievements of a country's foreign policy in exactly quantifiable terms. With this as a qualification, it would be a fair assessment to make that Indian foreign policy has sought to preserve, with conviction and consistency, the principles that were enunciated by the founding fathers of the Republic, both in the development of bilateral relations, and in international forums, where our views have won recognition and respect. A significant factor underlying this achievement has been the consensus, cutting across political divides, within the country, on what the basic aims and objectives of Indian foreign policy should be.[80]

Germany: Foreign policy

In the age of globalization, foreign policy is, more than ever before, the world's domestic policy. States, societies and economic zones are all becoming networked. The end of the East-West conflict has opened up new opportunities for German foreign policy – both within Europe and worldwide. Germany has accepted the international responsibility that has evolved for the country in the wake of dramatic changes with regard to world politics, and, together with partners worldwide, is deeply committed to the causes of democracy, human rights and the dialog

---

[80] Embassy of India, Washington D C

between cultures. The prime objective of Germany's foreign policy is to maintain peace and safety in the world.

Germany – a partner worldwide

The 20th century was characterized by quite unprecedented disruption. Three global conflicts, namely the two World Wars and the Cold War as well as a series of revolutionary upheavals left a deep mark on nations and peoples alike. This is especially true of Germany, if only because the country at the heart of Europe, was both decidedly responsible for the developments that led to the outbreak of both world wars, and was affected to an unusual degree by the Cold War and the gradual dissolution of the bipolar world order at the end of the 1980s.

When the post-War order collapsed, Germany faced a new situation as regards domestic and foreign policy. Here, the country benefited from the dynamism that culminated in the disbanding of the Soviet Union at the end of 1991. For this led in 1990 to the unification of East and West Germany and thus, for the first time in almost 50 years, to complete sovereignty.

With their approval of German unification, its former victims and opponents not only honored the German catharsis of the previous forty years, they also associated with it the hope that the efforts the Germans had channeled into reconstruction and integration in this period would build a viable bridge for the future. The fact that this realignment was successful was due not least of all to the manner in which German foreign policy had developed and established itself since the founding of the Federal Republic of Germany in 1949. The reaching of a broad-based consensus with regard to foreign policy and certain areas of continuity was and indeed still is one of the most salient characteristics of its political culture. These include, since the era of Konrad Adenauer, the first Federal Chancellor (1949–1963), the transatlantic partnership and European integration, and the desire for good neighborly relations – primarily with France, which German foreign policy was striving for in the early 1950s – just as much as the difficult process of reconciliation with Israel, which it began early on.

That may sound a matter of course, though given German politics and warmongering in the first half of the 20th century, and in view of the rigid constellations of the Cold War, it in fact represented a considerable challenge.

As of the end of the 1960s, in particular since Willy Brandt's chancellorship (1969–1974), these fundamentals of German foreign policy have been supplemented and advanced by a policy of conciliation with Poland and the other countries of East and Eastern Central Europe.

The bedrock of German foreign policy, as steadily created by all the different Federal Governments, has been the country's comprehensive integration into multilateral cooperation. This was fostered after the experience of two world wars by the unequivocal will of the country's neighbors to include and control it, and thus deter the Germans from breaking out or going it alone; and it was also fostered by the Germans' elementary need for peace, security, prosperity and democracy, as well as the recognition that the integration of their country formed the basis for its unification.

In the 1990s an era of extraordinary challenges began for the now united Germany. On the one hand the new domestic situation had to be mastered, while on the other the Germans saw themselves confronted with a new, unfamiliar role in foreign policy. That is the one side of the coin. There is another: German reunification contrasts significantly with the general trend of dissolution, decay and destruction in the world. The end of the Soviet Union, Yugoslavia, and Czechoslovakia, and the dismantling of Ethiopia, Somalia and Sudan, perpetrated in some cases internally, in others from outside the country – to mention just a few examples – led to a rapid increase in the number of players, even though these were not in all cases recognized states, and at the same time to a swift rise in complex problem situations.

Being the result of different conflict constellations, these represented hitherto unknown challenges for German foreign, security, economic, financial, development, and environmental policy: Ethnic and religious conflicts, border and resources issues, food and hygiene emergencies are frequently connected and create a complex that can no longer be solved without outside aid. At the end of the first decade of the 21st century Africa alone has 16 million refugees and internally displaced persons. In solving the problem the Germans are particularly called upon, because Germany is not only a wealthy country, in comparison with other European states it only has a short tradition as a colonial power, one that as abandoned shortly after WW I. As such Germany is an in-demand partner with regard to economic cooperation and development. Annual payments of almost US$ 14 billion make it the second biggest international donor – after the USA and in front of Great Britain, France, and Japan.

Commitment to European integration

From the very outset, the Federal Republic of German has been a driving force in European integration, which is doubtless one of the success stories of the post-War era. What began in 1951 with the founding of the European Coal and Steel Community by six states is today a European Union (EU) with 27 members. Despite all the setbacks and regression that also make up its history, the Maastricht, Amsterdam, Nice, and primarily Lisbon Treaties signed between 1992 and 2007 document the will of the participating states to adapt their community to the rapid changes in global politics and to stand out as an independent political force. Just how the European economies would have survived the global economic and financial crisis of 2008-09 without the euro as a monetary is another matter. At any rate, the price Germany paid for giving up the Deutschmark, at the time Europe's strongest currency, was not too high.

It was the commitment of the German chancellors that ultimately helped secure the signing of the Treaties of Nice and Lisbon. It was also Gerhard Schröder and Angela Merkel who emphatically and indeed successfully championed the appropriate representation of the new eastern European states, specifically neighboring Poland, in the committees of the European Union. In terms of foreign policy this commitment remains important, if only because there were considerable worries about the collaboration between Germany and Russia, for which there were good historical reasons. In fact this strategic partnership is aimed against no one; rather it is expressly geared to pan-European interests. This also applies to the energy relations, the nucleus of the partnership. Germany is poor in natural resources and procures 41 percent of its natural gas, 34 percent of its oil and 21 percent of its coal from Russia, while also serving as a transit country.

The fact that even during the Cold War German-Soviet economic and energy relations continued and were expanded without any noteworthy interruptions is an indication that they are a sound basis for a strategic partnership. And because this is not a one-way street, there are further political opportunities – for both sides. Something similar applies to the still young energy partnership with Central Asia.

Foreign policy in the age of globalization

Under the conditions that prevailed in the old world order it would have been inconceivable for German foreign policy to make such a clear and independent mark. For this Germany was too dependent on American guarantees of security. Over the course of the last 20 years this has changed noticeably. In 2002 and 2009 respectively, Chancellors Schröder and Merkel pointed out – before the German Bundestag and directed at the USA – which "decisions about existential questions relating to the German nation be made in Berlin."

This is an indication of how Berlin expects dealings among partners to be. It is not a rejection of the transatlantic relationship in general and NATO in particular, nor does it signal the announcement of a withdrawal from international and military commitments. With it Germany has, however, moved closer to the limitations of what is possible. For this reason, in its coalition agreement the Federal Government made up of C D U / C S U and F D P, which has been in power since October 2009, agreed on a "culture of restraint", which is traditional in German foreign and security policy. Nonetheless, since the turn of the century up to 10,000 Bundeswehr soldiers have been deployed worldwide at all times, and since 1999 in combat missions against aggressors, terrorists and pirates as well. Germany participates directly as well as part of the EU and NATO in United Nations (UN) peacekeeping missions.

In the case of NATO and EU operations under UN mandate the focus of military and police involvement is on the Balkans (KFOR, EUFOR, ALTHEA, and EULEX) and in Afghanistan as part of the difficult ISAF mission. As the third largest financial contributor to the regular UN peacekeeping budget Germany also plays a significant role in financing the "blue helmet" missions.

Coveted international partner

Germany is emphatic in its efforts to overcome global challenges such as climate change, scarce resources and a world without atomic weapons. The fact that in June 2007 the 33rd summit of the seven leading industrial nations and Russia, hosted by the Germans, succeeded in getting the Americans to agree to "seriously consider" a clear reduction in pollutant emissions and to recognize the United Nations as the platform for climate protection, was seen as remarkable. The Heiligendamm Summit also set new standards with the temporary increase in the number of participants. There can be no way forward in the future without countries such as Brazil, China, India, Mexico, and South Africa, which are growing rapidly, catching up swiftly in industrial terms, hungry for resources and not least of all of relevance with regard to the environment. Since the Pittsburgh Meeting in 2009 it is quite clear that the Group of Twenty, which also includes Argentina, Australia, Indonesia, Saudi Arabia, South Korea and Turkey, is the decisive economic forum.

German foreign policy also promotes expanding civil society structures; it is committed to helping overcome natural disasters, asserting democratic and human rights, and champions dialog among equals.

The fact that Germany can live this role stems from the trust carefully nurtured over the decades. German politics is today measured not against the yardstick of the destructive apparatus of the Third Reich, but against its achievements in development and integration. Reunited Germany has demonstrated that it can handle international responsibility and open up other perspectives.

Twenty years after the collapse of the old world orders the states and peoples on Earth are beginning to adapt to the conditions in the new, globalize world. For all the competition, they will only achieve this if they see each other as partners. The Germans, whose country is integrated in the international communities to an extent hardly, any other can boast, are well aware of the opportunities this offers.

Germany in Europe

Can a country that shares borders on all sides with other European countries, namely Germany with its nine neighbors, afford not to actively pursue a European policy? The answer is self-evident: With its central location at the heart of today's European Union (EU) Germany enjoys a special benefit from living in peace and harmony with its neighbors.

It is in Germany's interest for Europe to be a vibrant continent, in economic terms as well. The integration process has proved to be a suitable basis for ensuring peace, prosperity and security.

In 1957 the signing of the Treaty of Rome on establishing a European Economic Community spelled the beginning of the success story of European integration. It focused on developing the economies of Western Europe by strengthening and deepening cooperation and promoting trade among the founder nations.

Without wanting to play down how important it is that Europe grows together politically, we should no doubt consider the economic dynamism triggered by integration and the attractiveness of the major market to be the key driving force prompting other European states to accede. This applies to the accession of Great Britain, Denmark and Ireland in the 1970s, that of Greece, Spain and Portugal in the 1980s, and of Austria, Sweden and Finland in the

1990s. Likewise, it also applies to the magnetic appeal, which in 2004 and 2007 the EU had on the new democracies in the emerging market economies of Eastern Central Europe and South-East Europe. Just as was the case for the fledgling Federal Republic, the young democracies in the south and east of Europe rightly see accession to the EU as due recognition and assurance of the political achievements they have made in overcoming dictatorship and despotism.

The coming into power of the Lisbon Treaty in December 2009 saw the intensive negotiations come round full circle. German European policy played a pivotal role at all stages of this process: It was the concept of a European union initiated by Germany that in addition to an economic and currency union had as its goal an extended Political Union that was capable of acting. The Treaty of Maastricht was a major political step forward and put the first binding pillar in place; for the most part, however, the Political Union remained a vision. In the ensuing period it became clear that it would have to be created in stages, steps, and on another basis. For this reason, in the negotiations on the Treaties of Amsterdam and Nice, as well as in the European Convention Germany championed a gradual adaptation and advancement of the institutional structure, the clarification of areas of responsibility and the corresponding expansion of the democratic quality of EU decisions.

Consolidation and expansion initiatives

Parallel to this one of the focal points of German efforts and initiatives was the formulation of foreign, security, and defense policy within the scope of the EU Treaties, as well as a gradual increase in collaboration in the fields of justice and home affairs policy, as well as internal security. Considerable progress has been made in both areas, though it did not follow the classic integration method of communitization or a "major step". From the point of view of German European policy the Lisbon Treaty bundles together what is in practice possible in an EU, whose current 27 members appear to be clearly more different in terms of their economic and political situation, more diverse with regard interests and needs and more open in their ideas as to the future of integration than in all earlier stages of the European unification process.

With the process having ground to a halt in 2007, under the German Presidency of the EU success was scored in coming up with new grounds for a consensus on a Treaty reform. The results reflect important German concerns: The expansion of qualified majority decision making in the Council and EU Parliament co-decision making, the integration of the Charter of Fundamental Rights and the introduction of citizens' initiatives are important steps in the strengthening of the EU's decision-making capabilities and in securing democratic involvement. With the "High Representative for Foreign and Security Policy", who chairs the Council of Foreign Ministers, the establishment of a "European Foreign Service" and the associated combining of foreign policy duties of the Commission and Council of the EU the Lisbon Treaty considerably strengthen the international presence and role of the EU.

German European policy has unconditionally supported the ever-deeper integration process, its extension to the North, South and East as well as the establishment of the relevant institutions. The strength of German foreign policy has laid in ensuring Franco-German relations were firmly aligned to EU policy, on the one hand, and the close ties specifically to the smaller member states, on the other.

The Germans desire a Europe that is capable of acting, democratic and transparent, with a strengthened European Parliament, and clearly defined areas of responsibility. Incidentally, in line with their country's gross domestic product, the Germans provide some 20 percent of the EU budget.

The European Union's future tasks

The globalize world will continue to be a challenge for Europe. The key coalitions and constellations will change, and a new balance of interests will test the ability to forge compromises. The European Union must therefore field a trustworthy policy of development and partnership, not least for the countries on the Mediterranean rim. For years now there has been a stable majority in German public opinion in favor of tackling questions of foreign and security policy together with others. This applies in equal measure to the demanding agenda of global sustainability. Acting together in a European Energy and Climate Policy and in the response to the financial crisis is the prerequisite for safeguarding the interests and concerns of Germany and the other Member States.

Europe is not the place for small ideas. Without the European Union, welfare and security, those elementary services provided by the state, would no longer be possible. As such the policy of integration, the processes and the institutions are all part of Europe's political fabric and not mere frills. Any major theme concerning European societies also addresses the EU's contribution to the issue, as there is hardly any issue that does not involve the European level.

Coveted international partner

Germany is emphatic in its efforts to overcome global challenges such as climate change, scarce resources and a world without atomic weapons. The fact that in June 2007 the 33rd summit of the seven leading industrial nations and Russia, hosted by the Germans, succeeded in getting the Americans to agree to "seriously consider" a clear reduction in pollutant emissions and to recognize the United Nations as the platform for climate protection, was seen as remarkable. The Heiligendamm Summit also set new standards with the temporary increase in the number of participants. There can be no way forward in the future without countries such as Brazil, China, India, Mexico, and South Africa, which are growing rapidly, catching up swiftly in industrial terms, hungry for resources and not least of all of relevance with regard to the environment. Since the Pittsburgh Meeting in 2009 it is quite clear that the Group of Twenty, which also includes Argentina, Australia, Indonesia, Saudi Arabia, South Korea and Turkey, is the decisive economic forum.

German foreign policy also promotes expanding civil society structures; it is committed to helping overcome natural disasters, asserting democratic and human rights, and champions dialog among equals. The fact that Germany can live this role stems from the trust carefully nurtured over the decades. German politics is today measured not against the yardstick of the destructive apparatus of the Third Reich, but against its achievements in development and integration. Reunited Germany has demonstrated that it can handle international responsibility and open up other perspectives.[81]

Twenty years after the collapse of the old world orders the states and peoples on Earth are beginning to adapt to the conditions in the new, globalize world. For all the competition, they will only achieve this if they see each other as partners. The Germans, whose country is integrated in the international communities to an extent hardly, any other can boast, are well aware of the opportunities this offers.

---

[81] Josef Janning and Gregor Schollgen, Facts about Germany, 2011

SWEDEN: Foreign Policy

Sweden has maintained a policy of neutrality throughout the 20th century, avoiding both world wars and remaining nonaligned during the postwar period. Unlike Denmark and Norway, Sweden declined membership in the North Atlantic Treaty Organization (NATO) in 1949, wanting to remain outside of all military alliances. Moreover, Sweden's decision not to join the European economic alliance was based on a concern that membership would undermine its traditional policy of neutrality. Sweden has, however, participated actively in many international organizations, including the United Nations (UN), the International Monetary Fund (IMF), the Organization for Economic Cooperation and Development (OECD), and the General Agreement on Tariffs and Trade (GATT). With the end of the Cold War and the necessity to strengthen its economy, Sweden officially joined the European Union (EU) on 1 January 1995.

Persson's new government will depend on parties skeptical of membership in the EU, opposed to Swedish participation in the European Monetary Union (EMU), and opposed to closer ties with NATO. Along with Denmark and Britain, Sweden has chosen to remain outside of the EMU but reserves the right to join later. Sweden is committed to keeping its economy and currency closely tied to the EMU. With the economic improvements of recent years, it is now in substantial compliance with the criteria for EMU participation. Sweden has historically allowed its currency to depreciate significantly in order to maintain international competitiveness. EMU membership would close that option.

Sweden has modified its nonalignment policy to include participation in the NATO-sponsored "Partnership for Peace." As NATO expands into central Europe, Swedes have discussed closer ties to the alliance. While a majority of Swedes support NATO membership, the Left and Green parties, as well as more traditional SAP circles, are opposed. Persson will continue to maintain an activist role in peace-keeping operations, assertive diplomacy, and generous foreign aid programs.

Persson first took a moderate stance on the U.S. Iraq policy, but in March 2003, he called for a demonstration against the war in an attempt to win back the support of his own party's left wing. In 2001–2003, Sweden held the presidency of the Barents Euro-Arctic Council, a cooperation of Nordic and Baltic Sea countries. During that period, the focus on the economic development of the region based on its rich natural resources was emphasized.

After his electoral triumph in September 2002, Persson announced that Sweden would hold a euro referendum in September 2003. His own party continued to be divided and Persson clamped down on anti-euro notables in his cabinet. The public, however, also seemed skeptical and support for the euro hovered at 34% in the late spring of 2003, signaling that the referendum might end in defeat. In general, in European affairs, Sweden has been supportive of enlargement and of the EU convention although its main concern is to create a more transparent and accountable governance system.[82]

FRANCE: Foreign Policy

France's foreign policy is founded on several centuries of diplomatic tradition and some fundamental principles: the right of peoples to self-determination, respect for human rights and democratic principles, respect for the rule of law and cooperation among nations. Within this framework France's concern is to preserve its national independence while at the same

[82] Encyclopedia of the Nations

time working to foster regional and international solidarity.

The construction of Europe

From as early as 1945 European construction has been at the heart of French foreign policy. There have been several major reasons for this: the desire to restore peace and guarantee the security of the States, strengthen democratic government and build an integrated economic and monetary area able to ensure prosperity for the people of Europe. Given this, General de Gaulle and Presidents Pompidou, Giscard d'Estaing, Mitterrand and Chirac have striven unceasingly to make the European edifice a reality and develop it into an economic power and respected political forum.

On May 1, 2004, ten new members joined the European Union. They were followed by Bulgaria and Romania on January 1st, 2007. Strengthened by 27 countries, the European Union forms the third largest grouping on the planet, occupying 3 percent of its population and a quarter of global wealth.

International Security

In the area of security, the Cold War years and the succeeding period of instability have placed heavy responsibilities on all the democratic nations, including France. Party to the North Atlantic Treaty (NATO), France also belongs to the Organization for Security and Cooperation in Europe (OSCE) and the Eurocorps, in which France has nearly 13,000 troops.

As one of the five nuclear powers - alongside the United Kingdom, the United States, Russia and China - France is ensuring the maintenance of its deterrent force and its adaptation to the new strategic realities, taking into account the European dimension of its defense, while working towards a total ban on nuclear testing and committing itself to arms control and disarmament.

Action at the U N

France's foreign policy is conducted in accordance with the purposes and principles of the United Nations, purposes and principles, which in fact comply with the ideals underlying France's republican tradition. Thus, since 1945 France has constantly supported the UN, to which it is the fourth largest contributor. In 2007, it contributed a total of €101 million to the UN's regular budget.

As a permanent member of the Security Council, France has participated directly in many UN peacekeeping operations (in the Middle East, Cambodia, the former Yugoslavia, Democratic Republic of Congo, Côte d'Ivoire etc.). French contributions to peacekeeping operations stood at €240 million in 2006. France also supports UN development aid action, in particular through contributions and technical assistance that it provides to the main programs for fighting poverty (UNDP), child protection (UNICEF), fighting drugs (UNDCP) or food aid (WFP).

International Cooperation

France's international cooperation policy relies on the exercise of both influence and solidarity. The Directorate-General for Development and International Cooperation (DGCID) implements this policy around four main lines:

Development aid through cooperation

France intends to sustain its effort of solidarity towards the poorest countries. The major part of the funds provided by France for development aid is devoted to bilateral assistance provided directly to the beneficiary countries by French government departments of those acting for them. In 2003, development in Africa continued to be a priority for French foreign policy. The proportion of bilateral aid going to sub-Saharan Africa thus rose from 49 percent in 2002 to 57 percent in 2003.

Encouraging Cultural Exchanges and the Use of the French Language France has 151 French cultural establishments abroad, located in 91 countries, and a network of 283 Alliances franchises. The policy for promoting the French language concerns 82 million learners in 130 countries and relies on 900 000 teachers. The Agency for French Studies Abroad (AEFE) coordinates the activities of the 268 French schools in the world.

Promoting scientific and academic cooperation

France intends both to support the internationalization of French research and to disseminate information on the scientific systems of partner countries. The Science and Technology Observatory and the 28 French research centers abroad are responsible for implementing these objectives. As regards academic cooperation, France manages 200 French-speaking degree courses throughout the world and has been stepping up relations with partners such as Germany and the United States. An increasing number of foreign students come to study each year in France; today they total 220,000.

Ensuring a French presence on the world audiovisual scene The French audiovisual presence on the worldwide scene is increasingly strong and support for major operators in this sector, such as the French-speaking channel TV 5 and Radio France International (RFI) is now a government priority. France also supports the distribution of French films and documentaries.

Humanitarian action

France gives humanitarian action a specific place in its foreign policy, and also demonstrates its loyalty to the values it has inspired. France has played a vital role in the development of humanitarian action and international humanitarian law.

The French Foreign Ministry's Humanitarian Action Delegation implements the emergency humanitarian relief actions abroad decided by the government. The following institutions are its institutional partners, such as:

(a) The Sécurité civile (emergency services dealing with natural disasters, bomb disposal, etc),
(b) Samu mondial (mobile emergency medical service - international branch)
(c) The French Defense Ministry,
(d) Emergency NGOs and so on.

The funds earmarked for these programs totaled €9.3 million in 2004. French NGOs working abroad receive about 40 percent of theses funds in the form of grants.

In this area France also provides support to the activities of multilateral organisations. In 2004, €49 million was paid to various UN humanitarian agencies; Office of the High Commissioner for Refugees (UNHCR), UNICEF, World Food Program (WFP), United Nations Relief and Work Agency for Palestine Refugees (UNRWA), International Committee of the Red Cross (ICRC), etc. Finally France's contribution to programs implemented within the European framework amounts to more than €100 million. Through ECHO (European Community Humanitarian Office), France assists countries or peoples in need, suffering the effects of natural disasters or political crises.

The fight against terrorism

As a victim of international terrorism both at home and abroad, France has for many years shown its determination to combat terrorism in all its forms and irrespective of its source. France, which considers that an uncompromising fight to eliminate terrorism must be conducted without prejudice to human rights and public freedoms, has put in place specific anti-terrorism legislation.

Franco phony

While promoting cultural, scientific and technical exchanges, France is also keen to increase the use of the French language. Through Franco phony it intends to make the Francophone community (135 million people or 2.5 percent of the world's population) into a genuine forum for cooperation.

Since 1986, there have been twelve Francophone summits. The summit of Heads of State and Government of the countries having the French language in common, held in Hanoi (Vietnam) in November 1997, endorsed the Francophone community's political dimension with the appointment of a Secretary-General, a political spokesman for the community and coordinator of its economic, cultural and linguistic cooperation programs. Now including 55 States, the Francophone Community held its twelfth summit in October 2008 in Quebec.[83]

Sri Lanka Neglects Tamil Tigers

Two years after the elimination of the Tamil Tigers, President Rajapaksa is yet to fulfill his promise of meeting the aspirations of Sri Lankan Tamils.

---

[83] Profile of France printed by the French Ministry of Foreign Affairs

When Tamil Nadu Chief Minister J Jayalalithaa paid her first visit to New Delhi after assuming office, she forcefully articulated her concerns on Sri Lanka. Two issues concerning Sri Lanka Tamils stir passions in Tamil Nadu.

The first is the conviction that ever since the elimination of the Liberation Tigers of Tamil Eelam in 2009, Sri Lanka Tamils have remained displaced from their homes and been denied basic human rights.

The second concern is the attacks on Tamil Nadu fishermen by the Sri Lanka Navy on grounds of their encroaching into Sri Lanka territorial waters, beyond the 285-acre, uninhabited, Kachativu Island.

Records of the British India Government have showed Kachativu as part of Ceylon since 1876. The Raja of Ramnad in the then Madras Presidency, however, laid claim to the island in the 1920s. Kachativu was recognized by India as Sri Lanka territory in agreements signed in 1974 and 1976. The demarcation of the maritime boundary, under which India acknowledged Sri Lanka sovereignty over Kachativu, was based on the internationally recognized principle of the median line and in consonance with Article 15 of the Law of the Seas.

After the LTTE took control of northern Sri Lanka, fishing in each other's territorial waters became contentious. The Sri Lanka Navy resorted to what can only be termed as excessive and indiscriminate use of force. But in 2008, New Delhi and Colombo agreed that excluding what Sri Lanka considers as "sensitive areas", there would be "practical arrangements" to deal with bona fide Indian and Sri Lanka fisherman crossing the international boundary line.

Sri Lanka would be well advised to see that its Navy respects the spirit of this agreement. And those raising public passions in Tamil Nadu should remember that the objections to fishing in Sri Lanka waters by Indian fishermen come primarily from Sri Lanka Tamils. The exchange of letters accompanying the 1976 agreement makes it clear that fishermen of either country shall not engage in fishing in the other's "historic waters, the territorial sea and the exclusive economic zones".

Inevitably, but sadly, triumphal, rather than reconciliation, has characterised a section of public opinion in Sri Lanka ever since the bloody ethnic conflict ended in 2009. There is broad agreement and substantive evidence, which has been endorsed by a UN panel set up by the Secretary-General, of gross human rights violations by both the Sri Lanka Government and its armed forces on the one hand and the LTTE on the other, particularly as the ethnic conflict drew to a close. Both sides were found to have resorted to summary executions and disappearances.

The LTTE had adopted the policy of using civilians as human shields extensively during the IPKF's operations in 1987. There should, therefore, be no reason to doubt, as the UN panel acknowledges, that V Prabhakaran, a confirmed psychopath who brutally killed virtually all politically influential Tamil leaders, cynically did likewise when the Sri Lankan Army closed in on him in 2009.

The ethnic conflict has left over 300,000 Tamils, described as "Internally Displaced Persons", in refugee camps. India has committed 10 billion INR ($ 220 million) for rehabilitating them, including provision of construction material like cement and GI sheets for rebuilding homes. Large-scale medical assistance has also been extended. A programme to reconstruct 50,000 houses was commenced in 2010 and Tamil farmers were assisted with seeds, tractors and agricultural implements. A similar approach has marked India's commitment to broaden ties across the island nation.

India is Sri Lanka's largest trading partner, with the Indian private and public sectors widely having a significant presence there. India has extended Lines of Credit of around $960 million for the improvement of the tsunami-damaged Colombo-Matara rail link and for rolling stock and wagons for the northern railway line. In a longer-term perspective, India would be well advised to assist the Tamil population in Sri Lanka by setting up educational and vocational training institutes in northern and eastern Sri Lanka.

The 13th Amendment to the Sri Lanka Constitution, enacted pursuant to the Rajiv Gandhi- J R Jayawardene Accord of 1987, provided for the devolution of powers to the Provinces, including to the Tamil-dominated Northern and the multi-ethnic Eastern Provinces. President Mahinda Rajapaksa had averred that he would be prepared to go even beyond this framework to meet Tamil aspirations. Sri Lanka's Foreign Minister GL Peiris, while visiting India, agreed, "a devolution package, building upon the 13th Amendment, would contribute towards creating conditions for such reconciliation". But Mr. Rajapaksa now seems to be having second thoughts on his past assurances. Doubts are being expressed about abiding by the provisions of the 13th Amendment on crucial issues like law and order and land. After having won a landslide electoral triumph for ending the ethnic conflict, Mr. Rajapaksa may end up losing the prospect of lasting harmony and amity if political expediency prevails over statesmanship.

Following reports of human rights violations by Sri Lanka's armed forces, 17 countries, including France, Germany, Mexico and Britain, had moved a resolution in the UN Human Rights Commission in May 2009, calling for an investigation into the charges. India, together with countries like Brazil, Russia, China, South Africa and others, had this move rejected.

These countries, instead, backed a resolution, which was passed by 29 votes for and 12 against, condemning the LTTE and calling on the Sri Lanka Government to proceed with efforts for national reconciliation and resettlement of the internally displaced persons. Given the contents of the recent report of the committee constituted by the UN Secretary-General, which alludes to large-scale violation of human rights by the Sri Lanka Government, the 2009 resolution will inevitably be revisited and reviewed internationally. India has spared no effort to assist and cooperate with Sri Lanka to eliminate the LTTE and to deal with foreign pressures mounted on its neighbour at international forums. Sri Lanka, in turn, will hopefully realize the importance of abiding by the solemn assurances it has given to India of going beyond the 13th Amendment to meet the legitimate aspirations of its Tamil population.[84]

While Tamil demands for the merger of the Northern and Eastern Provinces are untenable, objections to provisions of the 13th Amendment about the transfer of limited powers on law and order and on land were not countenanced by both former President Chandrika Kumaratunga and former Prime Minister Ranil Wickremesinghe. One hope Mr. Rajapaksa will do likewise.

NEPAL: **A vision for Nepal-India relations**

Dr. Baburam Bhattarai, the Prime Minister of Nepal says, "My visit to India, which begins today, has great historical significance."

---

[84] G Parthasarathy (2011), "Colombo must act now", the pioneer, Bhubaneswar, July 7 2011

Nepal is passing through a major political transition. We fought against feudal autocracy and monarchy, and for overall socio-economic transformation, for almost 60 years. At times, our movement was peaceful, and at times, violent. But the consistent goal was to abolish feudal autocracy and monarchy, and democratize the state and society. Ultimately, the major political parties — which included the Maoists and traditional parliamentary parties — reached an agreement in 2006 to overthrow the monarchy and institutionalize democracy through the Constituent Assembly (CA).

Peace, constitution and India

We succeeded in abolishing the monarchy, and ushering in a new democratic era in Nepal. We are now in the process of institutionalizing achievements through the CA, accompanied by socio-economic transformation, and federal restructuring of the state. According to the Comprehensive Peace Agreement (CPA), signed in November 2006, we are now trying to complete the specific task of army integration and other aspects of the peace process. We are also trying to complete the process of writing the Constitution through the CA. Only after wrapping up this entire process will these gains be institutionalized, and we will enter into a new era of democracy, change and development in Nepal.

The role of India in this process is crucial. Nepal and India share a very unique relationship. Nepal is sandwiched between two huge states of India and China. But we are virtually India-locked, as we have an open border on three sides. Most of our socio-economic interactions take place with India. Two-thirds of our annual trade is with India, while only 10 per cent is with China. Given this historic tilt towards India, our bilateral relationship is unique. When you have more interaction, you have more problems and more friction. At times, there are misgivings and misunderstandings on various issues — some are genuine, while others are born out of skepticism.

India played a positive role in the peace process in Nepal, and during our transition towards democracy. My visit, at this juncture when we are at the last stage of completing the peace process, assumes special significance. While the peace process is basically conceptualized and led by Nepali political forces, the goodwill of international forces, particularly our neighbours, is very important for its success.

Security and development

An important bilateral issue between Nepal and India is related to politics and security. Nepal virtually lies in the southern lap of the Himalayas, and shares borders with two huge states of Asia. This geopolitical reality has to be taken into account. Naturally, there would be political and security concerns of our neighbours which Nepal is committed to observe keeping in mind mutual interests. Nepal will not allow its soil to be used against the security interests of any of its neighbours. Another key issue is economic development and development of resources. In the present day world, the economy of every country is interlinked with that of others, especially neighbours. If we have to prosper, we can only prosper if we cooperate with each other. Poverty and underdevelopment in the neighbourhood will have fallout, and hamper your own development.

India and China are developing at a fast pace. Nepal, lying between two fast-growing economies, cannot remain backward and under-developed. We will seek the cooperation of both our neighbours, especially India.

We have to find areas of economic co-operation for mutual benefit of India and Nepal. One major field is the exploitation of water resources for mutual benefit. The next is drawing in Indian investment to Nepal — we are committed to creating conducive environment for investors and providing them security. The trade balance between our two countries has been quite skewed. Our trade deficit with India is quite huge. The import-export ratio is about 7:1, which is not sustainable. That is another area where we have to deepen our economic cooperation.

Personally, I have had the opportunity to get my education in India, and my area of interest has been economic development. I will try to utilize my relations developed over the years to enhance bilateral relations, especially designed towards maximizing economic benefits for both sides. If Nepal can develop faster, it can become a development partner for India. For India also, a more developed Nepal will be a better guarantee of its security as only with development, peace, and stability, there can be security. Security concerns cannot be treated in isolation, but must be viewed in totality. Security and economic development must be seen together.

Trust and goodwill: The visit to India is basically directed towards building a better understanding between the two countries and two peoples. In that sense, it is a goodwill visit.

My personal thrust would be to have a very free and frank discussion with my counterparts so that we can upgrade the relationship according to contemporary needs. The relations and agreements institutionalized in the 20th century may not be enough to meet the needs of the 21st century. Hence, the emphasis would be to develop our relations further, clear misgivings and misunderstandings that we have against each other, and sort out the problems left by history. When the subcontinent was colonized by the British, they left behind a legacy which has created friction among the nations of South Asia. We have to overcome that, and develop mutual relations in the changed time and context. Instead of harping on old disputes, Nepal would like to look forward, and create an atmosphere of cooperation.

There are certain political issues, which would need more discussions. We can engage on it freely and frankly, but they can be postponed for the future. The major thing is to build trust between our two countries, two governments, and two peoples. Once there is trust, and we are sensitive and empathize with each other, even the most difficult issues can be resolved amicably. To reiterate, instead of pushing any specific agenda, I want to talk about all the issues in a friendly spirit, with the aim of conveying and understanding bilateral concerns. This will also be an opportunity to interact with those outside government, especially civil society, media, and intelligentsia. Given my long association with Delhi, I have several personal acquaintances there and look forward to renewing those relationships.

It is my strong conviction that my current visit to New Delhi will usher in a new era in our bilateral relations. Nepal is in the last phase of completing its peace process, and is about to enter a new phase of peace and development. Our new bilateral relationship, which will be based on a strong development dimension, can bring about peace and prosperity.

My dream is to have an inclusive democracy, sustainable peace and prosperity in this part of the world. Nepal will try to contribute its best to foster that relation among all the countries of South Asia. Nepal-India relations can be developed as a model of cooperation between neighbours. I am quite confident that after this visit, traditional misgivings between the different actors in Nepal and India will substantially be cleared, and a foundation for better partnership for development in the 21st century would be laid.[85]

Conclusion

The United Nations should sincerely try and create an atmosphere of stabilizing peace among all nations.

There is no need to have '**War Associations**' and it can be converted into '**Peace Associations**' to award peace among member countries and it could be extended the whole humanity and all countries.

Democracy, Communism and military rule have assumed the major political philosophy in most of the countries. These philosophies have created family rule, one-man rule and have converted the administration to accept corruption, widening rich–poor gap and lawlessness among the frustrated voters.

The print media, TV and internet facility are attracting the mass to revolt against the government as they undertake direct telecast on 'fighting among the police force and irate voters'. The media highlights the wrong doings, killings, abduction of people each day to divert public opinion to wrong paths. There is no censorship on news channels and these institutions have no right to instigate people to take up stone throwing at the police force; these political parties paralyze the busy roads and try stop the government offices and banks.

The media should be politics- neutral. It should be a non-corrupt organization.

The media should prioritize achievements of boys, girls and people, who contributed to the growth of

---

[85] Baburam Bhattarai (2011)," A vision for Nepal-India relations", The Hindu, October 20, 2011

science, technology, research findings, or received international and national awards. The media covers fighting among different religions, groups and highlight rape and murder cases wth detailed information. Hence, these institutions must be advised to publish good news only. Rape, murder, muscle power, black money, conspiracy and gang war should be avoided by the media or simply one two sentence news might be used. Bad news multiplies in geometric progression.

Religion based war could be avoided when each government arranges "All Regions Meet" in each country each year. All religions are created by the Almighty, Omnipotent and Omniscient Lord and the teachings have super values for each one and for the country. We have abridged all religions in "WORLD PEACE Volume seven" and have opined that 'HUMANITY – A religion for World Peace' could strengthen world peace movement. Let the political parties, politicians and governments find time to read and analyze religious sermons. If a single sermon is uttered by an individual as a practice for all the days; he would be definitely blessed by the Almighty God.

A man needs peace. It is easily possible when politicians would swear in name of the Almighty that we would support the World Peace Program. World Peace is possible provided the rich – poor gap is reduced in each zone / region. The rush for power of politicians should be checked by the voters.

Let the world be free from hunger, illiteracy and war; it would stabilize world peace for ever.

The United Nations should be renamed as the United Nations Peace Organization (UNPO).

+++++

Chapter VII

WORLD PEACE IS POSSIBLE

Let there be peace on earth and let it begin with me. - Miller and Jackson, 1995

World Peace is a necessity for the survival of the human, animal and plant kingdoms. It is a necessity because we are civilized, educated and economically advanced. It is possible because 97 percent of people are God believers. When we have not created this Earth, we have no right to destroy the Earth created by the Nature or the Almighty Himself. World peace is possible if each one of us at least think for world peace.

Each person should say:

(a) I am a part of the Universe.
(b) I am a member of the world family.
(c) I need peace.
(d) I support the world peace movement.
(e) I believe in God.
(f) I must contribute to humanity.

People or soldiers do not cause wars – those people who consider them as super human beings cause it. Those countries, which think that we want to rule the planet, cause it; those people who are corrupt, obstinate and immoral cause it. But these people rule the state, people and aspire to rule the time, environment and even God.

The Almighty needs to save His creation, so world peace is possible and we can do it.

Let us remember the photo and sermons of our great divine people, who came to this world to teach us, to advise us and to bless us. They are Lord Rama, Lord Sri Krishna, Lord Trithankar Mahabir, Lord Buddha, Lord Jesus Christ and Prophet Mohammad. Their advices are printed, published, circulated and available though out the world.

The world is full of advices; full of Learning's and full of religious places. Let us devote only five-minutes a day for a great cause – world peace. It would award peace to us, to society, state and the whole world. Let us find time to read, practice and concentrate on their advices, sufferings and sacrifices during prayer time for the benefits of all of us, our forefathers and off springs.

If we could think for the humanity, we can build peace for the world and it is possible. Let us hear the speeches of a great soul; let us think and think. It could be possible if we the people just adjust our mind for a great cause. Let us know what His Highness the 14th Dalai Lama says:

A Human Approach to World Peace

When we rise in the morning and listen to the radio or read the newspaper, we are confronted with the same sad news: violence, crime, wars, and disasters. I cannot recall a single day without a report of something terrible happening somewhere. Even in these modern times it is clear that one's precious life is not safe. No former generation has had to experience so much bad news as we face today; this constant awareness of fear and tension through TV and Newspapers has created fear psychosis among the people of modern world.

It is ironic that the more serious problems emanate from the more industrially advanced societies. Science and technology have worked wonders in many fields, but the basic human problems remain. There is unprecedented literacy, yet this universal education does not seem to have fostered goodness, but only mental restlessness and discontent instead. There is no doubt about the increase in our material progress and technology, but somehow this is not sufficient as we have not yet succeeded in bringing about peace and happiness or in overcoming suffering.

We can only conclude that there must be something seriously wrong with our progress and development, and if we do not check it in time there could be disastrous consequences for the future of humanity. I am not at all against science and technology - they have contributed immensely to the overall experience of humankind; to our material comfort and well-being and to our greater understanding of the world we live in. But if we give too much emphasis to science and technology we are in danger of losing touch with those aspects of human knowledge and understanding that aspire towards honesty and altruism.

Science and technology, though capable of creating immeasurable material comfort, cannot replace the age-old spiritual and humanitarian values that have largely shaped world civilization, in all its national forms, as we know it today. No one can deny the unprecedented material benefit of science and technology, but our basic human problems remain; we are still faced with the same, if not more, suffering, fear, and tension. Thus it is only logical to try to strike a balance between material developments on the one hand and the development of spiritual, human values on the other. In order to bring about this great adjustment, we need to revive our humanitarian values.

I am sure that many people share my concern about the present worldwide moral crisis and will join in my appeal to all humanitarians and religious practitioners who also share this concern to help make our societies more compassionate, just, and equitable. I do not speak as a Buddhist or even as a Tibetan. Nor do I speak as an expert on international politics (though I unavoidably comment on these matters). Rather, I speak simply as a human being, as an upholder of the humanitarian values that are the bedrock not only of Mahayana Buddhism but of all the great world religions. From this perspective I share with you my personal outlook - that:

(a) Universal humanitarianism is essential to solve global problems;
(b) Compassion is the pillar of world peace;
(c) All world religions are already for world peace in this way, as are all humanitarians of whatever ideology;
(d) Each individual has a universal responsibility to shape institutions to serve human needs.

Solving Human Problems through Transforming Human Attitudes:

Of the many problems we face today, some are natural calamities and must be accepted and faced with equanimity. Others, however, are of our own making, created by misunderstanding, and can be corrected. One such type arises from the conflict of ideologies, political or religious, when people fight each other for petty ends, losing sight of the basic humanity that binds us all together as a single human family. We must remember that the different religions, ideologies, and political systems of the world are meant for human beings to achieve happiness. We must not lose sight of this fundamental goal and at no time should we place means above ends; the supremacy of humanity over matter and ideology must always be maintained.

By far the greatest single danger facing humankind - in fact, all living beings on our planet - is the threat of nuclear destruction. I need not elaborate on this danger, but I would like to appeal to all the leaders of the nuclear powers who literally hold the future of the world in their hands, to the scientists and technicians who continue to create these awesome weapons of destruction, and to all the people at large who are in a position to influence their leaders: I appeal to them to exercise their sanity and begin to work at dismantling and destroying all nuclear weapons. We know that in the event of a nuclear war there will be no victors because there will be no survivors! Is it not frightening just to contemplate such inhuman and heartless destruction? And, is it not logical that we should remove the cause for our own destruction when we know the cause and have both the time and the means to do so? Often we cannot overcome our problems because we either do not know the cause or, if we understand it, do not have the means to remove it. This is not the case with the nuclear threat.

Whether they belong to more evolved species like humans or to simpler ones such as animals, all beings primarily seek peace, comfort, and security. Life is as dear to the mute animal as it is to any human being; even the simplest insect strives for protection from dangers that threaten its life. Just as each one of us wants to live and does not wish to die, so it is with all other creatures in the universe, though their power to affect this is a different matter.

Broadly speaking there are two types of happiness and suffering, mental and physical, and of the two, I believe that mental suffering and happiness are the more acute. Hence, I stress the training of the mind to endure suffering and attain a more lasting state of happiness. However, I also have a more general and concrete idea of happiness: a combination of inner peace, economic development, and, above all, world peace. To achieve such goals I feel it is necessary to develop a sense of universal responsibility, a deep concern for all irrespective of creed, colour, sex, or nationality.

The premise behind this idea of universal responsibility is the simple fact that, in general terms, all others' desires are the same as mine. Every being wants happiness and does not want suffering. If we, as intelligent human beings, do not accept this fact, there will be more and more suffering on this planet. If we adopt a self-centred approach to life and constantly try to use others for our own self-interest, we may gain temporary benefits, but in the long run we will not succeed in achieving even personal happiness, and world peace will be completely out of the question.

In their quest for happiness, humans have used different methods, which all too often have been cruel and repellent. Behaving in ways utterly unbecoming to their status as humans, they inflict suffering upon fellow humans and other living beings for their own selfish gains. In the end, such shortsighted actions bring suffering to oneself as well as to others. To be born a human being is a rare event in itself, and it is wise to use this opportunity as effectively and skillfully as possible. We must have the proper perspective that of the universal life process, so that the happiness or glory of one person or group is not sought at the expense of others.

All this calls for a new approach to global problems. The world is becoming smaller and smaller - and more and more interdependent - as a result of rapid technological advances and international trade as well as increasing trans-national relations. We now depend very much on each other. In ancient times problems were mostly family-size, and they were naturally tackled at the family level, but the situation has changed. Today we are so interdependent, so closely interconnected with each other, that without a sense of universal responsibility, a feeling of universal brotherhood and sisterhood, and an understanding and belief that we really are part of one big human family, we cannot hope to overcome the dangers to our very existence - let alone bring about peace and happiness.

One nation's problems can no longer be satisfactorily solved by itself alone; too much depends on the interest, attitude, and cooperation of other nations. A universal humanitarian approach to world problems seems the only sound basis for world peace. What does this mean? We begin from the recognition mentioned previously that all beings cherish happiness and do not want suffering. It then becomes both morally wrong and pragmatically unwise to pursue only one's own happiness oblivious to the feelings and aspirations of all others who surround us as members of the same human family. The wiser course is to think of others also when pursuing our own happiness. This will lead to what I call 'wise self-interest', which hopefully will transform itself into 'compromised self-interest', or better still, 'mutual interest'.

Although the increasing interdependence among nations might be expected to generate more sympathetic cooperation, it is difficult to achieve a spirit of genuine cooperation as long as people remain indifferent to the feelings and happiness of others. When people are motivated mostly by greed and jealousy, it is not possible for them to live in harmony. A spiritual approach may not solve all the political problems that have been caused by the existing self-centered approach, but in the long run it will overcome the very basis of the problems that we face today.

On the other hand, if humankind continues to approach its problems considering only temporary expediency, future generations will have to face tremendous difficulties. The global population is increasing, and our resources are being rapidly depleted. Look at the trees, for example. No one knows exactly what adverse effects massive deforestation will have on the climate, the soil, and global ecology as a whole. We are facing problems because people are concentrating only on their short-term, selfish interests, not thinking of the entire human family. They are not thinking of the earth and the long-term effects on universal life as a whole. If we of the present generation do not think about these now, future generations may not be able to cope with them.

Compassion as the Pillar of World Peace

According to Buddhist psychology, most of our troubles are due to our passionate desire for and attachment to things that we misapprehend as enduring entities. The pursuit of the objects of our desire and attachment involves the use of aggression and competitiveness as supposedly efficacious instruments. These mental processes easily translate into actions, breeding belligerence as an obvious effect. Such processes have been going on in the human mind since time immemorial, but their execution has become more effective under modern conditions. What can we do to control and regulate these 'poisons' - delusion, greed, and aggression? These poisons are behind almost every trouble in the world.

As one brought up in the Mahayana Buddhist tradition, I feel that love and compassion are the moral fabric of world peace. Let me first define what I mean by compassion. When you have pity or compassion for a very poor person, you are showing sympathy because he or she is poor; your compassion is based on altruistic considerations. On the other hand, love towards your wife, your husband, your children, or a close friend is usually based on attachment. When your attachment changes, your kindness also changes; it may disappear. This is not true love. Real love is not based on attachment, but on altruism. In this case your compassion will remain as a humane response to suffering as long as beings continue to suffer.

This type of compassion is what we must strive to cultivate in ourselves, and we must develop it from a limited amount to the limitless. Undiscriminating, spontaneous, and unlimited compassion for all sentient beings is obviously not the usual love that one has for friends or family, which is alloyed with ignorance, desire, and attachment. The kind of love we should advocate is this wider love that you can have even for someone who has done harm to you: your enemy.

The rationale for compassion is that every one of us wants to avoid suffering and gain happiness. This, in turn, is based on the valid feeling of '1', which determines the universal desire for happiness. Indeed, all beings are born with similar desires and should have an equal right to fulfill them. If I compare myself with others, who are countless, I feel that others are more important because I am just one person whereas others are many. Further, the Tibetan Buddhist tradition teaches us to view all sentient beings as our dear mothers and to show our gratitude by loving them all. For, according to Buddhist theory, we are born and reborn countless numbers of times, and it is conceivable that each being has been our parent at one time or another. In this way all beings in the universe share a family relationship.

Whether one believes in religion or not, there is no one who does not appreciate love and compassion. Right from the moment of our birth, we are under the care and kindness of our parents; later in life, when facing the sufferings of disease and old age, we are again dependent on the kindness of others. If at the beginning and end of our lives we depend upon others' kindness, why then in the middle should we not act kindly towards others?

The development of a kind heart (a feeling of closeness for all human beings) does not involve the religiosity we normally associate with conventional religious practice. It is not only for people who believe in religion, but is for everyone regardless of race, religion, or political affiliation. It is for anyone who considers himself or herself, above all, a member of the human family and who sees things from this larger and longer perspective. This is a powerful feeling that we should develop and apply; instead, we often neglect it, particularly in our prime years when we experience a false sense of security.

When we take into account a longer perspective, the fact that all wish to gain happiness and avoid suffering, and keep in mind our relative unimportance in relation to countless others, we can conclude that it is worthwhile to share our possessions with others. When you train in this sort of outlook, a true sense of compassion - a true sense of love and respect for others - becomes possible. Individual happiness ceases to be a conscious self-seeking effort; it becomes an automatic and far superior by-product of the whole process of loving and serving others.

Another result of spiritual development, most useful in day-to-day life, is that it gives a calmness and presence of mind. Our lives are in constant flux, bringing many difficulties. When faced with a calm and clear mind, problems can be successfully resolved. When, instead, we lose control over our minds through hatred, selfishness, jealousy, and anger, we lose our sense of judgement. Our minds are blinded and at those wild moments anything can happen, including war. Thus, the practice of compassion and wisdom is useful to all, especially to those responsible for running national affairs, in whose hands lie the power and opportunity to create the structure of world peace.

World Religions for World Peace

The principles discussed so far are in accordance with the ethical teachings of all world religions. I maintain that every major religion of the world - Buddhism, Christianity, Confucianism, Hinduism, Islam, Jainism, Judaism, Sikhism, Taoism, and Zoroastrianism - has similar ideals of love, the same goal of benefiting humanity through spiritual practice, and the same effect of making their followers into better human beings. All religions teach moral precepts for perfecting the functions of mind, body, and speech. All teach us not to lie or steal or take others' lives, and so on. The common goal of all moral precepts laid down by the great teachers of humanity is unselfishness. The great teachers wanted to lead their followers away from the paths of negative deeds caused by ignorance and to introduce them to paths of goodness.

All religions agree upon the necessity to control the undisciplined mind that harbours selfishness and other roots of trouble, and each teaches a path leading to a spiritual state that is peaceful, disciplined, ethical, and wise. It is in this sense that I believe all religions have essentially the same message. Differences of dogma may be ascribed to differences of time and circumstance as well as cultural influences; indeed, there is no end to scholastic argument when we consider the purely metaphysical side of religion. However, it is much more beneficial to try to implement in daily life the shared precepts for goodness taught by all religions rather than to argue about minor differences in approach.

There are many different religions to bring comfort and happiness to humanity in much the same way as there are particular treatments for different diseases. For, all religions endeavour in their own way to help living beings avoid misery and gain happiness. And, although we can find causes for preferring certain interpretations of religious truths, there is much greater cause for unity, stemming from the human heart. Each religion works in its own way to lessen human suffering and contribute to world civilization. Conversion is not the point. For instance, I do not think of converting others to Buddhism or merely furthering the Buddhist cause. Rather, I try to think of how I as a Buddhist humanitarian can contribute to human happiness.

While pointing out the fundamental similarities among these world religions, I do not advocate one particular religion at the expense of all others. I do not seek a new 'world religion' too. All the different religions of the world are needed to enrich human experience and world civilization. Our human minds, being of different calibre and disposition, need different approaches to peace and happiness. It is just like food. Certain people find Christianity more appealing, others prefer Buddhism because there is no creator in it and everything depends upon your own actions. We can make similar arguments for other religions as well. Thus, the point is clear: humanity needs all the world's religions to suit the ways of life, diverse spiritual needs, and inherited national traditions of individual human beings.

It is from this perspective that I welcome efforts being made in various parts of the world for better understanding among religions. The need for this is particularly urgent now. If all religions make the betterment of humanity their main concern, then they can easily work together in harmony for world peace. Interfaith understanding will bring about the unity necessary for all religions to work together. However, although this is indeed an important step, we must remember that there are no quick or easy solutions. We cannot hide the doctrinal differences that exist among various faiths, nor can we hope to replace the existing religions by a new universal belief. Each religion has its own distinctive contributions to make, and each in its own way is suitable to a particular group of people as they understand life. The world needs them all.

There are two primary tasks facing religious practitioners who are concerned with world peace. First, we must promote better interfaith understanding so as to create a workable degree of unity among all religions. This may be achieved in part by respecting each other's beliefs and by emphasizing our common concern for human well-being. Second, we must bring about a viable consensus on basic spiritual values that touch every human heart and enhance general human happiness. This means we must emphasize the common denominator of all world religions - humanitarian ideals. These two steps will enable us to act both individually and together to create the necessary spiritual conditions for world peace.

We practitioners of different faiths can work together for world peace when we view different religions as essentially instruments to develop a good heart - love and respect for others, a true sense of community. The most important thing is to look at the purpose of religion and not at the details of theology or metaphysics, which can lead to mere intellectualism. I believe that all the major religions of the world can contribute to world peace and work together for the benefit of humanity if we put aside subtle metaphysical differences, which are really the internal business of each religion.

Despite the progressive secularization brought about by worldwide modernization and despite systematic attempts in some parts of the world to destroy spiritual values, the vast majority of humanity continues to believe in one religion or another. The undying faith in religion, evident even under irreligious political systems, clearly demonstrates the potency of religion as such. This spiritual energy and power can be purposefully used to bring about the spiritual conditions necessary for world peace. Religious leaders and humanitarians all over the world have a special role to play in this respect.

Whether we will be able to achieve world peace or not, we have no choice but to work towards that goal. If our minds are dominated by anger, we will lose the best part of human intelligence - wisdom, the ability to decide between right and wrong. Anger is one of the most serious problems facing the world today.

Individual Power to Shape Institutions

Anger plays no small role in current conflicts such as those in the Middle East, Southeast Asia, the North-South problem, and so forth. These conflicts arise from a failure to understand one another's humanness. The answer is not the development and use of greater military force, nor an arms race. Nor is it purely political or purely technological. Basically it is spiritual, in the sense that what is required is a sensitive understanding of our common human situation. Hatred and fighting cannot bring happiness to anyone, even to the winners of battles. Violence always produces misery and thus is essentially counter-productive. It is, therefore, time for world leaders to learn to transcend the differences of race, culture, and ideology and to regard one another through eyes that see the common human situation. To do so would benefit individuals, communities, nations, and the world at large.

The greater part of present world tension seems to stem from the 'Eastern bloc' versus 'Western bloc' conflict that has been going on since World War II. These two blocs tend to describe and view each other in a totally unfavourable light. This continuing, unreasonable struggle is due to a lack of mutual affection and respect for each other as fellow human beings. Those of the Eastern bloc should reduce their hatred towards the Western bloc because the Western bloc is also made up of human beings - men, women, and children. Similarly those of the Western bloc should reduce their hatred towards the Eastern bloc because the Eastern bloc is also human beings. In such a reduction of mutual hatred, the leaders of both blocs have a powerful role to play. But first and foremost, leaders must realize their own and others' humanness. Without this basic realization, very little effective reduction of organized hatred can be achieved.

If, for example, the leader of the United States of America and the leader of the Union of Soviet Socialist Republics suddenly met each other in the middle of a desolate island, I am sure they would respond to each other spontaneously as fellow human beings. But a wall of mutual suspicion and misunderstanding separates them the moment they are identified as the 'President of the USA' and the 'Secretary-General of the USSR'). More human contact in the form of informal extended meetings, without any agenda, would improve their mutual understanding; they would learn to relate to each other as human beings and could then try to tackle international problems based on this understanding. No two parties, especially those with a history of antagonism, can negotiate fruitfully in an atmosphere of mutual suspicion and hatred.

I suggest that world leaders meet about once a year in a beautiful place without any business, just to get to know each other as human beings. Then, later, they could meet to discuss mutual and global problems. I am sure many others share my wish that world leaders meet at the conference table in such an atmosphere of mutual respect and understanding of each other's humanness.

To improve person-to-person contact in the world at large, I would like to see greater encouragement of international tourism. Also, mass media, particularly in democratic societies, can make a considerable contribution to world peace by giving greater coverage to human interest items that reflect the ultimate oneness of humanity. With the rise of a few big powers in the international arena, the humanitarian role of international organizations is being bypassed and neglected. I hope that this will be corrected and that all international organizations, especially the United Nations, will do more active and effective deeds in ensuring maximum benefit to humanity and promoting international understand. It will indeed be tragic if the few powerful members continue to misuse world bodies like the UN for their one-sided interests.

The UN must become the Apex institution for world peace. This world body must be respected by all because the UN is the only hope for small oppressed nations and hence for the planet as a whole.

As all nations are economically dependent upon one another more than ever before, human understanding must go beyond national boundaries and embrace the international community at large. Indeed, unless we can create an atmosphere of genuine cooperation, gained not by threatened or actual use of force but by heartfelt understanding, world problems will only increase. If people in poorer countries are denied the happiness they desire and deserve, they will naturally be dissatisfied and pose problems for the rich. If unwanted social, political, and cultural forms continue to be imposed upon unwilling people, the attainment of world peace is doubtful. However, if we satisfy people at a heart-to-heart level, peace will surely come.

Within each nation, the individual ought to be given the right to happiness, and among nations, there must be equal concern for the welfare of even the smallest nations. I am not suggesting that one system is better than another and all should adopt it. On the contrary, a variety of political systems and ideologies is desirable and accords with the variety of dispositions within the human community. This variety enhances the ceaseless human quest for happiness. Thus each community should be free to evolve its own political and socio-economic system, based on the principle of self-determination.

The achievement of justice, harmony, and peace depends on many factors. We should think about them in terms of human benefit in the long run rather than the short term. I realize the enormity of the task before us, but I see no other alternative than the one I am proposing - which is based on our common humanity. Nations have no choice but to be concerned about the welfare of others, not so much because of their belief in humanity, but because it is in the mutual and long-term interest of all concerned. An appreciation of this new reality is indicated by the emergence of regional or continental economic organizations such as the European Economic Community, the Association of South East Asian Nations, and so forth. I hope more such trans-national organizations will be formed, particularly in regions where economic development and regional stability seem in short supply.

Under present conditions, there is definitely a growing need for human understanding and a sense of universal responsibility. In order to achieve such ideas, we must generate a good and kind heart, for without this, we can achieve neither universal happiness nor lasting world peace. We cannot create peace on paper. While advocating universal responsibility and universal brotherhood and sisterhood, the facts are that humanity is organized in separate entities in the form of national societies. Thus, in a realistic sense, I feel it is these societies that must act as the building-blocks for world peace. Attempts have been made in the past to create societies more just and equal. Institutions have been established with noble charters to combat anti-social forces. Unfortunately, such ideas have been cheated by selfishness. More than ever before, we witness today how ethics and noble principles are obscured by the shadow of self-interest, particularly in the political sphere. There is a school of thought that warns us to refrain from politics altogether, as politics has become synonymous with amorality.

Politics devoid of ethics does not further human welfare, and life without morality reduces humans to the level of beasts.

However, politics is not axiomatically 'dirty'. Rather, the instruments of our political culture have distorted the high ideals and noble concepts meant to further human welfare. Naturally, spiritual people express their concern about religious leaders 'messing' with politics, since they fear the contamination of religion by dirty politics.

I question the popular assumption that religion and ethics have no place in politics and that religious persons should seclude themselves as hermits. Such a view of religion is too one-sided; it lacks a proper perspective on the individual's relation to society and the role of religion in our lives.

Ethics is as crucial to a politician as it is to a religious practitioner. Dangerous consequences will follow when politicians and rulers forget moral principles. Whether we believe in God or duty (karma), ethics is the foundation of every religion.

Such human qualities as morality, compassion, decency, wisdom, and so forth have been the foundations of all civilizations. These qualities must be cultivated and sustained through systematic moral education in social environment so that a more humane world may emerge. The qualities required to create such a world must be inculcated right from the beginning, from childhood. We cannot wait for the next generation to make this change; the present generation must attempt a renewal of basic human values. If there is any hope, it is in the future generations, but not unless we institute major change on a worldwide scale in our present educational system. We need a revolution in our commitment to and practice of universal humanitarian values.

It is not enough to make noisy calls to halt moral degeneration; we must do something about it. Since present-day governments do not shoulder such 'religious' responsibilities, humanitarian and religious leaders must strengthen the existing civic, social, cultural, educational, and religious organizations to revive human and spiritual values. Where necessary, we must create new organizations to achieve these goals. Only in so doing can we hope to create a more stable basis for world peace.

Living in society, we should share the sufferings of our fellow citizens and practise compassion and tolerance not only towards our loved ones but also towards our enemies. This is the test of our moral strength. We must set an example by our own practice, for we cannot hope to convince others of the value of religion by mere words. We must live up to the same high standards of integrity and sacrifice that we ask of others. The ultimate purpose of all religions is to serve and benefit humanity. This is why it is so important that religion always be used to cause happiness and peace of all beings and not merely to convert others.

Still, in religion there are no national boundaries. A religion can and should be used by any people or person who finds it beneficial. What is important for each seeker is to choose a religion that is most suitable to him or her. But, the embracing of a particular religion does not mean the rejection of another religion or one's own community. In fact, it is important that those who embrace a religion should not cut themselves off from their own society; they should continue to live within their own community and in harmony with its members. By escaping from your own community, you cannot benefit others, whereas benefiting others is actually the basic aim of religion. In this regard there are two things important to keep in mind: **self-examination and self-correction.** We should constantly check our attitude toward others, examining ourselves carefully, and we should correct ourselves immediately when we find we are in the wrong.

Finally, let me speak a few words about material progress. I have heard a great deal of complaint against material progress from Westerners, and yet, paradoxically, it has been the very pride of the Western world. I see nothing wrong with material progress per se, provided people are always given precedence.

It is my firm belief that in order to solve human problems in all their dimensions, we must combine and harmonize economic development with spiritual growth.

However, we must know its limitations. Although materialistic knowledge in the form of science and technology has contributed enormously to human welfare, it is not capable of creating lasting happiness. In America, for example, where technological development is perhaps more advanced than in any other country, there is still a great deal of mental suffering. This is because materialistic knowledge can only provide a type of happiness that is dependent upon physical conditions. It cannot provide happiness that springs from inner development independent of external factors.

For renewal of human values and attainment of lasting happiness, we need to look to the common humanitarian heritage of all nations the world over. May this essay serve as an urgent reminder lest we forget the human values that unite us all as a single family on this planet?[86]

I have written the above lines
To tell my constant feeling
Whenever I meet even a 'foreigner',
I have always the same feeling:
I am meeting another member of the human family.
This attitude has deepened
My affection and respect for all beings.
May this natural wish be?
My small contribution to world peace
I pray for a more friendly,
More caring, and more understanding
Human family on this planet
To all who dislike suffering or

---

[86] His Holiness Dalai Lama on " A Human Approach to World Peace

Who cherish lasting happiness? This is my heartfelt appeal.

His Holiness Dalai Lama Addresses Chinese Conference

About Tibetan-Chinese Relationship
July 11th 2011

On July 10 His Holiness left the hotel in the morning for the Verizon Center to continue with the preparatory rituals. Later in the morning, His Holiness departed to the venue of the conference on Democratic China and the Future of Tibet to address its participants. Dr. Chen Kuide of Princeton China Initiative, the organizer, introduced His Holiness at the conference. In his address, His Holiness mentioned that the Tibetan-Chinese relationship goes back to thousands of years during which there were occasions when ties were cordial as well as occasions when there were disputes.

He said in modern times, when he visited Beijing in 1954-55 he experienced a positive feeling that gave him confidence. He recalled his meeting Chinese general Zhang Guohua on his return journey to Lhasa from Beijing in 1955 during which he told General Zhang that when he left for Beijing the year before he went with trepidation but he was now returning full of hope and confidence.

His Holiness[87] told the gathering about his interest in Marxism and socialism and while in China he had in fact expressed a desire to join the Communist Party of China. However, Liu Geping, then head of the State Nationalities Affairs Commission, had told him that there was no need to hurry on this issue. His Holiness joked that his friend Liu may have known

---

[87] His Holiness Addresses Chinese Conference About Tibetan – Chinese Relationship, July 11, 2011, Washington DC, USA, 10 July 2011 -

how the Communist Party would fare in coming years. His Holiness said today the Chinese Communist Party is confronted with problems like corruption and that the party had become a capitalist communist party. There were problems not just with regard to Tibet, but in China in general. These problems need to be solved by the people, His Holiness said:

He added that just as the world belonged to humanity, similarly China belonged to the people in China and the ultimate owner of the country is the people.

His Holiness said that in the initial years of the People's Republic of China, the Communist Party did enjoy widespread support among the people, particularly among the working class. However, he wondered what would be the outcome if there were an independent survey of the views of the people in China on the Communist Party. He said he had always maintained that the 1.3 billion of people in China have every right to know the reality and that 1.3 billion people in China also have the ability to judge what is right and what is wrong. He added that implementing censorship and spreading distorted information were immoral.

His Holiness said that force and violence could not stop the problems from continuing. He referred to the demonstrations in Tibet in 2008, in Xinjiang in 2009 and now in Inner Mongolia. His Holiness said what was needed is for truth to be understood and addressed.

His Holiness said that even on the issue of Tibet the reality was not being seen and that there were distorted information being spread. He recalled the Chinese authorities terming him as a demon in 2008. Saying that the Chinese brothers and sisters should assist in resolving the Tibetan problem, His Holiness said that it was important to understand the truth about the Tibetan issue.

His Holiness then talked about his devolution of authority to the elected Tibetan leadership. He said that since 2001 when the process of direct election of the Kalon Tripa began, he had been in a state of semi-retirement. After the changes this year, he said the rule by Gaden Phodrang government had come to an end. His Holiness said that this year the Tibetans had an election for Kalon Tripa and introduced Dr. Lobsang Sangay, who was also sitting on the stage, as the winner. His Holiness said he was born in India, did schooling in Tibetan schools, did higher studies in Delhi University and Harvard University. His Holiness joked that he did not know Dr. Sangay's ability in Tibetan, but said that he enjoyed his full trust and he was confident that he would do well.

Thereafter, His Holiness answered some questions from the conference participants.

In response to a question about his Middle Way Approach, His Holiness said that it came about after thorough deliberations on the short-term and long-term impact with people both in exile and in Tibet and that it was formalized through majority support of the people. His Holiness said that intellectuals in China had also supported his approach.

His Holiness said that the new Tibetan leadership has also publicly affirmed its support to the Middle Way Approach.

On another question, His Holiness said that henceforth all political responsibilities would be shouldered by the elected leadership. He added that the Chinese authorities, who accuse him of being a separatist, and specifically the United Front Work Department, who consider him a problem, should know that he had fully retired. His Holiness clarified that the issue of Tibet was not that of the Dalai Lama. He recalled his rejection of the five points of message that the Chinese Government sent to him in the 1980s to resolve the Tibetan issue because all these points dealt with his personal matters. He said in the past he had not worked for any personal status and will not do so in the future, too.

To a question about any change of policy away from the Middle Way Approach, His Holiness let Dr. Lobsang Sangay respond. Dr. Sangay said that he had campaigned for the position with the platform of Middle Way Approach and the people had voted for him showing their support for this approach. He added that it is a hypothetical question on what would happen in the future but it is up to the people to decide.

His Holiness added that when he first laid out his Middle Way Approach he had maintained that ultimately, it would be up to the Tibetan people to decide.

Talking about China's responsibilities, His Holiness said that the country had the potential to contribute to the development of the world and be an important player. He said what was required was respect and trust by the international community towards China, which was missing currently.

Talking about development of democracy in China His Holiness said that he thought a more gradual path towards democracy was more appropriate as any overnight change could result in chaos. What were needed in China in the immediate future was transparency, end to media censorship, and a system of rules that meet international standards. He said that today whether it was laws or the Constitution they were all connected to the Party.

His Holiness also talked about the gradual degeneration of the Chinese Communist Party. During the time of Mao Zedong, His Holiness said the Party leaders were sincere individuals. He said he wondered what Mao would say if he saw today's Chinese Communist Party. His Holiness said in the past, Mao had termed the Russian Communist leader Khrushchev as a revisionist. Today's Chinese Communist Party had become a greater revisionist, His Holiness added.

To another question, His Holiness talked about his interest in democracy from his childhood. He said that while in Tibet he saw that the existing political system was not benefiting the poor and the needy section of the society. Even though he had set up a Reforms Commission in 1952 the Chinese officials in Tibet posed obstacles to implementing the reforms. It was only after coming to India in 1959 that he was able to launch the democratization of the Tibetan society. Through gradual development beginning in 1960, we reached the stage in 2001 where the political leadership began to be directly elected by the people. This has further developed to the situation that we are in today. Thus, His Holiness said that Tibetan democracy was something that was based on over 60 years of experience and not something thought of suddenly.

The two-day conference began on July 9, 2011 and is being participated by around 100 Chinese writers and democracy proponents as well as Tibetans and others.

His Holiness then left for the teaching venue, where he continued teaching on the Stages of Meditation by Kamalashila as well as the 37 Practices of a Bodhisattva by Thokmey Sangpo. Before going to the actual texts, His Holiness gave an introduction to Buddhism. Today's session began with the recitation of the Heart Sutra in Chinese. On July 9, the session began with the recitation of the Heart Sutra in Pali and Sanskrit.[88]

In Search of Peace

Accumulation of wealth and conspicuous consumption are not enough. Humankind has to think and live differently to be truly happy.

It has long been a commonplace that wealth does not necessarily mean happiness. On the contrary, apart from the fear of losing it, its possession fuels what can only be called competitive acquisitiveness and competitive consumption, which in turn leads to relative deprivation. As opposed to absolute deprivation, which pertains to actual lack of necessities, relative deprivation refers to what one does not possess but others do. For an aspiring upwardly mobile person who, for example, lacks a motor, which his neighbor has, it can cause greater anguish and bitterness than any experienced by victims of absolute deprivation.

Besides, opportunity brings its own frustrations. Eric Hoffer writes, "Unlimited opportunities can be as potent a cause of frustration as a paucity or lack of opportunities. When opportunities are apparently unlimited, there is an inevitable deprecation of the present. The attitude is: 'All that I am doing or possibly can do is chicken feed compared with what is left undone'." Clearly, happiness depends on what one seeks in life and how one goes about getting it. That again depends a great deal on one's social conditioning since birth.

While competitiveness is scripted in the dynamics of life as an instrument of survival in a shortage-ridden,

---

[88] Note: The teachings are being translated into English, Chinese, Russian, Vietnamese, Italian, Spanish, French, Japanese and Mongolian. They are also being webcast live on www.dalailama.com.

hostile and insecure world, it had been contained in the West by the ethical cannons of religion until the advent of the Reformation. RH Tawney writes, "When the age of Reformation begins (in the 16th century), economics is still a branch of ethics and ethics of theology; all human activities are treated as falling within a single scheme, whose character is determined by the spiritual destiny of mankind ... the legitimacy of economic transactions is tried by reference less to the movements of the market, than to the moral standards derived from the traditional teachings of the Christian church..."

The Reformation and the secularization of society that followed destroyed the hegemony of ecclesiastical authority. Capitalism established the sovereignty of economic utility and necessity. The market economy, with advertising as its cutting edge, is enshrining consumption as the new religion and a human being's possessions as the measure of individual worth. Its impact is being felt in post-liberalisation India as the market casts its net far and wide. The rich criminal is a celebrity; the poor schoolmaster, dirt under one's feet. The rich and ennobling spiritualism of the *Upanishads* and the *Bhagavad Gita*, and the wisdom of the *Vedas, Mahabharata* and the *Ramayana* have been thrown to the winds.

Understandably, there is anger, depression and violence everywhere and in especially acute forms in India because of its massive inequalities and increasingly corrupt and criminalized bureaucracy and political class, which enables the powerful to plunder the country virtually at will, riding rough shod over the rights of the poor and the vulnerable and raping the environment. Animals suffer the most. As Erich Fromm points out in Fear of Freedom, one of the ways in which humans try to overcome their feeling of insecurity is by resorting to sadist behavior, which consists of physically torturing and psychologically dominating and manipulating others, which gives them a sense of power.

The ultimate power one can exercise over living beings is that of life and death. Genocide is the most extreme form of its exercise. A person demanding the genocide of a particular segment of human society would be labelled a mass murderer. On the other hand, one demanding the mass killing of stray dogs, in an act of transference of the genocidal urge, might be called a hero in a sick society. Not surprisingly, animals who, in violation of the basic ethos of the Indian heritage, are excluded from the moral universe of the humans, are particularly vulnerable.

It is goes to the credit of the organizers of the Gurgaon dialogue that they invited animal rights activists to participate. Animal and plant welfare is an integral part of human welfare, as the extinction of non-human living species will destroy the delicate ecological balance whose evolution over millennia made human life possible on Earth. Once animal exploitation was institutionalized and accepted as a part of the natural order of things, it opened the door to similar ways of treating human beings.

The global explosion of aggression in the form of crime, terrorism and violence to the environment will end only if people begin to live and think differently. Happiness is subjective; a state of mind that depends on how one reacts to the world as well as the condition of the world itself. No short answers are available. One must begin by identifying factors that lead to aggression and trying to control or eliminate them. It is a long haul.[89]

---

[89] Hiranmay Karlekar (2011), " In search of Happiness", The Pioneer, July 30, 2011

Let's keep religion out of politics

There can be no bigger an embarrassment to a secular democracy than a live and much-publicised rip-off of its citizens' democratic rights on the pretexts of religion, caste, sect and region. The very recent, disturbing incident in Muzaffarnagar, in Uttar Pradesh, is one such crying instance. The communal riot in Muzaffarnagar — in the backdrop of a weak economy — not only adds to the woes of the economy but also forces both internal and external minds to perceive our nation as a 'failed state'.

As is easily understood, the impact of the flare-up is not confined to the western Uttar Pradesh district that is home to over 41 lakh individuals from many religions and castes (and has a literary rate of under 60 per cent as per the 2011 Census). The violence in Muzaffarnagar has impacted thoughts and processes in other locations like Baghpat, Unnao, Bulandshahr, Bahraich, Bijnor, and other towns in the vicinity of the district. One can almost sense that some of these poisoned minds are working tirelessly to steadily disturb social stability in the entire nation.

What is worse is that such a fomented communal unrest as this, only ends up lending the upper hand to anti-social elements. That eventually creates a rift between various social groups in many belts across the nation. And what we could — and would — witness is many-a-magnified repeats of the 'blood and fire drama' that unfolded in Muzaffarnagar this September. What's the panacea to eradicate this social plague? A re-drafted and powerful Communal Violence (Prevention, Control and Rehabilitation of Victims) Bill is a must.

Without any iota of doubt, we immediately need to re-work and clear the Bill. But what should rightfully precede — in terms of importance or value — the passage of the new Bill is a need to incorporate a few fundamental changes in our political system.

Violence pitting one community against another has been an indisputably striking feature of Indian politics since we really severed all ties with Pakistan 66 years back. It's been religion. And it's been caste. Look at communal riots that have put this nation to shame in the past six-plus decades. Almost all of them bear this one peculiar characteristic: That fanning such disturbing fires have often benefitted political parties — those that claim to play the messiah to certain religious or caste groups that become their vote-banks during elections. Either these riots were, are (and will be) politically ignited or were, are (and will be) later used at political forums.

We are one of those few nations where religion and politics work hand in glove. Many nations have adopted policies that separate their organised religious groups from their political systems and at no point do these two groups cross paths. In 1802 that Thomas Jefferson iterated the importance of separation of the Church from the state. In fact, much earlier in The First Amendment to the United States Constitution, was it clarified that, "congress shall make no law respecting an establishment of religion..."

Along the same lines, even before we pass and convert the communal violence Bill into a law, we need to ensure that other supporting laws are secular and do not favour any particular religion or group per se. The incumbent Government is busy with other Bills for many years now and has paid literally no heed to the communal violence Bill. Seems today, the file has been put on 'dormant' mode.

What can be more ironical than our Union Minister for Home Affairs delivering a statement on the decaying conditions of communal harmony of the nation, but not taking any stern step to get the Bill in place? Due to lack of such a Bill, the Union Government and Central authorities are not authorized to take action and interfere in State-related matters even during communal riots. The communal violence Bill would empower the Centre during such disturbing situations and would allow it to help the States keep the fire under check and subsequently douse it.

It would further ensure the inception of a specialised task force called the National Authority for Communal Harmony, Justice and Reparation (by the Centre) that could come into action whenever required. 451 cases of communal violence between January and August, 2013, took place in our country as compared to 410 in the 12 months of last year (as put across by our Home Minister). Aren't these numbers enough to substantiate the importance of such a Bill most urgently?

At present, the police and Rapid Action Forces are handicapped as they are not permitted to take remedial action during processions and during gatherings where venomous speeches are delivered. Obviously, in its current form, the Bill does provide for special courts (for trails) and empowers the victims while further providing protection to witnesses during the trial period. But the next big issue that makes the Bill flawed is the demarcation line that it draws between the 'majority' and 'minority'.

The Bill silently favours the latter group. Under no circumstance should a secular country have special laws for a particular religion or a separate trial system for a religious group. The provisions of the communal violence Bill should apply to the Hindu and Muslim victims alike. Differentiated provisions and laws based on religion or caste or any such element, are in themselves non-secular and communal and only encourage anti-social elements to customize it politically and take undue advantage.

Where do we begin? Separate religion from legislation and make sure that laws that differentiate individuals on the ground of religion (especially for crime) and caste are not allowed to breathe the Indian air. The Bill, then, should be passed immediately after removing the clauses of majority and minority and adding clauses that provide for excellent provisions to all victims irrespective of their religion, caste, sect and region.[90]

In short, the communal violence Bill should be passed at the earliest after removing the clauses on 'majority' and 'minority' and adding provisions that provide justice to victims, irrespective of their religion, caste, sect and region.

World Peace Is Possible

Only the governments cannot establish world peace. These public institutions have rather polluted the peace atmosphere in their countries and forced the citizens of the world to feel and calculate the consequences of wars.

The world peace organizations have tried to find out the ways for prevalence of permanent peace in all states and countries. A number of authors have also hypothesized to stop wars at any cost. Each individual would be the actor in world peace activities. Each person should say that I could bring world peace for the benefits of humanity. But he / she should adopt the following steps:

(a) **Change your way of thinking:** Changing us to resolve conflict peacefully plays a part in world peace. We need to understand our own anger, aggression and desire for revenge. We can always learn more

---

[90] Arindam Chaudhuri (2013), "Let's keep religion out of politics", the Pioneer, Friday, September 13, 2013

about controlling these basic with a reasoned logical approach. We can choose to value and respect others no matter what their religion, ethnic background, class and nationality.

We can choose to make world peace a priority and get educated. Find an international news service that avoids national bias. See yourself as a global citizen first then a member of your nation second. Try to find out what is really happening in world conflicts, and learn to detect western propaganda that becomes increasingly subtle as we become more educated. Discuss all these issues with family and friends. Give a damn.

(b) **Family and community initiatives:** The average western child watches thousands of murders on television before they reach their teens. Parents have a responsibility to teach nonviolence. Make a point of having no firearms in the household and demonstrate conflict resolution skills in your relationships. Violence in local communities can provide a foundation for conflict on a national level. You can support any strategies that assist marginalized people in your community. Violent behavior has strong links with poverty and lack of opportunities.

(c) **Promote and educate for world peace:** Every nation needs to overhaul their education systems to promote world peace and nonviolent strategies, and global cooperation. Education would have a strong focus on human rights, democracy, tolerance and understanding of other cultures, religions and genders. Education is a vital link to achieve a culture of peace when every person can understand global issues, respect human rights, appreciate diversity, and respect others.

(d) **Strengthen the United Nations:** Despite criticism and mistakes, the United Nations has played a role in preventing or limiting wars around the world. Many dream of the day when all nations can be warned that any invasion of another country will be met with a speedy response from all UN members. This approach minimizes spending on arms as the armies of 40 countries should suffice to stop an invading army. The reform of the United Nations Security Council is needed to make it more representative and its decision-making process more transparent.

International laws still need improvement, as the Declaration of Human Rights by the UN still does not prohibit killing. These laws still need stronger backing by international courts and UN sanctioned military force.

The UN is in a unique position enact and enforce laws that prevent anyone supplying terrorists or repressive leaders, minimize nuclear arsenals, outlaw mines and biological weapons and propose weapons inspections of any country.

(e) **Religions can promote peace and justice:** Religions have caused many wars, but parts of their beliefs can promote peace and justice. The major religions should be able to make firm commitments to this and adopt firm positions on major conflicts. The churches should work closely with the UN to promote world peace. The major religions can still do much more to promote links with each other and tolerance of other faiths.

(f) **Promote global democracy and government:** Nations find it more difficult to go to war when there is representative and a democratic decision-making process. Non-violent promotion of democracy in authoritarian regimes is a long-term goal toward world peace. Support the reform and democratization of the United Nations. Get involved in movements like Amnesty International who seek to make repressive regimes more accountable. Speak out and get involved if you think your country is being unjust.

(g) **Encourage just use of resources**: Poverty and injustice have clear links with war, revolution and terrorism. The West consumes far more than the third world, while the third world suffers much more the effects of this in terms of pollution and weather changes. We can get involved in agencies promoting conservation, sustainable development, equitable trade patterns, provision of food and clean water supplies.

(h) **Political activism:** There are many organizations you can join who are working toward world peace. Some are sensible, some tend to be a bit extreme but they all play their part in the move toward world peace. Get on the Internet and do a search for any that you feel you could join.[91]

Politics can promote World Peace

Why a man behaves as an animal? Why a man kills another man? Why a country wages war against another country even in twenty-first century? When truth is known to both parties, both countries, and to the mediators, why all disputes are not solved through discussions? How a country could hate another country? Why a government challenges another government?

The Twentieth century was the bloodiest century ever! 27,000,000 soldiers and 170,000,000 civilians were killed in 1900 – 1999.

How can we boast that we are civilized, when 197 million of people were killed without their faults? A

[91] World Peace / world - peace 110 - mb Com, world – peace—personal-action Html

soldier is an employee of the government; he fights against the enemies as he is paid for it. Is it correct to say that hire killing is justified and morally correct? The military is the strength of the country; this does not mean that governments would use them as per their whims. The governments must be scanned by the world organizations – godly persons do not form the governments – they are simply corrupt politicians who boast that all people are sub-ordinate to them. The justice system could control the governments, if they find the governments adopt anti-people policies. But they are also silent.

Perhaps we are advanced to boast that we have property, land, gold, buildings, and enough bank balance; but we lack in sympathy, forgiveness, humanity, friendship, goodness and godliness. All misunderstandings could be solved. Let the United Nations Organization act as a non-controversial and highly esteemed organization to award justice to the mankind.

Perhaps we are again drifting to pre-historic period. Why a government would fight against its own voters with guns, bullets and other sophisticated war equipments in the name of fighting against Maoists, Naxalites and Terrorists? Why the government fears these persons carrying arms?

We feel that the planning and implementing machinery are moving in wrong direction that does not help the victims. The government is corrupt, inefficient and anti-people.

(a) We suppose that head of the government is more ambitious to remain in power for the life.
(b) We are in doubtful that democracy, the best form of governance, needs improvement. The 'vote-buying' democracy must be changed with a new formula.

(c) None should be permitted to the legislature more than eight years in his / her lifetime.

The Election Commission must see that there should be a maximum of 10 political parties with difference in ideology or objectives. And only the presidents of the political parties would contest for all assembly or parliament elections. Of course, all registered political parties would submit the names of persons suitable for at least 50 percent of parliamentary seats in the country. The percentage of votes realized for each party would determine the percentage of berths of that party in the parliament. In other words if the All India Kisan Party gets 24 percent of votes in the Election, it would have 24 percent share of total number of Members of Parliament (M. P.) in the Parliament. There are 543 MPs in the Lower House of the Parliament in India, so the All India Kisan Party would have 130 Members of Parliament in the Lower House of Parliament. The South Africa model of election should be followed in each democratic country.

The President of the country must call for the President of the highest vote pulling party to form the government. After 60 days of swearing ceremony, the party would face division in the parliament to prove majority in the House. If he / she fail to prove majority in the parliament, the second highest vote puller would be requested to form the government. He/she must prove majority in the House within 30 days of swearing ceremony. Similarly, if the second highest party fails to prove majority, the third best political party should prove majority within 30 days from the swearing ceremony. If the government fails again, it is advisable to hold fresh elections.

Political alliances among political parties to form the government with opposite views and political philosophy after the election lead to corruption and no-governance.

The President or the Governor should follow the constitution in all matters. They must see that the administration moves as per rules.

The President, Prime Minister, Governors, Supreme Court or High Court Justices are not superior citizens of the country; they are awarded top jobs by the constitution to do justice to the whole country and people. So all misdeeds incurred by them should be enquired after they retire or leave the posts like other citizens.

No policy or program of the government should be named after the departed or retired politicians. This is done to blackmail the hungry people in vote politics.

All politicians should register their names as politicians in the government. These registered politicians can take part in elections. Non-politicians or political followers are the root causes of corruption, black money, contract business and anti-social activities. If politics becomes clean, governance is ought to be clean.

Mahatma Gandhi's 5 Teachings to Bring about World Peace

If humanity is to progress, Gandhi is inescapable. He lived, thought, acted and inspired by the vision of humanity evolving toward a world of peace and harmony.

- Dr. Martin Luther King, Jr.

Have you ever dreamed about a joyful world with peace and prosperity for all Mankind – a world in which we respect and love each other despite the differences in our culture, religion and way of life?

I often feel helpless when I see the world in turmoil, a result of the differences between our ideals. This leads to grief and sorrow being inflicted on millions of innocent victims by a few who abuse the power of their convictions.

How can I make difference so that I may bring peace to this world that I love and cherish so much? A name flickers instantly in my mind.

- Mahatma Gandhi

Mahatma Gandhi inspired the world with his faith in truth and justice for all Mankind. He was a great soul who loved even those who fought against his ideals to bring about peace with non-violence.

How could a meek and fragile person of small physical stature inspire millions to bring about a profound change in a way the mightiest had never achieved before? His achievements were nothing less than miracles — his creed was to bring peace to not only those who suffered injustice and sorrow but to espouse a new way of life for Mankind, with peace and harmony. His life was a message — a message of peace over power, of finding ways to reconcile our differences, and of living in harmony with respect and love even for our enemy.

Teaching 1: Power is of two kinds. One is obtained by the fear of punishment and the other by acts of love. Power based on love is a thousand times more effective and permanent then the one derived from fear of punishment.

— Mahatma Gandhi

The force of power never wins against the power of love. At this hour of greatest unrest and turmoil in our world; the greatest force to be reckoned with lies within our hearts — a force of love and tolerance for all. Throughout his life, Mahatma Gandhi fought against the power of force during the heyday of British rein over the world. He transformed the minds of millions, including my father, to fight against injustice with peaceful means and non-violence. His message was as transparent to his enemy as it was to his followers. He believed that, if we fight for the cause of humanity and greater justice, it should include even those who do not conform to our cause. History attests to his power as he proved that we can bring about world peace by seeking and pursuing truth for the benefit of Mankind. We can resolve the greatest of our differences if we dare to have a constructive conversation with our enemy.

Teaching 2: What difference does it make to the dead, the orphans, and the homeless, whether the mad destruction is wrought under the name of totalitarianism or the holy name of liberty and democracy? — Mahatma Gandhi

A war always inflicts pain and sorrow on everyone. History has witnessed countless examples of dictators, including Hitler, Mussolini, and Stalin to name but a few, who inflicted sorrow and destruction on our world. A world of peace can be achieved if we learn the power of non-violence, as shown by the life of Mahatma Gandhi.

Mahatma Gandhi has proven that we can achieve the noble causes of liberty, justice and democracy for Mankind without killing anyone, without making a child an orphan, and without making anyone homeless with the damage caused by war.

Teaching 3: There are many causes that I am prepared to die for but no cause that I am prepared to kill for. — Mahatma Gandhi

We live for our values and passion but at the core of our existence lies our innate desire to live a peaceful life. The greatest noble cause is to display our desire to bring about peace in this world by our own sacrifice and not that of those who oppose our views. The strength of cowardice is in using power to cause death and destruction for others. The strength of courage is in self-sacrifice for the benefit of all.

Mahatma Gandhi sacrificed his own lucrative law practice in Durban, South Africa to lead a simple life and to share the pain of the powerless and destitute. He won over the hearts of millions without ever reigning power over anyone — simply with the power of altruism. We too can bring peace to our world by showing our willingness to sacrifice our self-centered desires. Our utmost cause in life should be to win the hearts of others by showing our willingness to serve causes greater than ourselves.

Teaching 4: An eye for an eye will only make the whole world blind — Mahatma Gandhi

History can attest to the fact that most human conflicts have been as a result of a stubborn approach by our leaders. Our history would turn out for the better if our leaders could just learn that most disputes can be resolved by showing a willingness to understand the issues of our opponents and by using diplomacy and compassion. No matter where we live; what religion we practice or what culture we cultivate, at the heart of everything, we are all humans. We all have the same ambitions and aspirations to raise our family and to live life to its fullest. Our cultural, religious and political differences should not provide the backbone to invoke conflicts that can only bring sorrow and destruction to our world.

Teaching 5: We must become the change we want to see in the world. — Mahatma Gandhi

A great leader always leads with an exemplary life that echoes his ideals. Mahatma Gandhi sacrificed his thriving law practice and adopted a simple life to live among the millions who lived in poverty during his freedom struggle. Today, we see modern leaders cajoling the masses with promises that they never intend to keep – let alone practicing what they preach in their own lives. One cannot bring world peace to all unless a leader demonstrates peaceful acts of kindness daily. Mahatma Gandhi believed that we are all children of God. We should not discriminate amongst ourselves based on faith, caste, creed or any other differences.

An outstanding example of Mahatma Gandhi's leadership was his famous Salt March, which brought about a profound change. On March 2nd 1930, as a protest at tax on salt, Gandhi wrote a remarkable letter to Lord Irwin, the Viceroy of India. He wrote, "Dear Friend, I cannot intentionally hurt anything that lives, much less fellow human beings, even though they may do the greatest wrong to me and mine. Whilst, therefore, I hold the British rule to be a curse, I do not intend to harm to a single Englishman or to any legitimate interest he may have in India..." With these words, he inspired millions to fight for this righteous cause and eventually forced the British to leave India without inflicting harm to any Englishman. Such were the quintessential qualities of justice and peace that made Mahatma Gandhi the man who changed our world for the better with his ideals of faith, love and tolerance.

Generations to come, it may be, will scarce believe that such one as this ever in flesh and blood walked upon this earth.

- Albert Einstein on Mahatma Mohandas K. Gandhi

Mahatma Gandhi taught us that we can bring harmony to our world by becoming champions of love and peace for all. The task is daunting, but he has shown that a fragile, meekly man of small physical stature can achieve feats of incredible magnitude with a staunch belief to practice peace through non-violence. Will you make a pledge to become the change that you would like to see in this world? I have.

Let the first act of every morning be to make the following resolve for the day:
I shall not fear anyone on Earth.
I shall fear only God.
I shall not bear ill will toward anyone.
I shall not submit to injustice from anyone.
I shall conquer untruth by truth. And in resisting untruth, I shall put up with all suffering. [92]

- **Mahatma Gandhi**

Conclusion

The politicians, Governments, world organizations and people of all the countries should observe silence and pray God on New Year's Day (January 1) at 11 AM local time for five minutes only for WORLD PEACE. Powerful people might cause the whole world blind. Yet, there is hope for amity, freindship and love among people and races of all countries. We have no right to destroy the world created by the Almighty. Politics can strengthen 'world peace' provided government of each country accepts and adopts the following TEN suggestions:

1. Each country should declare:

The government accepts and pledges that the country is a zone of peace and it would not cause or wage war against another country. It would approach the United Nations instantly in case of urgency. Each country should honor the verdict of the boundary commission to solve boundary problems. It can appeal to the United Nations, if the verdict is not favourable to the country.

(2) A corrupt government raises war because war creates panic in the country. The President or Prime

---

[92] Shilpan Patel of the Success Soul Blog, – Smile, Breathe and Go slowly, Zenhabits.net

Minister or the military ruler gets ample scope to convert more defense funds as personal funds. This fund is deposited in foreign banks for future use. Absolute power corrupts a man absolutely.

(3) The United Nations should have three functions:

(a)**To create and stabilize Peace in all countries,**

(b)**To stop war anywhere in the world by request, order, or by challenging a war against the country, which causes a war;** and

©To promulgate international laws to solve problems on: Black money, defense production, boundary issues, terrorism, military rule, and conversion of religion, debt reduction, and environment protection.

(4) Each country must plan, execute, and monitor an appropriate budget for the income-poor people of the country. The government must ensure food security, employment opportunity, safety and peace environment to all the inhabitants. Government can't issue false reports and can't mislead people with false promises. All court cases must be finalized within a year.

(5) Each government must not violate the guidelines of 'Environmental Laws'. A corrupt government changes the 'law of the land' for vested interests. A corrupt government sells or leases out land to the industrialists, foreign companies and builders through kickbacks. Forestland must be protected by Law. In no case, forestland, agricultural land, common land and public land should be squeezed. Countries like Afghanistan and Pakistan are exporting terrorism and are running parallel administration as forest area has come down to 4 per cent.

(6) Free gifts to voters, high subsidies, cheap rice and wheat, high budget and foreign funding do not help the people and country. The Terrorists, Naxalites and Maoists are anti-government but not anti-national. The governments should pardon them and bring them to society. Easy money creates more number of greedy politicians. The government must admit that some of the state policies need change to check corruption.

(7) Politicians must be honest, truthful and sincere. They should be knowledgeable and must possess the capacity to assist in law-making for the benefits of the country and people. They should have the capacity to think for tomorrow and for the humanity. A shortsighted politician is corrupt, and anti-national.

A politician with police cases must be asked for political holiday till he is free from all charges. How can a suspected murderer be a Lawmaker?

(8) To err is human. Every one has a price. The auction value of a politician or a cricketer varies. Corruption is deep rooted in the society because politics has become a business. So, the Presidents or Prime Ministers should hold the coveted posts for **two terms.** The bureau of investigation should enquire their assets after retirement from the posts. A long-time political leader is more prone to corruption, mis-use of power, bossism, groupies, and black money.

(9) The Presidents of Political parties should contest election for the entire country with dummy candidates for each constituency. The percentage of votes secured by the political party would determine the percentage of seats in the parliament or senate or assembly.

If a single party does not prove majority in the house, all party government must be ensured.

There cannot be regional political parties in the country.

(10) A citizen with clean activity and character should be permitted to contest in election. Persons, who have been awarded punishment by courts or have been elected to the Parliament, Assembly or Senate for two times, should be debarred to contest election. Moreover, citizens with money laundering court cases may be disallowed for contesting elections.

(11) A corruption-free election process and government would reduce corruption; decrease the number of political workers, anti-socials and terrorists in the country. This would strengthen peace in society, state and country and ultimately we would live in the safest world where WORLD PEACE would monitor our life and activity. And it is possible.

(12) There should be PEACE ORGANIZATIONS in each settlement. The government should organize these clubs. The government should declare Peace prizes for peace workers in each C. D. Block area, in each district, in each state and in each country each year.

World Peace is not a dream; it is possible if politicians forget war and concentrate on 'food security to all'. Even a strong handshake and true friendship between the Presidents, Prime Ministers or External Affairs Ministers of neighbouring countries could make the world 'free of war' for decades and decades.

The United Nations should declare 'The UN Peace Prize' for 100 peace workers each year.

We feel that the governments could convert the morbid environment into a peace environment provided politics is clean. And it is possible.

THE END

AUTHOR INDEX

+++++

SUBJECT INDEX

+++++

A MOVEMENT FOR A PEACEFUL WORLD

AUTHORS

Professor Suresh Chandra Mallick (b 1944) was a faculty member of the OUAT, Bhubaneswar (India) during 1968 - 2004. He is a researcher, writer, thinker and social worker. He is an Agricultural Economist with specialization in Agriculture, Poverty, Marketing, Policy and World Peace to motivate people's involvement in peace process. He held the post of Vice President, Indian Society of Agricultural Marketing during 2003 - 05. At present, he is the Chairperson of the Institute of Development Studies & Policy Research, Bhubaneswar.

Pritam Mallick (1975–2006) was extremely noble, friendly and knowledgeable and possessed extraordinary memory. He received B.A. (Honors) from Utkal University, M.A. from Central University, Hyderabad and M. Phil. Degree from Jawaharlal Nehru University and completed Ph. D. courses in JNU. He was a specialist in Monetary Economics and Econometrics. He remembered the Oxford Dictionary and Roget's Thesaurus to master English literature. He acquired deep knowledge in Astrology, Palmistry, Mathematics and Statistics. He contributed enormously for WORLD PEACE manuscripts as co-author. But his heavenly demise occurred on August 4, 2006.